(RE)BORN IN THE USA

ALSO BY ROGER BENNETT

Men in Blazers Present Encyclopedia Blazertannica
And You Shall Know Us by the Trail of Our Vinyl
Camp Camp
Bar Mitzvah Disco

(RE)BORN IN THE USA

AN ENGLISHMAN'S LOVE LETTER
TO HIS CHOSEN HOME

ROGER
BENNETT

DEY ST.
An Imprint of WILLIAM MORROW

DEY ST.

Some names and identifying details have been changed.

HarperCollins books may be purchased for educational, business, or sales promotional use. For information, please email the Special Markets Department at SPsales@harpercollins.com.

FIRST EDITION

Designed by Michelle Crowe

Library of Congress Cataloging-in-Publication Data
Names: Bennett, Roger, 1970- author.
Title: (Re)Born in the USA / Roger Bennett.
Description: First Dey Street edition. | New York: Dey Street, 2021.
Identifiers: LCCN 2021000545 (print) | LCCN 2021000546 (ebook) | ISBN
   9780062958693 (hardcover) | ISBN 9780062958716 (paperback) | ISBN
   9780062958723 (ebook) | ISBN 9780062958747 | ISBN 9780062958730
Subjects: LCSH: Bennett, Roger, 1970- | British—United States—Biography. |
   Immigrants—United States—Biography. | Sportscasters—United States—
   Biography. | Popular culture—United States. | Jews—England—Liverpool—
   Biography. | Liverpool (England)—Biography.
Classification: LCC E184.B7 B38 2021 (print) | LCC E184.B7 (ebook) |
   DDC 305.9/06912073—dc23
LC record available at https://lccn.loc.gov/2021000545
LC ebook record available at https://lccn.loc.gov/2021000546

ISBN 978-0-06-295869-3

21 22 23 24 25 LSC 10 9 8 7 6 5 4 3 2 1

To Jamie Glassman, with eternal thanks for his lifelong patience, love, humor, and friendship. And willingness to run up his parents' phone bills.

CONTENTS

TIMELINE **viii**

PROLOGUE: **Of Hot Wings and Fast Cars** **1**

INTRODUCTION: **A Room Full of Strangers** **5**

BOOK ONE: THE DARKNESS/ENGLISH ROG

CHAPTER ONE: **Amber Waves of . . . Rain** **13**

CHAPTER TWO: **Spaghetti Scarlet Letter** **23**

CHAPTER THREE: **Bullshit Baffles Brains** **31**

CHAPTER FOUR: **Feathered Hair Fantasies** **41**

CHAPTER FIVE: **"Just Locker Room Talk"** **49**

CHAPTER SIX: **Think Once, Think Twice . . . Duck** **61**

CHAPTER SEVEN: **The Other American Revolution** **67**

CHAPTER EIGHT: **Bar Mitzvah Disco** **73**

CHAPTER NINE: **The Pepsi Choice** **87**

BOOK TWO: THE HALF-LIGHT/TRANSATLANTIC ROG

CHAPTER TEN: **The King Takes America** **101**

CHAPTER ELEVEN: **Fat Knacker's Words of Wisdom** **107**

CHAPTER TWELVE: **The Funky Chicken** **113**

CHAPTER THIRTEEN: **Like a Rolling Stone** **123**

CHAPTER FOURTEEN: **Crockett's Theme** **135**

CHAPTER FIFTEEN: **My American Twin** 147

CHAPTER SIXTEEN: **Super Bowl Shuffle** 159

CHAPTER SEVENTEEN: **The Goers Go** 163

BOOK THREE: THE LIGHT/AMERICAN ROG

CHAPTER EIGHTEEN: **Beef, Democracy, and Freedom** 175

CHAPTER NINETEEN: **Game Show Winner** 179

CHAPTER TWENTY: **On Glencoe Beach** 185

CHAPTER TWENTY-ONE: **Don't You . . . Forget About Me** 191

CHAPTER TWENTY-TWO: **Midnight with the Fridge** 195

CHAPTER TWENTY-THREE: **The End Is the Beginning** 203

CHAPTER TWENTY-FOUR: **New Rog in Town** 209

CHAPTER TWENTY-FIVE: **The Transformation of Titty Thomson** 217

CHAPTER TWENTY-SIX: **Leveling Up** 223

CHAPTER TWENTY-SEVEN: **Bigmouth Strikes** 231

CHAPTER TWENTY-EIGHT: **Liverpool College Breaking Crew** 243

CHAPTER TWENTY-NINE: **The Big Show** 257

CHAPTER THIRTY: **The Wake-up Bell** 269

CHAPTER THIRTY-ONE: **The Beastie Boys and the Liverpool Welcome** 279

CHAPTER THIRTY-TWO: **We've Got to Make a Decision** 291

EPILOGUE **301**

ACKNOWLEDGMENTS **313**

TIMELINE

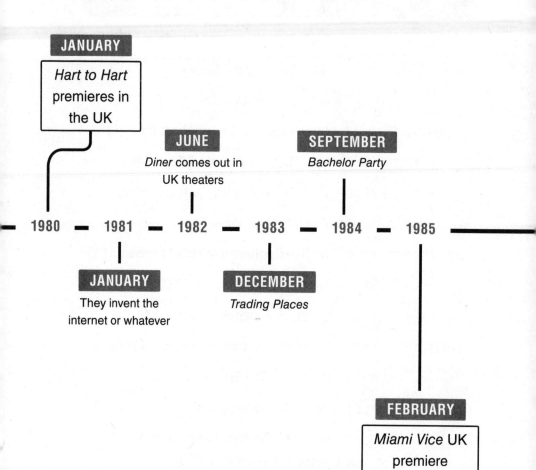

JANUARY

Hart to Hart premieres in the UK

JUNE

Diner comes out in UK theaters

SEPTEMBER

Bachelor Party

1980 — 1981 — 1982 — 1983 — 1984 — 1985

JANUARY

They invent the internet or whatever

DECEMBER

Trading Places

FEBRUARY

Miami Vice UK premiere

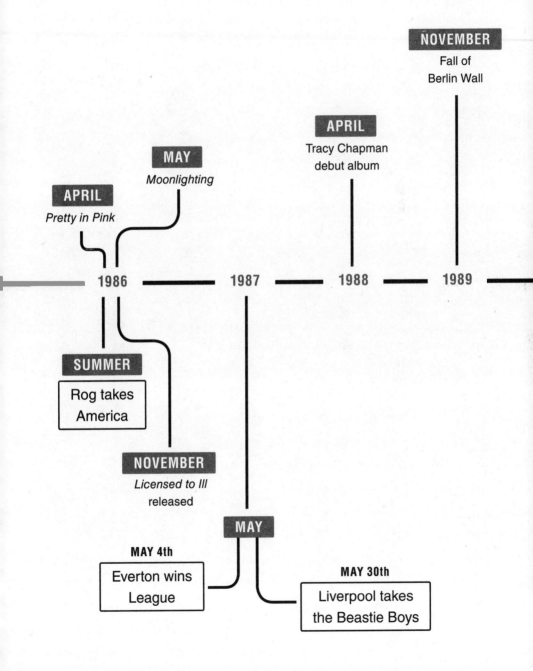

APRIL
Pretty in Pink

MAY
Moonlighting

APRIL
Tracy Chapman
debut album

NOVEMBER
Fall of
Berlin Wall

1986   1987   1988   1989

SUMMER

Rog takes
America

NOVEMBER
Licensed to III
released

MAY

MAY 4th

Everton wins
League

MAY 30th

Liverpool takes
the Beastie Boys

"O, let America be America again—
The land that never has been yet—
And yet must be"

—*Langston Hughes*

"I used to want to be a real man
I don't know what that even means"

—*Jason Isbell*

Of Hot Wings and Fast Cars

I was born, reared, and raised on American soft power. A bloke who grew up in the murk of 1980s England inhaling everything American I could lay my hands on—the movies, television, music, books, clothes, and occasional pair of knock-off Ray-Bans that made the United States my light in the darkness. America existed almost as an alternate planet to me, a place filled with possibility and promise, where life seemed to be lived with a different gravitational pull. One that could not only sustain existence, but empower joy, hope, love, and laughter, even if much of that laughter was clearly of the canned variety.

All of this fueled an inner life that had a substantial influence on my identity. At different times in my youth, I have tried to boost my fragile self-confidence, or at least minimize my deep sense of self-loathing, by persuading myself:

"I am Don Johnson."

"I am Walter Payton."

"I am John Cougar Mellencamp."

"I am the Beastie Boys' Ad Rock."

"I am Tracy Chapman."

Notions I made real in a way, by moving here, and becoming not only a citizen, but a gent who in his own mind loves

America more than Bruce Springsteen loves America. Someone who adores nothing more than to travel across this great nation, reveling in every regionally specific hot chicken wing, barbecued rib, or corn dog it can provide. New York. Louisville. Charlottesville. Nashville. I savor all the 'villes.

I know some of this will sound trite. A love of a nation based on the largely fictional stories, images, and myths it peddled about itself. Having lived in the United States for more than half my life now, I am keenly aware that *The Love Boat, Pretty in Pink*, and *Miami Vice* are not the real America. I also understand the real America has flaws, like every nation. But that knowledge does not diminish the awesome power these images held over me as I was growing up, because they were so vastly different from the grim everyday reality I was exposed to. This was the power I acted upon, moving here, shaping my life, and changing my family's destiny.

All of this feels almost implausible now from the perspective of the America in which I now write. Over the past year, the coronavirus pandemic, Black Lives Matter movement, and the toxicity of the 2020 election have created the impression we are a nation that is divided, chaotic, and racked by fear. I reeled upon reading a Pew Foundation study that discovered only 46 percent of Western Europeans currently hold a favorable view of the United States. At a time when the world cries out for the kind of global leadership that once enchanted me, America's soft power has imploded.

Months lived in lockdown give plenty of time for the mind to wander. I have spent a lot of mine digging deep into memories of an era when the United States felt very different. Looking on from across the ocean, the United States appeared to me a beacon of such courage, tenacity, and wonder that it changed everything I thought was possible about the world, and gave me the confidence to chase those possibilities with the passion Tracy Chapman once sang about fast cars. As such, this book is a love letter to America, a place that has played roughly the same role in my life as ballet dancing did for Billy Elliot. It is also an investigation into whether it is possible to be what you are not, to be shaped throughout adolescence by a country you have never set foot in.

Ultimately, I attempted to write this book in the spirit of the love, hope, and optimism I believe will prevail. I came of age with the Stars and Stripes and the Manhattan skyline painted as a mural on my bedroom wall and ended up moving here. I still believe the act of becoming an American citizen is the single greatest achievement of my life. I now live on the Upper West Side of New York City. On my dining room wall is a photo of my great-grandfather Harris, clad in the uniform of the Russian army, in which he had been forced to serve. He is the man who had first boarded a boat believing he was setting sail for the United States, only to end up in Liverpool, England, by mistake, setting off my family's obsession with the United States. Alongside it is another photograph, a black-and-white image of a thick-necked, savage-looking bloke whom family lore has as my great-great-great-grandfather. No one can remember his name. The photograph used to be one of dozens that graced my grandfather Sam's living room. I loved to point to it when I was a kid and listen to my grandfather tell me all he knew about this man, the sum of which amounted to "He was the one who once fended off a murderous Cossack to save our family. He was 'the Cossack Killer.'"

My greatest hope is that in five generations' time, my NBC network head shot will similarly hang on one of my descendants' dining room walls. They will look up occasionally during family meals shared together and when asked, point at it with mouths still full. "We can't remember his name," they'll say, "but we do know he's the one who first moved the family to the United States of America."

Roger Bennett
New York City
December 2020

A Room Full of Strangers

NEW YORK CITY, MARCH 8, 2018

The drabbest of surroundings can often conjure the most magical of scenes.

I say this to myself as I slump into a cracked plastic seat in the bowels of a government building in the southern tip of New York City along with close to four hundred other unfortunates. A veritable United Nations of races, ethnicities, backgrounds, and classes. All of us are at different points of the patience-grinding bureaucratic labyrinth that is the United States citizenship process.

U.S. Citizenship and Immigration Services' waiting rooms are designed to control people who have to wait a very, very long time. Practical. Functional. Purpose-built to numb the senses and control and command through boredom. Every room smells of stale sweat and cleaning product. Each is a different shade of shabby beige, broken up only by the reds, whites, and blues of the randomly scattered eagle-filled posters screaming "Securing America's Promise" battling for attention alongside those that bark "No Cell Phones" in handwritten Sharpie.

Although there are several hundred people waiting, the entire room is almost silent. There is the sound of muted feet on government-issue linoleum. A can of soda clattering out of some nearby vending machine. A pencil being ground in an automatic sharpener. Despite the humdrum vibe, there is a palpable feeling of nerves and fear. To be a visitor in this room is to have survived countless rounds of interviews, background checks, and fingerprinting biometrics in the two years or more of the American citizenship process. We are so close to our personal promised land, yet as everyone is intensely aware, one mistake, slip of the tongue, or wrong answer and it could all end.

I am, I hope, at the last step of the naturalization process, the Citizenship Test, and have been ushered into an antechamber cordoned off from the bigger waiting room, a holy of holies open to the dozen or so candidates who are similarly at the final stages. I am wearing a suit and tie in a craven effort to project as much polish as is humanly possible while being perched on an orange plastic seat, alongside two fellow applicants—a pair of Mexican gents in grease-stained chef smocks, one sporting a hairnet, as they whisper, giggle, and occasionally take turns to knuckle-punch each other's biceps. We all snap to attention the moment a harried-looking, plump Department of Homeland Security employee lollops into the room. He reaches the doorway, and after slowly pulling out a lectern that had been hidden there, wedges himself in behind it. "De Roon . . . Leenaert De Roon" he calls out, while flicking lazily through a sheaf of papers.

Behind me, a pair of elderly Belgians struggle to their feet in unison and shuffle forward toward the lectern from the back of the room. One sports a well-worn, slightly faded black beret, the other a fraying purple scarf, bedecked with the logo of Belgian football club Anderlecht. The jaded caseworker cannot mask his impatience as they amble in his direction. "Leenaert De Roon?" he inquires again in a weary tone that causes the beret wearer to speed up his step and, in a thick Flemish-accented English, intercede on his compatriot's behalf. "He speak only the Flemish," he explains.

"Can you translate?" snarls the caseworker impatiently.

"Ja," the old man nods.

"Okay. Tell him to put his right hand over his heart and repeat after me."

The old Belgian does as he is told and the caseworker begins.

"Leenaert De Roon of Anderlecht, Belgium. You have completed the naturalization process and will now be sworn in as a citizen of the United States of America."

Those last fourteen words totally transform the energy in the room. All eyes immediately lock onto the scene unfolding before us. I had been feverishly reviewing the answers to Citizenship Test questions that stumped me the night before, but in an instant stopped whispering "Benjamin Franklin was also the nation's first postmaster general," and "the number of amendments that have been proposed to the Constitution is thirty-three." A Sikh student pulls his eyes away from his geophysics textbook. An African mother in beautiful colors tilts her head to the side. Even the Mexican boys call a truce on their play fight and stare.

After clearing his throat dramatically, the caseworker begins the Oath of Allegiance with a flourish. "I hereby declare, on oath, that I absolutely and entirely renounce and abjure all allegiance and fidelity to any foreign prince, potentate, state, or sovereignty . . ." then pauses to allow beret-Belgian to whisper into his companion's ear and translate.

"Ik verklaar hierbij, onder ede, dat ik absoluut en volledig afstand doe van alle loyaliteit en trouw aan elke buitenlandse prins, potentaat, staat of heerschap . . ." wizened purple-scarf guy declares, seeming, almost magically, to stand a little taller with every word.

The immigration caseworker's demeanor also changed. It was as if, for him, the Oath of Allegiance is a beloved song on a classic oldies radio station. No longer fatigued, he begins to deliver his lines with an oaky baritone timber.

"I take this obligation freely," he sings with heft, enjoying every possible drawn-out syllable until he comes to the final phrase . . . "So help me God."

For a beat, there is an awkward silence. Something so human and profound has just occurred, but in a room full of strangers. The caseworker is by now totally committed.

"Yes, you should clap," he says, summoning a solemn tone befitting of the moment.

And we do. Every single one of us. Bonded in our shared desire to become American.

A tough-looking Eastern European fellow clutching a man purse is the first. Everyone quickly follows suit. As that applause becomes a standing ovation, the old man turns around and faces us. Abashed at first, but then, like a veteran flyweight boxer who has survived a grueling twelve rounds and been awarded the decision, he slowly raises his hands above his head and begins to punch the air with his thin, frail arms. As he does so, a single tear runs down his cheek and I realize I am crying, too. I want what he just received—American citizenship—to my very core.

And then a voice rings out from the reception's public address system. "Bennett . . . Roger Bennett . . . Citizenship Test. Room Forty-Two."

BOOK ONE

THE DARKNESS/ ENGLISH ROG

LIVERPOOL, ENGLAND, 1980–1984

"Stars hide your fires; let not light
see my black and deep desires."

—*Macbeth*

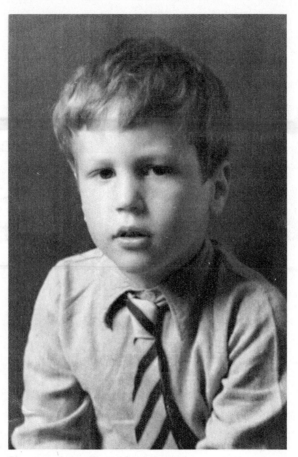

Six years of age. Braced for darkness.

CHAPTER ONE

Amber Waves of . . . Rain

One of the earliest beliefs that I still cling to in life is that I was born an American trapped in an Englishman's body. That is the kind of story you manufacture about yourself when you grow up in a place like Liverpool in the 1980s. Back then, the city was apocalyptic. A rotting, dilapidated carcass in grim decline. When I first watched *Mad Max,* I thought the wasteland Mel Gibson braved appeared like an upgrade in comparison. When you live somewhere like Liverpool, you ask yourself a simple, yet powerful question on an almost daily basis: How on earth did I land here?

There are fewer than three thousand Jews in Liverpool. A gaggle of doctors, accountants, and lawyers with the occasional dentist thrown into the mix for variety. Every family has some variation of a similar explanation to the above question. The tale generally begins with a great-grandparent fleeing whatever inhospitable, frigid, rotting-potato-stenched Eastern European shtetl they had tried to pass off as home, hotfooting it onto the steerage level of an ocean liner. Chased right up to the gangplank, in almost every telling, by a rabid band of Cossacks with murder on their mind. When that vessel stopped briefly to refuel along the way, their ancestors had been among the simpler-minded, dimmer ones who glimpsed the one tall building on the Liverpool skyline and believed they were staring right at New York City, their intended destination. Fatally mistaken, they disembarked and were left to eek out pennies in the English North West, rather than undoubtedly make their fortunes in that promised land filled with bounty and possibility, the United States of America.

The myth was certainly true for my family. My great-grandfather was a kosher butcher from Berdychiv, a textile town in northern Ukraine.

His escape plan was rational: to flee to Chicago, Illinois. A city that made sense for a meat man as it was the self-professed "Hog Capital of the World." Liverpool not so much. A paucity of clients made it hard to earn a living as a kosher meat whole-saler. Improvisation was necessary, which ultimately meant also servicing the need for halal beef among the growing Muslim population scattered across the gloomy declining mill towns of the north of England.

Back then, Liverpool was a place large on lore, low on qual-ity of life. In the high-rolling days of the British Empire, it had indeed been one of the world's great port cities. In the eigh-teenth century the waterfront became a hub of the slave trade, as Liverpool-based vessels stole one and a half million Africans across the Atlantic in unimaginably cruel conditions, while the textiles, coal, guns, and steel once produced in vast quantities across the industrial north were dispatched in the opposite di-rection to pay for them. The banks of the River Mersey became weighed down by warehouses, commercial power, and mercan-tile wealth. Yet the Second World War laid waste to Britain's industrial might and the establishment of Europe instead of the United States as our primary trading partner stripped Liverpool of its geographical raison d'être almost overnight. The docks fell silent. The city spiraled into decline, beset by the degrading forces of unemployment, poverty, and crime, like a British Baltimore without the steamed crabs upside.

Thanks largely to the vicarious prestige cast on the city by the Beatles and its two powerhouse football teams, Liverpool remained well known around the globe despite the general decay of the surroundings, a reality accentuated by the fact that few towns boast more raconteurs, romantics, and deluded self-aggrandizers per square mile. To this day Liverpool remains defiantly proud, a city often quite literally drunk on its own sense of self. Yet no amount of romantic truth-stretching could bring back the hemorrhaging jobs or quell the sense that when you stood still on a street corner, you could witness the industrial carcass of a town actually rotting away before your eyes.

It was amid this sodden wasteland of a city with its moldy terraced housing, drab chip shops, and cheap booze houses that a handful of Jews had accidentally marooned themselves. A land with a low-grade fear hanging over it. A place as dispiriting as the sunless sky and the all-pervasive dampness you could not shake no matter how many layers of clothing you put on.

Certainly, the most infertile ground to sew escape-fueled romantic dreams of freedom, acceptance, and success.

The Jews stayed put because they were exhausted and relieved and, after escaping the Russian bloodlands, had pretty low standards. Any place offering more than immediate death and destruction was an upgrade. And because adaptation is in the DNA of the Jewish people, they always attempt to make sense of the world around them.

I often wondered what early encounters between these bewildered Yiddish speakers and local Liverpudlians must have been like. One group with their spigot of broken Yiddish-inflected English, sounding like a constant moaning complaint. The other snorting Scouse words angrily out of their nasal passages. A local dialect so baffling, it's as if the sentences have somehow been recorded and then replayed backward. One way or another, the new arrivals worked out how to raise their synagogues, open their delis, and break ground on their cemeteries, striking out to pursue the best Britain could offer its accidental citizens—the security of grinding their way to middle-class comfort.

That vaunted middle-class status had been attained by the time I came into the world at Broadgreen Hospital in 1970. My older brother, Nigel, was already two years old. I was given the birth name Roger. There is perhaps no greater sign that we were still a family in search of acceptance than my parents anointing us with the least Jewish names possible. Their unspoken hope was to help us fit in by choosing what they perceived to be the Englishiest, most Christian identities. Yet they were either too eager, oblivious, or willing to overlook that my name was also a synonym for anal sex (as in "Sir Roderick Wigbert Stourton loved to roger his butler"), and perhaps for that reason had long faded out of fashion by the time I was of schooling age. Thus, I was always the only, lonely Roger in a classroom sea of Waynes, Garys, and Jeremies, or as Liverpudlian naming conventions dictated, "Wazzas," "Gazzas," and "Jezzas."

Alas, my name was the least of my challenges. As a Liverpudlian middle-class Jew, I was already an outsider in a working-class, heavily Catholic city that did not cope well with even a whiff of the other. For the first ten years of my life, my best friend was my grandfather Samuel Polak, who lived right across the road from us with my grandmother Rita in the house they had raised my mum in. Almost every night, I would run over the moment

I finished my schoolwork, and spend the evening being doted on in a house that perpetually smelled of chicken soup, honey cake, and the peculiar odor emitted by heavy velvet curtains.

My grandfather Sam was my best mate. We are at the race track here. On my sweatshirt are four Adam and the Ants buttons he'd just bought me with his winnings.

My grandfather continued the family meat line, but grudgingly. I learned not to blame him after accepting an invitation to experience his job for a day. At the abattoir where he plied his trade, I watched him wander into a pen of defeated cattle and insert his fist into one unfortunate cow's anus after another. My grandfather's arm would thrust deep into the animal, disappearing right up to the armpit, a feat that somehow empowered him to assess the ultimate quality of the meat. With a grimace, he would slowly retrieve his limb, and murmur "Good anus" or sometimes "bad cow, that" to a silent, melancholy note-taking assistant before moving on to the next. My grandfather was an intellectually curious, quiet, dapper man. The whole ordeal seemed to make him suffer more than it did the cows.

At home, with slippers on, reclining on a throne-like mahogany and leather couch in his living room, my grandfather was altogether more content. We would play game after game of chess. Evenly matched, the two of us were a great pair. I was hungry for company. He was eager to talk about the things that really interested him. With a pot of tea and an endless supply of chocolate-covered digestives to dunk into our cups between us, we would engage in serious man talk about the important things in life: war movies, history books, and Everton Football Club. My nightly goal was to relax my grandfather sufficiently so I could coax him into telling me the stories of his life as an infantryman during the war. Startling tales about shooting at, or being shot at, by Germans, whom he referred to as "Jerries," during the Siege of El Alamein, an experience he generally preferred to keep to himself.

But by far his favorite topic of conversation was the United States of America. Or rather, recounting random memories born of his frequent pilgrimages to the American shores. This was the destination my grandfather had repeatedly traveled to for vacations since the 1950s, an intrepid decision back in an era when British vacationers rarely ventured far from home. The way he described it, he had felt compelled to journey to those gold-paved streets his father had once dreamed of moving to, like a sockeye salmon programmed by nature to swim upstream and spawn.

These adventures started way before transatlantic flight was a regular facet of travel life. Alongside the couch, on a small matching side table on which he placed his most vital lounging items—a packet of Senior Service cigarettes, a family-sized slab of Cadbury's Fruit & Nut chocolate, and a brick-sized, primitive television remote control—was a black-and-white photograph of him bound for New York City, standing proudly beside a plucky propeller plane, refueling in some remote snow-filled airfield in Goose Bay, Labrador, or Gander, Newfoundland, clad in the same trilby hat and three-piece suit he wore to the slaughterhouse.

The instant the topic turned to America, the chess game was forgotten. My grandfather would sit back, cigarette in hand, and the tales flowed as if he had entered a fever dream. Fragments of memory from expeditions to Florida, New York, California, and all points in between would tumble out of his mouth. "Did you know in Vegas, they serve you breakfast *while* you play the slot machines?" he would say with an undiminished sense of astonishment. Or "In Times Square, there are diners where they refill your coffee cups the second you have finished them." Or "Miami is a land *filled* with Jews, and the restaurants grill steaks that are bigger than the plate that carries them." There were stories of plenty, of service, of perceived luxury and wonder from a land that still seemed as magical, distant, and exotic to me from the perspective of 1970s Liverpool as it had to my Cossack-fleeing ancestors at the turn of the century.

Indeed, as he spoke, many of those relatives would stare down at us from their vantage point in heavy-framed sepia-tinged photographs on the walls around the room. Formal turn-of-the-century portraits of sickly-looking groups gazing austerely at a Ukrainian photographer, or head shots of terrified-looking uniformed teenage boys who had been forcibly conscripted into the Russian army. Scattered between these heirlooms, though, was an arsenal of tourist trinkets. Once his stories had picked up a sufficient head of steam, my grandfather would incorporate them into the telling as visual aids with a dramatic flourish.

With eyes frantically scanning the room he would locate a tin tray, proclaiming "Golden Nugget Casino, Vegas," and stab his cigarette toward it while beginning a tale about a spectacular evening spent watching Sammy Davis Jr. in concert. The pottery ashtray with "Virginia Is for Lovers" glazed into the rim could trigger a rumination about either a walk across Civil War battlefields, or a particularly unforgettable "kosher" hot dog he had procured from the snack bar. To my grandfather, these and countless other objects in his collection were no mere tchotchkes. Their importance lay in the sense memory they triggered, and he afforded them the reverence archaeologists bestow upon Stone Age relics.

Pride of place was reserved for a miniature Statue of Liberty replica made of diecast metal, which sat on the mantel above the fireplace alongside a similar souvenir of the Empire State Building. My grandfather treated it with the pride I imagine explorer Francisco Pizarro afforded to the first potato he had sailed back from the Americas to present to the Spanish court in 1532. Such was its power that even though my grandpa carried some girth—an adorable potbelly stomach honed over many hours spent watching television on the couch—one look at Lady Liberty would compel him to spring up to his feet so we could marvel upon her together. After sweeping it off the mantel into his meaty hand, Grandpa would shunt his spectacles back onto his forehead, squint his eyes, and read the inscription on the base in a unique English accent that combined inflections of both Yiddish and Scouse. "Give me your tired, your poor, your huddled masses yearning to breathe free," he'd slowly intone. "The wretched refuse of your teeming shore." We would then stand together in a reverent silence. A grandparent, a grandson, and a cheap tourist souvenir, contemplative until my grandfather would inevitably whisper, "We should have lived there."

Because of those shared moments, I loved that statue and worked to bless it with the kind of covetous gaze that let a grandparent know a grandchild wanted it for himself, an unspoken request to which my grandfather ultimately relented. But back when it was still a fixture on his fireplace, my grandfather would eventually drag himself back to the sanctuary of his couch with heavy legs. After taking out his false front teeth and placing them on his side table, he would chew meditatively on a packet of nougats in silence until he dozed off, head tilted to the left, with mouth ajar.

I would gaze at him across the chessboard with its game unfinished and wonder what he could be dreaming about in those moments.

With our evening clearly over, it was time to head home. I would locate my grandmother baking somewhere in her kitchen, kiss her goodbye, and skip across Menlove Avenue, a once grand, yet still well-trafficked road that separated my home from my grandparents'. The central divide was pockmarked by oily puddles filled with orphaned crisp packets and crushed, empty beer cans. I trooped through them, most often in a light drizzling rain, past leafless beech trees whose trunks had been brutalized by penknife-wielding vandals unable to resist the urge to carve "Jez luvs Caz B" or "MANCHESTER DIE!" into the bark.

Once back home, I would quickly pop my head into the living room, where my family would inevitably be glued to the television; I preferred to charge upstairs into my room and voluntarily put myself to bed. After hauling a giant volume from my bookshelf, I would lie under the covers, alone with my copy of *Alistair*

Cooke's America, a grand, hardback tome that my grandfather had gifted me for my seventh birthday. The book traced the arc of America's history from founding to present day. I mostly loved it because it was identical to the one my grandfather kept by his own bed.

Under the warm glow of my bedside light, I would flip through the pages, ignoring the words and feasting on the color plates. While staring at a stock photograph of an empty highway in the middle of Utah, I'd hear my grandfather's voice from nights when we had savored the book together. "Look at that road," he'd marvel. "Now, that's a road." The image titled "Bison in Montana" would remind me of him gasping "That's a big unit," a comment that automatically conjured images of him ill-advisedly attempting to drive his arm up the bison's anus. Quickly turning to "Farmland in Kansas" I could hear his voice filled with longing. "Have you ever seen such wheat, Rog?"

CHAPTER TWO

Spaghetti Scarlet Letter

My parents were best understood whenever they recounted their respective dreamlives. My father, Ivor, loved to initiate conversation about this topic at the breakfast table first thing in the morning. He would excitedly lower the newspaper, behind which he typically shut out the rest of the world, and ask out loud to no one in particular: "Do any of you have a recurring dream where you are able to fly, glide up over the city, and soar into the clouds?" He would then pause wide-eyed, brows furrowed for effect, and add, "It's simply marvelous."

Before my brother and I could barely even have begun to process the question, my mother, Valerie, would respond from her traditional position, standing by the side of the table in her dressing gown and slippers, weighed down by an iron skillet filled with scrambled eggs that she was ladling onto everyone's plates but her own. "The only recurring dream I have is where I am falling," she would mutter. "Falling without stopping. Tumbling out of the sky."

As in dreamlife, so in reality. My father and mother were a devoted unit, composed of two very different, almost opposing parts. My dad was a naive, eternal optimist who had stubbornly clung to a sense of English middle-class decency that had long been kicked out of most Liverpudlians by the city's postwar economic implosion. For my father, that decency was epitomized by a golden vision of Britain as empire and an absolute commitment to the Protestant work ethic that was surprising for a Jewish gent. In Ivor Bennett's mind, questioning authority ranked somewhere between pillaging and serial killing in a man's moral code. His entire life revolved around a passion for rule-following, a value he had ultimately managed to monetize by becoming a judge. It was a profession from which he derived immense personal pride, reveling in the arcane detail of the British legal system and the sense of moral integrity the duty of judging others refracted back upon him.

Dad believed in working hard, and playing hard, relying on an eclectic set of classically English hobbies—bird watching, stamp collecting, model railroading, and winemaking—to fill the crevasses of downtime in his weekend. Never happier than when drinking a rare Lapsang Souchong tea, he used perpetual action to avoid having to contemplate life's complex nuances that he could not tolerate.

As my father was almost entirely consumed by his own passions—whether they related to a complex legal argument, the relative merits of 1960s vintage Bordeaux, or the breeding habits of the white-cheeked bullfinch—my mother was his perfect mate. She was an adoring, faithful homemaker drawn to service, suffering, and sacrifice. Mum was rarely more fulfilled than when attending a friendless stranger's funeral, caring for an elderly neighbor by volunteering to clean out their surgically implanted feeding tube, or breaking awkward silences in our house by offering to put the kettle on and make some tea. One of her cardinal rules in life was to avoid saying a bad word about anybody—a commitment that meant she spoke in code. If my mother credited someone with having a "heart of gold" or said that they "mean well" it was her way of saying they were truly shitty human beings.

The two had grown up as next-door neighbors. The eight-year age difference between them, though initially chasmic, was slowly eroded by the passage of time until it was appropriate for them to begin courting the moment my mother turned seventeen. That was marrying age back then in 1960s Liverpool. Family lore has it that after nine months of romancing, my impatient grandfather, Sam, became anxious my mother would be "left on the shelf" if no proposal was imminent. So, when my father came round to pick her up on a routine date, he was intercepted at the doorstep by the father of his girlfriend gruffly throwing down an ultimatum:

"You're either going to marry Valerie, or you are going to break up with her."

My father, who never did anything in life rashly, without the aid of vast amounts of research and several copies of *Consumer Reports*, chose the latter option. I spent many hours as a kid wondering how devastated my mother must have been in that moment, powerless at having her future so crudely negotiated on her behalf. Yet my father merely proceeded to date at a dizzying clip until twenty-four months later, when word spread across the Liverpool Jewish grapevine that one of his rivals had proposed to my mum. It was a moment of reckoning that compelled young Ivor to speed round to her home in his bachelor-cliché MG convertible. I always imagined him screeching into her driveway with a handbrake turn, leaving the sports car's engine running, as he charged into the house and found my mum (most probably in the vicinity of the kitchen) before dropping to one knee and breathlessly pleading, "Don't marry Victor! Marry me!"

The two were wed within seven months, on October 26, 1966, which also happened to be my mother's twenty-first birthday. This was a symbolically fitting act for our family's origin story: from the very beginning, my mum surrendering individual joy to the good of the collective. My dad eventually traded the roadster for a family car, as the two settled into a detached house on Calder Drive, a quiet street straddling the border between the Jewish neighborhood of Childwall and the slightly more aspirational area of Allerton, a block away from the homes they had grown up in.

My mum and dad circa 1966. Regretfully, I inherited my dad's hairline, not my mum's.

Like the majority of middle-class Jewish abodes I ever set foot in as a kid, our home was warm, functional, and an explosion of early seventies decor, leaning heavily on umber and avocado floral wallpaper, macramé knickknacks, and pendant lighting. By Liverpool standards, our house was comfortable, yet my parents' decision to send both my brother and me to private school strained family finances. We had just one television in the Bennett household, a giant, boxy set, with matte teak finish. It weighed a ton. I knew that because there were two rooms we watched it in: our den (which in England is starchily known as "the morning room") on weekdays, and our more formal, fancy "lounge" for weekend use. Rather than shell out the extra cash to purchase a second television for both environs, my parents simply mounted the appliance on wheels and forced my brother and me to push the box between rooms every Friday night.

Once our cumbersome nemesis had successfully been dragged into the lounge, my family, eternal creatures of habit, would take our assigned seats. My brother and I recovered from our toil in a pair of armchairs positioned on either side of a chessboard with heavy brass pieces. My mother splayed out on the couch utterly exhausted, a position from which she would drift between waking and sleep states. My father liked to sit stiffly upright in his rocking chair, holding a copy of the *Daily Telegraph* out in front. I would stare at the two of them. Even at rest, they remained a study in contrast. My father was an impatient man, quick to fury. My mother was filled with love and always struggled to give me the benefit of the doubt. As such, she acted as my moral guide. While Dad tended to blow up at every minor infraction, only when my behavior caused my mum to break down was it the indicator I had truly and severely transgressed the bounds of socially acceptable norms and needed to dial myself back. To this day, few things reduce me to tears quicker than witnessing my mother cry. A point of no return at which she would unleash her go-to phrase of disappointment in me, the gut punch of "you are worse than a murderer" from in between sobs, as she sped off toward the healing sanctuary only a bath filled with bubbles can provide.

In times of crisis like these, I would always turn to my brother, Nigel, for counsel. He was two years older than me, and coincidentally, also the coolest person I knew in real life. Nige was everything I was not. Whereas I was short, impulsive, and mouthy, he was tall, artistic, and a master withholder, able to control social situations with an unnerving silence, which combined with his carefully cultivated haircut, a floppy fringe that he kept flicked over one eye, to give him an air of self-possessed mystery. A shrewd operator, Nige always knew how to handle my parents, mostly by keeping them an arm's length from his inner life at all times. He achieved this by maintaining a catlike silence at family gatherings, while also quietly goading me to cross the line. It was a masterful double-pronged strategy guaranteed to pay off, my inevitable misbehavior acting as a smoke screen for whatever misdeeds he quietly wanted to indulge in.

Older brothers can coast through life like that. Little brothers not so much. In many families, a single story often cements your entire place in family lore. Mine was "The Night of the Plate of Dropped Spaghetti." A borderline national catastrophe struck one evening when I was seven or eight years of age. I had been casually tasked by my mother with taking a plate of steaming spaghetti Bolognese from the stove to my seat at the dinner table. An epic journey from pot to my Queen Elizabeth Silver Jubilee Souvenir placemat. Twenty-seven steps. Somewhere on that brave odyssey, with my little legs churning, and hand sinews straining to keep the plate balanced, I must have tilted the pasta at a perilous angle, inviting the still-oily concoction to slide clean off. One second, my plate bore a feast fit for an

Emilian prince. The next, the dish had rearranged itself, meat first, all over the beige carpeting. "Ohhhh Roger," my mother groaned as if she had just witnessed me crash the family car, or accidentally push an old man onto a track in the London Underground.

From that moment on, this story defined me in my family's eyes. It was constantly introduced as evidence of my inherent inability to meet any responsibility or to reinforce how unreliable, flaky, or physically incompetent I was. For years, and I mean *years*—one of my parents even incorporated the story into their toast at my engagement party—if a plan was discussed in which the notion of me playing a lead role was floated, the case of the spilled spaghetti was inevitably resurfaced to quash that idea. As in:

"Shall we have Roger do it . . . ?"

"No, he'll drop it/lose it/forget to do it. Remember the Bolognese?"

It did not surprise me I could never shake this spaghetti-inflected Scarlet Letter. As anyone who knows my family would acknowledge, Bennetts are quick to judge and slow to forgive. If remembering slights and human wrongdoing was an Olympic pursuit, we would definitely medal. We cling to perceived insults like other families treasure happy memories. My grandfather Sam had three brothers and four sisters and fell out with all of them over minor personal and business grievances. As a kid I accompanied him to the funeral of the second oldest, whom he had not spoken to in nearly forty years. He wept all the way on the drive home. I asked him why they fell out in the first place. "Can't remember," he muttered. I asked him if he regretted that, and the blood flowed back into his face as he perked up and said, "Never, Rog. Hate with reason!" He paused at a stoplight, turned to me, and added, ". . . and always make sure you write that reason down."

Hence, that plate of Bolognese hounded me through life. Yet, I have often wondered how my world would have been different—my family's sense of me, my persona, and ultimately my self-image—if that plate had made it safely table-side without incident and not ended up facedown on the nylon carpet fibers, soaking in and permanently staining them.

So that morning, after my dad wondered if anyone had ever dreamed about flying, I did not answer. I had fantasized about neither soaring nor falling. The only recurring dream I ever had was of meat-based tomato sauce and slender strings of flailing pasta tumbling through space in agonizing slow motion, and an awareness I was powerless to stop it.

CHAPTER THREE

Bullshit Baffles Brains

Your 1982 Liverpool College chess champion.

I was schooled at Liverpool College for Gentlemen, a centuries-old, all-boys institution that was the last bastion of traditional English values in a city that had decayed around it. My father, the consummate conformist, had enjoyed many of his most treasured childhood moments within the College's strict confines. As an adult he was willing to invest an enormous chunk of disposable income to ensure my brother and I received a similar moral education. Yet the school had barely changed since he left. Nor had the cane-wielding faculty. And so, my experience was akin to being locked inside an educational Grey Gardens. Within the College's walls, the Churchillian spirit lived on: England still had an empire, the monarch was beloved, and all boys were to be seen and not heard as they strictly followed orders. Any challenge to one of these "truths" would quickly earn the violator a savage thrashing of the bare buttocks courtesy of a teacher armed with a bamboo cane, cricket bat, or whatever aide de memoire was to hand.

Despite the frequent spankings, Liverpool College prided itself as being an oasis of civility within a city that was a seething cauldron of vice, a fact we were reminded of whenever we dared venture from the safe confines of our school's ivied buildings and lush playing fields. The formal college-blazer-and-tie uniforms we were forced to wear singled us out for a kicking at the hands of agitated oppressors from the surrounding educational institutions. When out in the open, fear and habit taught us to move only in packs.

My dad during his College days. A sepia-tinged, nobler time and the high-water mark for cravat wearing.

Back in the more innocent days when my dad had attended the College, the pupils were Liverpool's best and brightest, the vaunted sons of the region's merchants, bankers, and privileged fleshy wallets, eager to immerse themselves in the Latin, Greek, and classics education on offer, while striving for glory on both rugby field and cricket pitch.

By the time I rolled around, the school's hefty fees meant the student body was a motley crew comprising the sons of the few who could still afford it: the dying embers of the city's receding well-off; successful local gangsters and nightclub owners hungry for legitimacy they believed the College conferred; the local Nigerian consulate-general, who had government oil money to burn; and Chinese, Asians, and Jews—first-generation chip shop owners, curry house proprietors, and accountants—whose ethnic traditions meant they would sacrifice everything to invest in the best education available for their children. Or in our case, to attend a school where we were commonly referred to as "Chinks, Pakis, and Yids" for the duration of our educational experience.

Those insults were just a tiny particle of the overall sense of menace that hung over all of us like the hole in the ozone layer. There was the enduring threat from the world outside. Local schoolkids lurked on the other side of the school's walls like mutant zombies who seemingly lived just to pick off College stragglers. I once had the misfortune to play cricket in the outfield of a pitch that ran alongside the road marking the College's perimeter, making me the perfect target for rocks flung by miscreants from the local Catholic school. My terror at the prospect of incoming fire from either side—a cricket ball from the field, or a stone from the rear guard—was paralyzing until Jez Knight, the son of a local midlevel gangster, a boy who was essentially no different than the stone-throwers, swooped in alongside me. He picked up one of the rocks and hurled it back whence it came with astounding velocity, while bellowing, "Fuck off, youse," in his Liverpool accent so thick, it was impervious to the College's best efforts to educate it out of him. "We're rich and you're poor."

But the external threat was nothing compared to that which lurked within. Corporal punishment or "canings" doled out with fury by our teachers were a savage yet accepted part of life. I would estimate that approximately two-fifths of the conversations I shared with school friends between second and seventh grade related to the same long-running debate that bordered upon the theological: Was it better to be punished by a regular disciplinarian or a weaker tutor who rarely waved a cane in anger? I was of the firm opinion that it was preferable to be thrashed by an experienced beater like Mr. Bosworth, a biology teacher, who dispensed up to a dozen spankings a day, with seething yet expertly controlled blows from a metal ruler whose precision limited the damage. True suffering was to have sufficiently goaded a meek teacher like Mr. Weakstone, the aging English master who was rarer to anger but delivered a scatter-shot thrashing up and down your thighs. Yes, some blows would miss altogether, but others would land haphazardly with an unbridled, uncontrolled fury, unleashed at what felt like the risk of accidental manslaughter.

The everyday barbarity emanating from the faculty infected the entire school culture, one that made the challenge of the *Lord of the Flies* desert island survival seem relatable, and occasionally preferable. School custom dictated we were all called only by our last names. Until I was sixteen, even the first names of the classmates I was closest friends with remained a mystery to me. This was but one dehumanizing step that reduced the entire student body to a sea of body-odor-ridden Smiths, Needham-Joneses, Chans, and Chowdhurys.

Weakness and vulnerability were despised and preyed upon. Even the perception of frailty was unforgivable. A sweet-natured rake of a boy named Brewer once had the misfortune to lay a crap in Phys Ed while attempting a through-vault over a pommel horse. One minute he was an innocuous, relatively popular kid and a solid rugby player to boot. The next, he hit that springboard, placed his hands into correct position on the horse, raised his legs, and to his horror, involuntarily relieved his bowels as his body flew over the gymnastic apparatus.

Full credit: The lad had the accuracy of a B-17 Flying Fortress and was able to deposit a perfect, almost delicate turd pile, dead center atop the leather horse. I initially thought it was stuffing coming out of the aging equipment but then the stench of shit hit everyone's nostrils at the same second and the whole class started retching. A humiliated Brewer charged toward the locker room in tears, leaving a snaking trail of turd behind him. He knew full well that his life was over in that moment, and he was right. He lasted less than a year before crumbling in the face of relentless daily teasing, which forced him to leave the school, never to be seen again.

Worse than the violence, though, was the learning. The College's curriculum had last been modernized sometime between the Normandy landings and VE-Day. Our education, combining classics, a military cadet force, and a punishing rugby regimen, was designed to pump out a supply line of midlevel managers, army officers, and local government technocrats who adhered to the values of discipline, blind obedience, and conformity, none of which were my strong suit. While a beleaguered faculty member prattled on about Virgil's *Aeneid* or *Gawain and the Green Knight,* all I wanted to do was listen to my Walkman, watch football, and as soon as I was physically able, masturbate. Preferably all three at the same time.

Our teachers' common room was a Star Wars cantina of humanity, a musty-tweed-blazered gaggle of embittered men whose only commonality was that they had shed the idealism that once propelled them to become educators in the first place. They were all victims of a daily fight to demand respect from a student body who were intuitively aware their teachers had long ago lost their own self-respect.

There was the tiny, bitter, bearded Mr. McCullough, a feared German teacher with a savage temper, known to all as "Pixie." Every pair of shoes Pixie owned squeaked, like an un-oiled door hinge. Just the whine of his footsteps approaching from a nearby hallway was enough to fill even the toughest pupil with a sense of terror and impending doom.

Not every teacher was similarly able to maintain control. Mr. Jowell was a shatteringly depressed chemistry teacher whose nickname, "Dobbin," was perfect because, facially, few humans have ever resembled a horse more. Dobbin spent a daily losing battle to retain his sanity against students who would pour hydrochloric acid on his desk and wait for him to howl in agony the second it began to burn through his skin.

Mr. Stonehead, a computer teacher, had a birthmark covering the right side of his face, which earned him the cruel nickname "Patch," a moniker you could not even dare whisper in his presence without receiving an instant caning. Mr. Stonehead spent much of his life banging away angrily at a keyboard, attempting to teach us rudimentary coding. None of it felt like it was going to change our life, but possibly it would make it a little more fun. We once placed a thumbtack on Patch's chair before class, only to be disappointed once he sat on it without flinching for the next hour of a lecture. As the lesson wrapped up, he calmly explained, "I know you left a nail on my seat, lads. I am also painfully aware that I sat on it. But, if I am stupid enough to fall for that, then I deserve the punishment of suffering as a consequence." He rose from the seat but maintained complete control, aware the masochism of his behavior had given him the upper hand and stunned the entire class into silence. "British officers who survived Second World War prisoner camps teach us that life, lads, is about suffering," he said. "The whole point is the dignity with which you face up to that suffering."

Other teachers terrified us in more tangible ways, most horrifyingly of all Mr. MacDuff, an unkempt 320-pound Scottish gym teacher who stuffed himself into a red Adidas tracksuit that when viewed from behind made him resemble an overcooked bratwurst on the brink of bursting out of its casing. According to the school curriculum, "Porky" MacDuff was responsible for overseeing an array of what were deemed "minor sports"—gymnastics, handball, cross-country running. Yet the only one he ever chose to teach us was his version of wrestling in which he left the entire grade unsupervised, skirmishing on mats in the gym hall, while he took a single handpicked victim—always one of the smaller, blonder pupils—into the adjoining changing rooms to "wrestle" against himself, grinding his enormous, corpulent torso against his overmatched opponent, until a large stain covered the front of his tracksuit pants. Possibly the only good thing about being Jewish at Liverpool College was that MacDuff hated Jews and thus would not want to fuck you.

Yet the damage inflicted by Porky's physical transgressions was outstripped by that doled out by Mr. Stott, the chain-smoking, ruddy-nosed deputy principal who had taught for over fifty years at the College he had attended as a pupil. A life lived in a bubble allowed him to make believe and act as if the world outside the College walls had not changed and that British sea power still ruled the waves.

Peter Stott, known to the pupils as Q.P. or "Queer Pete," a nickname, like the rest, which was inherited without any questioning, was a man who delighted in entering every classroom by barking "Open all available oxygen inlet valves lads, smells like a Turkish brothel in here." His greatest pleasure was to entertain himself by forcing an entire class of eight- or nine-year-olds to memorize First World War poems about being gassed at the Somme, or slaughtered on Flanders Fields, sobbing quietly into a handkerchief as he ordered one boy after another to stand in front of his desk, look him in the eyes, and recite horrific lines about death, sacrifice, and defeat in their high falsetto voices. Occasionally he would snap upright and dispense random nuggets of wisdom, such as "Bollocks! Bolla! Bollum!" or "Bullshit baffles brains, lads, always remember that. Bullshit . . . baffles . . . brains."

Teaching may have been Q.P.'s job, but overt racism was his true avocation. He was an ever-present fixture on the sidelines of the school's senior rugby team, standing stoically amid huddles of college kids, and refusing to wear an overcoat, even in the icy winds of December. Stott rarely emoted, even when the College scored a try. Yet, if the opposing team fielded an Asian pupil, he lived for the moment that kid would leap to catch a high, punted ball as college players descended upon him. "There's a nip in the air, lads!" our deputy principal would shout to his own, very apparent, amusement. "There's a nip in the air!"

By far his favorite party trick was to begin class by commanding the nearest first-generation Pakistani-English pupil to read his book of choice out loud. The book was guaranteed to be literature about the days of empire, be it *A Passage to India* or *The Siege of Krishnapur*. The unfortunate pupil would begin to read earnestly in his Urdu-inflected accent, only for Stott to interrupt him within a minute, gleefully screaming, "Speak English, boy, we are not in Karachi now! No need to make all of this so damned authentic for God's sake," and then inevitably turn to me and bark "You! Jew! Read!" And I would calmly pick up where my classmate had finished off, striving not to flinch so as to give this cane-wielding sadist pleasure.

All of the stories Q.P. would tell of his own college days were variations on one of two themes: being beaten by fellow pupils or beating fellow pupils. It was clear this man had tortured the lives of hundreds of boys, just as his own life had been tortured by his teachers back when he was a pupil in the 1930s. As I read those chapters with their cloying themes of colonialism and British triumph out loud, I did so with a heart that rooted desperately for the natives to wise up, rise up, and destroy their Anglo overseers, and throw off the soul-crushing yoke of empire.

CHAPTER FOUR

Feathered Hair Fantasies

How exactly did I survive? The human capacity to endure is remarkable. I knew that fact to be true because as a kid I loved to spend hours in the local library, immersed in a musty, crisp-paged volume entitled *The Will to Survive*, a book that transfixed me for its tales of tenacious Argentinian rugby players who ate their own teammates for nourishment after a plane crash in a remote part of the Andes, or sailors lost at sea for 436 days who were forced to devour their own fingernails to fend off hunger. Yes, Liverpool College occasionally made the prospect of being left for dead on a small boat in a large ocean and having to feast on your digits seem a more appealing option. But I learned to persist by finding happiness in the crevices: in debate club, where I could summon a fleeting burst of delight by making the case "This house believes ABBA are the greatest band ever"; on the school chess team, where I could lose myself through the release of the psychological battle to the death across the board; and through friends.

"Friends" is a slight exaggeration. I only had one true friend: Jamie Glassman, not coincidentally, the only other Jewish boy in my grade. He was a joyous, warm, curly-haired, chunky kid who was like a Care Bear in human form. Fate had brought us together as seven-year-olds on our very first day at the College. And by fate, I mean his inability to keep his lunch down. The nerves and anxiety inherent in all the disorienting newness that overwhelmed us had made him puke back up an entire plate of stew, carrots, and sprouts, all of which reemerged in large stocky chunks all over the polished wooden floor of the austere dining room.

Our class teacher, Mrs. Chadwick, a sour lady of undeterminable age, did not flinch as one of her new charges doubled over and retched a waterfall of green and orange cubes in her vicinity. She ignored his suffering and merely moved to damage mitigation, turning to the rest of the class to inquire, "Which of you pupils is a responsible boy?"—a question to which a class of anxious, barely post-toddlers desperate to prove their worth are almost programmed to raise their hands. We all fought for her attention, straining our arms skyward. To my nervous surprise, Mrs. Chadwick zoned in on me. "You, Bennett," she said, with thin lips quavering in an effort to suppress a smile. "There is a shovel and brush in the kitchen. Go back there, ask the janitor where to find it, and sweep up Glassman's detritus." She added under her breath, "You are, after all, both Jews," spitting out that last word in a style similar to the way Jamie had his Brussels sprouts minutes earlier.

Thus introduced, a lifelong friendship was born, one that though forged in vomit and casual racism, soon flourished. The two of us signed up to run the school's break-time candy store together, slinging Mars Bars, Smarties, and packets of Smokey Bacon crisps to the great unwashed—our fellow pupils—who would push, shove, and grunt their way to a table packed with our wares.

We volunteered to do this partially because it gave us the

opportunity to pocket more candy than could rot a thousand teeth, and because it offered us precious time alone, away from the muck of the student body, during setup. Behind our shop's yet-to-open doors, we could talk openly and freely. There was laughter at Liverpool College but most of it was cruel, aimed savagely at others' weaknesses. Alone, Jamie had an inner sweetness and almost celebrated his own shortcomings due to a radical willingness to make jokes at his own expense, a trait that would have been fatal if expressed openly.

Our conversations were animated by a singular passion we both shared: Americana. A love affair forged at an early age by the works of a shared foundational text: the Richard Scarry books. A classic series of brightly illustrated hardbacks written and created by this fine gent who dedicated his life to portraying the jobs, and stores, and cars of everyday American life carried out in detailed cityscapes populated not by humans, but by anthropomorphized animals. In such epic masterpieces as *Busy, Busy Town*, wide-eyed dogs, cats, raccoons, bears, owls, wolves, and leopards would go about their working day in groceries, butchers, and hardware stores on Main Street.

The collective effect of these books was to project a vision of the United States that emanated a joyous sense of harmony and unity. Richard Scarry drew Wolf and Sheep firemen working happily side by side polishing their truck in the warmth of their firehouse. Dr. Lion expressing a calm yet loving concern as he took Lowly Worm's temperature in his office. Perhaps above all, from an English perspective, the allure of Richard Scarry's world was the weather. A perpetual autumn—leaves were always being raked—that Rockwellian glow. What an inviting contrast to the frigid, deflating sogginess of Liverpool.

The golden hues of Richard Scarry's Busytown were just a

gateway drug leading us to television. For context, understand this: All of the British shows we came of age with could be filed into one of two categories. Grim and Grimmer. There were three massive English soap operas that captivated the nation in the 1980s. *Eastenders* depicted working-class struggles in London. *Coronation Street* reveled in its characters' working-class struggles near Manchester. *Brookside* followed the struggles in a working-class neighborhood in Liverpool. Each one was a vicarious tour of working-class misery, sadder than the last. The value proposition the three shows offered their massive viewership was essentially this: "No matter how depressing and hopeless your life is, Dear Viewer, just watch half an hour of this relentless misery and you will feel better about your own reality."

It was into this milieu that a wave of American prime-time soaps crashed onto our television screens and consciousness: *Dallas* and *Dynasty*. In stark contrast to their turgid, poverty-ridden English counterparts, they depicted lives lived around opulence, abundance, and luxury, where problems were caused by having too much money and there not being enough oil wells, silk lingerie, or crystal chandeliers in the world to spend it on. Watching them catalyzed an unusual brew of emotions deep inside me. In contrast to the English soaps, which were designed to foster an unconscious sense of superiority in the viewer, these American shows made me experience something between coveting and aspiration.

Dallas and *Dynasty* proved merely to be the amuse-bouche for a plethora of G-rated comedy-adventure series on which we truly feasted. *Fantasy Island* was first, a series about utopian escape where guests lived out their greatest desires for one weekend within the safe confines of a luxe resort. A nondescript man wanted to become irresistible to every woman he encountered.

At home, watching Everton lose against Liverpool
while recovering from a black eye and concussion.
A rugby injury.

A wealthy businesswoman dreams of being a secret, silent ob-
server at her own funeral. An elderly couple long to drink from
the fountain of youth. No matter their fantasy, the life lesson
gleaned from almost every episode saw the guests leaving the
mysterious island armed with a renewed appreciation for their
real life, which, in my mind, was the only unbelievable aspect
of the show. A narrative weakness was more than offset by the
dizzying performance of tiny star Hervé Villechaize, who played
Tattoo, the number two at the resort, whose job appeared to
consist of ringing a bell when the seaplane bearing new arrivals landed and listening patiently as the visitors described their

desires. He attacked the role with an enthusiasm for life I had to admire.

Jamie and I also revered *The Love Boat*, the nautical series that employed a similar conceit to *Fantasy Island*, lived out on the high seas. Every week, new passengers would check in on board to experience the doting care of a zany crew, bringing as much emotional baggage as they did actual luggage, all of which they would unpack over the course of the ensuing hour. Whether they were grappling with loneliness, crumbling relationships, or the hunger for an affair, the wound would be neatly healed while visiting secluded lagoons, white-sand beaches, and exotic ports of call, all of which radiated a sense of mobility, possibility, and escape.

My mum adored watching *Love Boat* along with me. When the show's perky theme song kicked in to signal the end of an episode, she could not help herself from emitting a sigh that was both appreciative and wistful in equal measure. I once asked her what she liked about the *Love Boat*. She thought for a moment, then said, "The 'let go of your inhibitions' attitude sea life seems to encourage." I asked her what "inhibitions" were. She defined them as the "things that hold you back." As my mum toddled off to go and put the kettle on for tea, I realized, as I was 90 percent composed of inhibitions, that without them I would be nothing.

The impact these shows made on Jamie and me transcended television. We treated them with the mystery and reverence ancient historians afforded *The Epic of Gilgamesh*'s hieroglyphics, dedicating our lives to analyzing their fragments, searching for deeper meaning. The experience of watching, then dissecting, their story lines was a weekly fiesta for the preteens we were. In seventh-grade English class, we were studying *Walden* by Thoreau, and when Mr. Weakstone read out aloud, "I went to the woods because I wished to live deliberately, to front only the essential facts of life, and see if I could not learn what it had to teach, and not, when I came to die, discover that I had not lived. I did not wish to live what was not life." While Weakstone added "Thoreau wanted to suck the marrow out of life, lads," in his monotone accent, I turned around to Jamie and whispered, "That is us and Fantasy Island."

Life without fantasy was not worth living.

CHAPTER FIVE

"Just Locker Room Talk"

The stench hit you first: a musty mix of damp moss, piss, and stale muscle rub. That stink was an assault on the senses, overwhelming any stranger who mistakenly wandered into Liverpool College's locker rooms. Less an odor. More a final warning to turn back now and save yourselves.

We doomed pupils had no choice but to step through that single door three times a week. Monday, Wednesday, and Saturday afternoons were the darkest blight on my existence: gamesday. Rugby in the winter, cricket in the summer. Regardless of the sport, gamesday was an excruciating psychological trauma that transformed that building into a torture chamber.

Design-wise, the locker room was the kind of brutalist eyesore commonly constructed by English architects in the 1970s whenever they were handed a brief to "build something cheap and quick, spare the aesthetics." Hence the long, windowless atrocity that ran like a scar alongside the entire length of the schoolyard. The construction was spartan. All cinder blocks and cheap poured concrete, which rather than provide refuge from the English weather, soaked it up and refracted it, acting like a giant meat locker during the permafrost of Liverpudlian winter, and a still, airless oven in the dry summer months. Pack two hundred middle school boys into those conditions, then force them to strip down naked, and prison rules apply.

Your average First World War trench was less dank than that locker room. Its inside was bereft of anything natural, be that light, air, or human decency. A thin line of bare electric bulbs cast a watery glow. Upon stumbling in, your eyes needed a moment to adjust before they were met by bank after bank of wire cage lockers stretching into the distance. Narrow benches hugged one wall, littered with the discarded flotsam and jetsam of boys' athletics. Disowned wet towels; squeezed-out tubes of Deep Heat; orphaned rugby socks; the occasional jockstrap flailing across the floor like a soldier killed in action, left where he had fallen.

Afternoons experienced in that locker room were proof of seventeenth-century philosopher Thomas Hobbes's assertion that human life is "nasty, brutish, and short." A torment that began straight after lunch when I joined two hundred other middle schoolers, boys aged eleven to fourteen, charging en masse to change into games attire. Ties, pants, and blazers swapped out for rugby equipment: a cotton-polyester sports shirt boasting proud red and black harlequin squares; tight bum-hugging shorts; saggy black socks tucked into heavy, metal-studded boots. It was meager protection against the bitter November winds whipping in off the Irish Sea to batter the wide-open expanse that was the school playing fields, to which we headed to face our collective fate.

Two hours of torment followed. On a lucky day, we would just play in a drizzle of rain, drops deepening the pits of mud caused by previous storms that already polka-dotted the spread of a dozen fields onto which we trundled. On more punishing days, the wind would slice over the train tracks that bordered the fields, forcing the rain showers to defy physics and fall horizontally upon us, accompanied by the stinging lash of sleet, or even snow.

The weather never stopped us. It was the ideal backdrop for rugby's misery. The whole ordeal was overseen by our coach, Mr. Gore, a pockmarked, handlebar-mustached geography teacher. He was one of the few masters to fully embrace the nickname that had been bestowed upon him—"Caner," earned for his predilection to spank boys first and ask questions later, if at all.

Caner Gore set a murderous tone from the outset, calling proceedings to order by violently barking, "Fatties on thinnies!" It was a command universally understood by the smaller boys to mean we were to put the bigger, more developed, or just plain obese lads on our backs and thus encumbered, attempt to struggle upfield. We did this not for the benefits of traditional pregame warm-ups, but more for the slapstick comedy that would ensue, delighting Mr. Gore, a man who never smiled, but rarely seemed more alive than while watching his undeveloped charges grunt and strain along the full length of a rugby field while being taunted and slapped by their chubbier, bulkier brethren.

The moment we mites had completed a barely passable attempt at this Herculean task, Caner would reverse the order; "Thinnies on Fatties, lads." This was, of course, the signal for the heftier kids to scoop up their physical lessers, and charge back down the field, flinging us around savagely to the point of whiplash with every step, before inevitably disposing of their load into one of the lake-sized puddles around the goal line.

Only when Caner had finally bored with the sadistic freak show that was his warm-up regimen would game play commence. For the next hour or more, we classmates would discard friendships, or prior alliances of any kind, dividing into two teams, then attempting to smite the opposition in near biblical fashion. At its best, rugby is a smashmouth game centered on blunt human force. But for the Liverpool College Under-14 team, the game's scrums, rucks, and mauls were less sporting maneuvers and more opportunities to vent for the larger, stronger, inherently violent pupils who lived for the chance it provided them to stamp, gouge, and bludgeon. There was a group of popular kids who were coincidentally more physically advanced than the rest of us and called themselves the Rugger Buggers. For them, the game was a release valve enabling them to discharge the metric tons of boredom that had built up over periods of double Latin and Religious Studies. I would watch on in horror from the wing—the position as far away from the action as was humanly possible—as the Rugger Buggers repeatedly clashed and fell together in piles. A tangle of limbs, akin to a homicidal game of Twister.

Caner Gore loved to stay close to the carnage, delighting in the slaughter, with a whistle always close to his lips. He never stopped the game for fouls or injury. That whistle would only blow if Caner had seen something that disappointed him, a boy he perceived to have shown fear while missing a tackle, or even more egregiously, forgoing an opportunity to "lay one on an opponent" by driving his head into an exposed belly, or a fist into a vulnerable limb. "What are you, a fucking poof?" he would demand of his chosen coward, with a volley of spittle emerging from beneath his mustache bush to reinforce his disdain.

Here is one of the most important educational lessons I learned during eleven years at Liverpool College: You should never underestimate just how much energy it takes to ensure you are not involved in a game of rugby while making it seem

Me (right) in a pair of tight shorts, looking up at the sky while eight other kids rip each other's arms off in an effort to grab the ball.

like you are perpetually primed for action. I became a master of *nearly* being there, a purveyor of well-intentioned, failed, last-ditch tackles, a player who was constantly faked out by his opponent's high-speed moves, diving full length the wrong way to tackle as if juked, allowing them to run on unhindered. "Nearly had him, sir," I would say to Caner Gore after the other team had scored, with appropriately sad eyes, jogging back to my station on the flank.

I achieved all of this while carefully monitoring the freezing of my extremities. Your fingers would be first to succumb to the raw, near-arctic chill. That was just the appetizer of suffering for the numbing of your crotch that was sure to follow, a physical and mental agony during which your penis shrank to the point it felt like it was in danger of being recalled into your midriff. The moment you could feel nothing below your waist came almost as sweet relief.

There were days when the fear of frostbite was so terrifying and my urge to survive too real, that I would take the most desperate measure of all: intentionally becoming involved in the game, allowing myself to actually be caught up in a mauling pile of bodies. The ecstasy of other people's limbs rubbing against my own and the body heat they temporarily provided overrode any fear of injury. Besides, being studded, bruised, or even punched in the teeth does not hurt so much when your entire body is numb.

How I longed for an end to the suffering signaled by the three long blasts with which Caner reluctantly brought the day's athletics to a close. That yearning, though, was akin to a prisoner begging to be executed just to be put out of his misery. However, a fate far worse awaited us in the locker room.

We walked back leadenly in clusters, bodies caked in mud, resembling a street gang of Victorian chimney sweeps after a

Flattened.

long day scaling sooty stacks. Neither exhaustion nor cold could stop the bigger lads from bonding and joking. I did not share those emotions. Like most of the smaller boys who lagged behind in silence, my muddy limbs were heavy, not from fatigue, but from fear of what was to come. The cold made my breath visible in the icy near-darkness, and I would stare at it rising up in a cloud then vaporizing, wishing I could make myself disappear along with it.

By the time I reached the locker room, it was well ablaze with the sound of mocking laughter, slamming lockers, and the muffle of punches being thrown and connecting somewhere in a distant corner of the vast bunker. It was a cruel empire now populated by two distinct classes: Boys who had "been through the changes" and those of us who had not. It was easy to tell the difference. The alphas who had gone through puberty stripped out of their games gear with abandon, standing around to talk to each other, buck naked, with pythons swinging, like cavemen planning a hunt around a campfire. They would swagger, dance, strut, any movement that would cause their proud, hairy cocks to swing side to side, showcasing the feeling of dominance they experienced and would occasionally accentuate by brazenly cupping their pride and joy, waggling them at each other as if heroically bringing out a fire extinguisher in a moment of pubic need.

Those of us who had not yet acquired such physical attributes, the weaker, smaller of my classmates, known collectively as "eunuchs," clung to the shadows, eyes downcast. Showering was compulsory, but we eunuchs would play for time, slowly unlacing our boots, finding some reason to fold a dirty shirt in painstaking fashion, or becoming fascinated by the zipping mechanism on a school bag.

I was a late bloomer. My tiny child-penis was a bald spigot, as close to puberty as a pure, trickling source of the river is to the powerful, free-flowing mouth. As much as I hated the manly scenes playing out before me, I could not help but stare at them, mesmerized. I took it all in with a mix of aspiration, jealousy, and self-loathing.

Patrols of teachers circled the lockers in pairs, seemingly immune to the towel-snapping tomfoolery around them. Their only concern was to ensure every student reached the showers at the back of the long room, a task they pursued with almost fascistic zeal. "Don't lollygag, Bennett." "Clean up, lad," said Mr. Pimmons, the ancient history teacher, as if impervious to the extent that the prospect of sharing my nude form in public filled me with sphincter-curdling angst. I knew two things: Showering was unavoidable, and timing was everything. Strip naked quickly, and there would be too many eyes paying witness and magnifying your humiliation. Leave it too late, and the cavemen would have showered, dried off, and been on the hunt for any lingerers to whip with a wet towel.

Upon sensing the perfect moment, I sprang into action, executing a series of sad yet well-honed moves. Step one: to whip off my rugby shirt while simultaneously wrapping a towel around my waist to protect my modesty. From that position, my shorts were next to go, yanked down from beneath the towel, as if I was changing in full view on a sunny beach. This was no simple task. The shorts were tight to begin with and the mud from the playing fields had turned them into a second skin. But fear brings the side benefit of adrenaline. A few tugs and accompanying muffled grunts and those shorts would be around my ankles. There would be no turning back now. I was in too deep, with no option but to commit: speed-walking, head down, towel around waist, athlete's foot be damned, toward my hell place. The showers.

History has perhaps seen more menacing shower rooms than those at Liverpool College. The Bates Motel. The "chain saw scene" in *Scarface*. Wherever Carrie had her "incident." Yet, none of these had Mr. Stott stationed at their entrance. Armed with a Woodbine cigarette in one hand and an old cricket bat in the other, he would smoke one while using the other to thrash the buttocks of every boy who skipped by him, displaying all the casual brutality of a cowherd driving his ignorant charges to market.

Mr. Stott's official duty was to check for clean legs on every boy exiting the shower area. He augmented this task with the additional, self-appointed role of color commentator, providing play-by-play on the physical status of all the boys who passed, as if announcing their arrival at a society ball.

"Goatcock," he bellowed as Kay, the rugby captain, strolled by early on, with towel brazenly draped around his neck.

A gleeful "All Hail Keenman-Jones and his cheese roll" was followed by a dismayed "Coleman, carrying two unshelled pistachios."

"Fresh forestation, well done, Tarrant," he marveled, salaciously appreciating the new hair growth while stubbing out his cigarette, and looking up, only to be filled with disgust. "Patel! What is that, boy . . . a urethra?"

Greek mythology imagined Cerberus, who guarded Hades as the ultimate gatekeeping monster, but Mr. Stott was far more fearsome than any fabled multiheaded hound. Cerberus merely ate his victims, a speedy death compared to Stott's slowly served yet still lethal approach, doled out one taunt at a time, like the cutting quip he always reserved for me. "Bennett. Incoming. Accompanied by Hitler's deformed micropenis." It was a crushing blow, far more painful than Stott's cricket bat sadistically crashing across the small target of my exposed ass cheeks.

There was no time for tears. They would not serve me. Biting my bottom lip, I pushed onward toward the shower area, filled with all the noise and panic of a slaughterhouse. Eight showerheads were evenly spaced along the wall, seven of which reliably piped out hottish water. The boys who had reached puberty monopolized them unashamedly, soaping up their nobs while singing oafish rugby songs and luxuriating in the shower heat's thawing qualities.

The eunuchs were left to cower miserably around a single showerhead on the far right. The one that for years had spat out nothing but cold water in a punishingly thin drip. Temperature be damned, our limbs had to be clean before the ordeal was over so, after stripping off our towels at the very last second, we would fight for position to jam our legs under the frigid, chilling spill, frantically scrubbing ourselves mud-free, every man—or boy—for himself. Rather than share a collective empathy, we had internalized the hatred and scorn our more physically advanced classmates slung toward us. Unable to look at each other, we were swamped by shame and disgust.

The cruelest part of the whole experience was that membership of the two groups was not permanent. Over time, more and more boys physically transformed into men. It was bewildering to see one fellow eunuch after another break ranks, ditching the sanctuary of the bench area, yanking down their Y-fronts, and proudly unveiling a newly throbbing member to the world. I would watch agog as their new cock flopped out, almost in slow motion, and would stare in jealous disbelief that they too now had downy hair, fluffy like a baby chicklet.

Witnessing a weaker kid, who had spent months by my side, cowering around the showers suddenly take flight like Dumbo for the first time felt like a personal act of betrayal. On the day even Weekes joined the master race, strolling up to Mr. Stott, towel in hand, schlong a-swinging, headed for the hot end of the showers, I could no longer bear it. Throwing on my school pants, shirt, and blazer over mud-scaled limbs, with hair still thick with muck, I wiped as much dirt off my face as I could with a towel and charged outside, standing alone in the middle of the empty schoolyard in the inky early-evening darkness, doubled over breathless as if sucker punched, while a shower of sleet fell down around me.

That night, I showered alone in my home bathroom. As the water cascaded down my body, and the mud pooled around my feet, I looked down at the smooth porcelain cherub's genitalia that was my boyhood. Tilting my head at every angle, I squinted my eyes until I had persuaded myself I could glimpse a microscopic, single baby hair taking sprout above my penis.

CHAPTER SIX

Think Once,
Think Twice . . . Duck

Britain in the 1980s often felt like it was tearing at the seams, pulled apart by violence, chaos, and fear. One minute we had a global empire, the next, even our own tiny island seemed to be crumbling all around us with the nation's industrial muscle, atrophying into a mass of unemployment and despair.

In 1979, Margaret Thatcher became the nation's first female prime minister. A polarizing figure, she attempted to modernize the economy by making London a global financial center, a move that turned the capital into a boom town, but as the industrial heartlands rotted away it only exacerbated the North-South divide. The nadir was the miners' strike in the middle of the decade when the coal unions struggled defiantly to save their ailing industry through a year-long nationwide uprising. A desperate, violent, yet doomed effort to prevent the government from closing down pits and to protect miners' livelihoods while Thatcher, fully embracing her nickname as "the Iron Lady," seemed to delight in suffocating their very being.

On a nightly basis, the national news was dominated by the

grim unfolding story lines, leading with graphic footage from across the country as thousands of working-class miners fought savage hand-to-hand battles against massed formations of police. I would watch with my mother as the screen filled with horrific scenes of bloodied, bewildered men from both sides. She would tut, then stumble off to make a cup of tea as if a cuppa would provide sweet relief from the dark spectacle that surrounded us. Yet, there was no escaping it. The entire nation was drawn into the sharpened political fray, and Liverpool, perched deep in the North West of England, with its dockland roots and proud working-class history, was at the forefront of the resistance.

The city elected a Trotskyist member as their representative in Parliament and the local council was not just left-wing, it was militantly so, going as far as to debate whether Liverpool should secede from the rest of the country and form an independent socialist republic. All of this would have felt right on if it were not for the fact that my father, a member of the judiciary, and a devout traditionalist, was one of the few men left in Liverpool who remained a card-carrying member of Margaret Thatcher's Conservative party.

To the rest of the city, Thatcher was Medusa, a three-times prime minister who sought to reshape the nation to the wishes of the financiers and bankers in the south, and slaughtering protections around the north's predominantly working classes. But in my father's mind, her ideology of personal responsibility and privatization was the only thing that could reverse decades of the social, economic, and moral decline he had witnessed from behind the judge's bench in his courtroom. This meant that in the run-up to every national election, my brother and I were forced to spend an inordinate amount of time accompanying my dad as he leafletted the city on behalf of the Conservative party, led by the woman known locally as "Attila the Hen." In a city as left-wing as Liverpool, this act was utterly futile, as courageous as Daniel walking into the lion's den, only with the opposite set of values.

I was too young to question my father's command to go canvassing for Thatcher, even though our politics were very different. Like many of my classmates at Liverpool College, I secretly wore a pro–miners' union "Coal Not Dole" sticker on the inside of my school blazer's lapel, a subversive act of protest that risked an instant caning if discovered by a teacher. Although I did not admire my father's decision, I could not disobey it. Being made to go door-to-door felt as dutiful and inconvenient as anything my brother and I were forced to do, be that tidy our rooms, turning down the volume on our record player after 9 P.M., or being prohibited from answering the telephone if it rang while the family sat for dinner. The latter was an idiosyncrasy of his with which we neither understood nor agreed, but complied simply because it was our dad's order.

I did learn this, though: There are few better ways of ensuring your offspring become bleeding-heart liberals than to expose them to the poverty and squalor rife in the low-income housing estates of England and force them to push right-wing literature through the mailboxes. No sooner had the leaflets left our hand than we were set upon by dogs. Turd, which I presumed to be human, was dropped from windows opened above our heads. We became deserving targets for generations of pent-up anger.

One night, I had been charged with leafleting a dank local library, a task that consisted of pinning large posters proclaiming "Don't just hope for a better future, Vote for One! VOTE THATCHER!" on any available public notice board. I knew they would be defaced at best, torn down within minutes at worst. When I made my way down the dark, detergent-drenched hallway, I could discern a tiny figure heading toward me from the opposite end. The hallway was so long it took three or four minutes for us to close in on each other, me weighed down by a heavy roll of Tory party posters tucked under my arm, him bearing all of the hallmarks of your average eight-year-old Liverpudlian: a seething expression covered by a buzz cut, sporting only a T-shirt in the damp cold. As we crossed, without breaking stride, he cleared his throat and coughed up an enormous glob of guttural phlegm that he expertly spat in my direction. This hate-propelled snot rocket spiraled toward me in slow motion, before landing square on the frames of my enormous spectacles. One of the many remarkable aspects of my oppressor's superlative athletic feat was that he never had to break stride. The kid kept walking and so did I. I actually saw his point. Frankly, I deserved it.

My father, though, would not be deterred. On election day, he dutifully hired a minibus from one of the few car rental outfits brave enough to allow him to fix protective steel-mesh grills over the windows. Partially out of curiosity and partially out of perverse horror, I agreed to keep my dad company as we drove the van over to pick up Howell Grimley-Jones, a dentist with skeletal features topped off with a fine comb-over, who was the chairman of the local Conservative club. Part of the reason Grimley-Jones held that position was the fact he owned a mobile public address system that he and my father struggled to mount on the minibus's roof. The speakers were wired to a microphone my father held as Grimley-Jones drove slowly around the perimeter of the voting district.

I sat on the long front seat in between the two men, as my father raised the microphone to his lips, and in his crisp middle-class accent took it upon himself to impart the following unsolicited advice: "Think Once, Think Twice, Vote Conservative." To this day, I challenge you to conjure six words that could so quickly and consistently trigger a more viscerally violent response. Pedestrians who one minute were innocently pushing infants in baby strollers, or perhaps rushing to the baker's to grab a hot pie for supper before it closed, were transformed into snarling, outraged aggressors, their faces contorted into furious scowls. Many flicked two fingers at our vehicle. A chorus of howling "Fuck offs" (pronounced gutturally in the Scouse dialect as "Fucchhhhhhhh off") was our sound track, punctuated only by the staccato thud of a beer can, rock, or whatever was quick to hand crashing off the minibus's window grates.

This fool's crusade went on for hours. Despite the sustained fury, the two men remained unperturbed and unmoved. Grimley-Jones hunched determined over the wheel, keeping his eyes grimly fixed on the road ahead as my father calmly and obediently repeated his mantra to the same effect until the moment the voting stations closed down. I stared not at the stone throwers but at my dad, with a sense of bewilderment, never truly able to understand whether he was oblivious to the hatred or fueled by it.

Back home our entire family sat around the television and waited for election results to filter in from across the nation. With school in the morning, I was sent to bed way before the final count was in. As I kissed my parents good night, my father, no doubt stressed about the outcome, involuntarily muttered something to the effect of "If Mrs. Thatcher loses tonight, we are all moving to Canada." This flooded me with hope. I had seen *The Kids of Degrassi Street.* Toronto seemed decent enough, and was close to America. Before I went to sleep, I theatrically put my palms together in front of my face as I had seen my class-mates do when worshipping in school assembly, and fervently, yet futilely, prayed for Thatcher's defeat.

CHAPTER SEVEN

The Other American Revolution

Every thirteen-year-old has four eternal secrets that must be unlocked:

Puberty

Homework

Music

Style

How anyone confronts these bewildering, chaotic challenges alone, without the guiding wisdom of an older brother, is one of the greatest human mysteries.

Thank God, I had one. Nigel. He was two grades ahead of me. A quantum leap of experience, insight, and worldliness that I loved to tap into. In our younger days, we were inseparable, the perfect duo, one brother lean, stylish, and unflappable, the other a tiny ball of manic energy. We were Liverpool's answer to an Arnold Schwarzenegger and Danny DeVito buddy comedy. Then Nige hit puberty, became interested in girls, and stopped hanging out with me in public. Yet, I still savored the inordinate amount of time we spent together behind closed doors during the week, playing snooker in the hour before bedtime on a flimsy collapsible table we set up in the cramped confines of my father's study. The game itself was really an excuse. It was something to do while we spun vinyl from our prized collection on a turntable that had been the jewel of his bar mitzvah gifts amid the less-useful deluge of fountain pens, atlases, and toiletry kits.

I relished these late-night moments when all homework had been dispensed with, and we could relax, shoot some stick, and listen to sounds that made me feel alive. Echo and the Bunnymen. Duran Duran. The Human League. All the while, my brother took my questions, unlocking the secrets of life to me in short, carefully doled-out portions. Subjects were as diverse as how to game a forthcoming Latin test on the periphrastic present subjunctive tense, impress girls by playing them at table tennis and confidently unleashing a high-toss forehand serve, or fold your shirtsleeves with a "master roll," a technique that looked effortlessly casual. Information I did not always understand or have use for at the time but stored away as I knew it would undoubtedly come in handy later.

My glacial pubic progress remained a simmering angst that perpetually sloshed around within me, but when I was with Nige, even that agony felt lessened. "Relax," he ordered me while casually chalking his cue. "Hairy bollocks are a journey. You are on that journey. You are afraid because you don't understand the destination." These words of mystical truth were grounded in our shared knowledge that my ignorance of the human body had been created by a root cause we had both experienced: Liverpool College's septuagenarian biology teacher, Dr. Rocksland, who had for the last half century been delegated with the task of providing sex education lessons to generations of confused, fearful, horny boys. "Roxy" was a tight-lipped yet furious man who had navigated life with one arm ever since one dark Second World War day when a German stick grenade found its way into his trench. In the face of danger, Rocksland instinctively unfurled the textbook sense of duty any public-school-educated Englishman should display in the circumstances. Without having to think, he took off his tin helmet, placed it over the bomb, then lay on top of both to smother the explosion and protect his trench mates. The stiff, prosthetic right arm he wore under his tweed blazer was the result. A symbol of both sacrifice and honor.

My knowledge of puberty and the technicalities of the reproductive process had been gleaned from this onetime war hero's lessons. They consisted of his energetic attempts to roll a condom over the end of the metal ruler he more typically trusted to swing around viciously to enforce discipline. While we watched on in confused horror, Roxy, with ruler jammed between his thighs, struggled to stretch rubber over metal, using his one good hand, while muttering "the importance of always putting a 'Johnny' on it" in a tone of vague, frustrated disgust.

On one of so many nights when I was crushed by a toxic combination of uncertainty and inadequacy that accompanied my lack of development, I summoned the courage to ask my brother to articulate what it felt like to have emerged on the other side of childhood. As if he had long been anticipating that very query, Nige calmly downed his cue, closed the study door, and strolled masterfully toward my father's bookcase. A heaving shelf lined the longest wall, stuffed with law casebooks, huge pleather-backed *Sprowtworthy on Torts*, twelve volumes of Churchill's autobiography, and bound copies of assorted works of Dickens. "How have you not found these yet?"

he asked, pointing with his sock-clad foot toward three books in the bottom corner of the bookshelf, all of which had their spines turned around the wrong way.

The mysterious trio were summarily yanked out by my brother with one hand, before he flung them with bravado onto the green baize of the snooker table before me. There were three books, of slightly different sizes, but all of which had gone in an almost identical direction with their art design, bearing similar white covers with some variation of a discreet photograph of a blissful, scantily clad woman hugging a hippy-looking man *incredibly* tight. *The Joy of Sex: A Gourmet Guide to Lovemaking*, proclaimed one. *Advanced Positions for Experienced Lovers*, announced the second. "Don't be afraid," my brother encouraged calmly. "Take a look." With trepidation I snatched up the book that had landed closest to my hand. *The Art of Sensual Massage* by Gordon Ikneles and Murray Todris was a midsized white paperback that had a sepia close-up photograph of an ecstatic woman having her neck rubbed by a powerful pair of male hands and in small font below it, the promise that the volume "will allow the reader to spread pleasure inch by inch."

My brother was wise enough to give me space and time to coexist with this alien material in silence. I leafed through its glossy images, my mind desperately attempting to compute what my eyes were seeing. The photos showed a progression of two couples, unabashedly savoring each other in what looked like the comfort of their own homes. The rooms were different but had both evidently been decorated by someone with a deep emotional attachment to enormous wicker chairs, sheepskin rugs, and sprawling ferns. Everything, human and not, appeared verdant and overgrown. In one image, a black bloke demonstrated a procedure apparently known as "Fast Buttock Rotation" on a white woman as a fluffy cat obliviously attempted to nibble on her upper thigh. In another photo, a skinny white man with long hair, a center part, and a droopy beard performed "Temple Strokes" on the forehead of a squat, short-haired woman who looked unnervingly like Miss Brownhead, our English teacher in second grade.

I was a bookish kid by nature, so to make sense of these images—the terra-cotta oil bowls, all that armpit hair, and the kind of human euphoria I had only encountered at football matches in the immediate aftermath of a goal—I instinctively began to read. The book's introduction was bold. It talked of "a revolution gripping the United States of America, emanating out of the East Bay in Berkeley," and turning a nation that had become a "cold place after 400 years of Puritan oppression" into one wrapped in "human feeling—we call it the sensual."

I do not know how long I read. I do not know exactly how much I understood. I had reached a paragraph that proclaimed "the body is a machine we must learn how to operate. Rub a fine spray of perfumed powder onto her lower body from head to toe. No kneading, no hacking, just fingertips. You know how your woman feels. . . ." Then my brother roused me from my reverie, using the end of his snooker cue to deliver a quick, emphatic lecture while pointing at a double photo spread of a thin hippie guy practicing a technique called "third eye kinetics." "That python is a nob with a boner," he said convincingly. Then moving the cue tip down toward the hair forest below the woman who looked like my English teacher's naked waist, he continued dispensing enlightenment: "And that's the fanny. Any questions?"

I had so many questions, I did not know where to start. I was thrilled, even awestruck, by what I had seen and both curious and eager to learn more about this "revolution gripping the United States of America." "What's a vibrator?" I burbled excitedly, repeating a word I had seen in the last chapter, titled "Expert Tools." "It's a kind of kitchen blender," my brother responded curtly with authority as he bent over his record player and placed an LP onto the turntable to signal that tonight's time for learning had come to an end.

The sound of a needle dropping on vinyl crackled through the speaker, followed by the jaunty keyboards and tinny hand-clapping that ease the listener into the majesty that is "Hurts So Good" by John Cougar. Judging from the record cover photograph in which he posed with feathered hair simmering and collars flipped, Cougar undoubtedly had the rasping, saucy soulfulness of an American who was a key part of the sensual massage revolution. Nige looked at me, flicked the collar of his own school shirt up, and began to sing along with the opening words of wisdom in a fake American drawl. "When I was a young boy, Said put away those young boy ways," he mouthed alongside Cougar. This was a man who sang with the confidence of a man who knew "how his woman feels." By the time the grinding guitar break kicked in, both my brother and I had raised our snooker cues to our hips as if they were a pair of matching Fender Stratocasters, looking over at each other as we thrust our hips dramatically and windmilled while making eye contact and shrieking in laughter. As we did so, my body began to surge with adrenaline. It was an emotion, not quite confidence, but more a fleeting sense that within the confines of that room, for at least that moment, everything felt okay.

CHAPTER EIGHT

Bar Mitzvah Disco

When I turned twelve, life finally gave me the opportunity to have an up-close relationship with a member of the opposite sex. Her name was Amy. And she was my newborn sister. Yes, her arrival was a shock. Until my mother's belly started to show earlier that spring, I was blithely unaware my parents had been trying to have a third child *forever*. Although I have little clear recollection of Amy's actual birth, I do remember the day before it well. My mum, aware she would not be able to take us shopping for some time, dragged her heavily pregnant self across Liverpool's crowded city center to buy winter coats for my brother and me, an odyssey that culminated in my exhausted mother, carried away by the weight of the moment, and ground down by our begging, treating us both to a pair of the fingerless gloves that were all the rage, and that we had long coveted.

JEWISH TELEGRAPH   W

Their big day

● BARMITZVAH at Childwall Synagogue on Shabbat was Roger Bennett, younger son of Valerie and Ivor Bennett, of Calderstones. Roger is the grandchild of Flora Bennett of Liverpool and the late Abe Bennett and Rita and Sam Polak of Liverpool. He has an elder brother, Nigel, 15 and a younger sister Amy, 10 months.

A pupil at Liverpool College where he is chairman of the Debating Society Junior Section, Roger has represented Liverpool at chess and his other interests include reading, tennis, golf, cricket and collecting records.

When a tightly swaddled Amy returned home from hospital two days later, I was initially thrilled by the idea of having a sister, even though, for the first few months, she looked like Mikhail Gorbachev. I also did not mind being woken in the middle of the night by her hungry late-night screaming. I would sit up in bed until the house quieted down again, picking strands of fraying wool out of the ends of my fingerless gloves.

It took some time for me to fathom the true seismic nature of the changes that had occurred the second my sister appeared. My identity had been transformed. One minute I was the extroverted youngest of two, fully playing the role of "baby of the family" in all its glory; the next I had been shunted to the dreaded middle child spot, exiled to life tinged with inadequacy, lived out of the spotlight.

Alongside my brother, Nige, I had been so comfortable being one of two kids. We were a duo versed in tussling with my parents and their well-worn, defined roles: Mum the carrot, Dad the eccentric stick. Now my mother was lost to the endless, selfless tasks of child-rearing, bottle-feeding, and diaper-changing while my forty-five-year-old father spent the first year of my sister's life chaffing as every stranger he encountered while pushing the stroller assumed he was her grandfather.

Molly Ringwald's breakout portrayal of a middle child's struggle in *Sixteen Candles* captured my rude awakening. Molly's family forgot her sixteenth birthday amid the chaos of her sister's wedding planning. Against the backdrop of the shifting Bennett family balance of power, we plunged into my bar mitzvah year.

Anyone who has had a bar mitzvah will know the experience is inherently stressful, a sleight of hand devised by some no doubt well-meaning biblical authority eager to persuade Jewish thirteen-year-olds to ignore the trauma of their early teens by unilaterally proclaiming them to be full-fledged adults overnight, even though all credible evidence points otherwise. With mouths full of braces, and puberty often light-years away, we wobble through this ritual act of self-deception with all the eagerness of infantrymen having to run through a minefield.

I was well aware of the peculiar havoc bar mitzvahs created. I had witnessed my older brother's experience and glimpsed the extent to which the tight-knit Liverpool Jewish community's best intentions cast him into a crucible of pressure. I enjoyed Nigel's big day far more than he did, mostly because of the cascade of gifts that spilled into our home. In the Bennett household, we never went without, but lived modestly compared to our family friends whose homes contained the extravagant twenty-four-inch televisions, front-loading video recorders, and Ataris we craved. So, the sight of the gifted gold-plated cuff links, Casio digital watches, and multiple copies of Roget's Thesaurus that now packed his bedroom was genuinely arousing.

So abundant was the incoming bounty that my brother had surplus with which to barter in return for my commitment to write all of his thank-you notes. I received a snazzy Anglepoise bedside light and a two-volume Oxford English Dictionary and faced up to the endless task, relishing in the opportunity to zing the notoriously cheap aunts and uncles on my dad's side of the family, who had dispatched minuscule cash gifts, by scrawling, "Thank you for your kind words and modest offering on the occasion of my bar mitzvah. I will buy a magazine with it," before signing my brother's name with a flourish.

How different it felt to experience my own bar mitzvah rather than just savor the benefits of Nige's vicariously. This time, it would be me up there performing in synagogue, chanting the

Torah portion in Hebrew and unfurling a sudden mastery of the ancient sacred texts. This song-and-dance act required months of grueling tutorials with a weary local rabbi because, as a Liverpool College boy, my own Jewish literacy was rudimentary. After all, Christian values were a bedrock of a college education, values that were reinforced at the beginning of every learning day, when the student body faithfully trotted down to the chapel on the edge of the school property for prayer and worship. While all of that went on, we were in a classroom popularly known as "Jewish room."

As the name suggests, the Jewish room contained about a dozen Jews. There were also twenty or so Muslims, a sprinkling of Sikhs, and Kerwin-Jones, the school's lone Bahai. No one ever really understood what that was, but he was always there, sitting on his own in the corner. While our fellow Christ-believing classmates savored chapel, communing through hymn and prayer with their Lord, we heretics used our time slightly less productively: forced to sit in total silence, with perfect upright posture, at risk of a requisite spanking from a master patrolling the classroom, cane in hand. The handful of Jews, vastly outnumbered by the Muslim kids, made it a mini–Middle East where a majority simmered, incensed once more at the injustice of having the Jews somehow screw them out of naming rights.

The quasi-penal nature of the whole experience neither upset nor surprised us. We were well aware of our difference. It was revealed when we stripped naked in the school changing room before rugby to widespread derision for lacking a foreskin. We Jewish boys hailed from another stock. Our ancestors had been chased across Poland and Russia's Pale of Settlement by Cossacks. Whereas they were hunters, our DNA made us forever the prey.

The one ripping yarn I emotionally connected to after several years of otherwise irrelevant Hebrew school education was that of the Spanish Marranos, Jews who in 1492 had been forced at pain of death to convert to Catholicism. Despite seeming like good Christians on the outside, they proceeded to devise ingenious strategies to maintain secret Jewish practice for generations. At great risk, they would light Sabbath candles in their basements, meet clandestinely in forest clearings to hold Passover seders, or become vegetarian so as to avoid eating unkosher meat. In many ways, we Liverpool College Jews were modern-day Marranos. We masked our Jewishness, relegating it to our homes, and shedding it the second we stepped on the bus to school, prepared to utter almost every Christian prayer or hymn that littered the average Liverpool College day.

Having a bar mitzvah meant having to remove that mask, and I experienced a sting of shame and fear in doing so. But, I had no choice. Part of the ritual was a party. Parties need guests. While Jamie, who could seamlessly move with me from school to synagogue, remained my one true soul mate, we were not loners. The problem was, playing football on the schoolyard or playfighting in the lunch line with a school mate was a very different proposition than casually inviting him to your synagogue and home for your bar mitzvah. That felt like exposing myself in a way that was more naked than the locker room showers.

My mother, ever empathetic, sensed my diffidence and tried to generate some positive energy around the event by encouraging me to select a theme for the party. This task was as anxiety producing as it was well-intended, because it demanded I delve into the question of who I was at my core. An Everton fan was the obvious answer. But half of my football-crazed city would have the same response, so it did not seem sufficiently singular.

Thirteen years old. Light-years away from manhood. Wearing an ill-fitting pair of women's spectacles.

As much as chess was a massive part of my inner life, Sicilian defenses and back-rank checkmates did not feel exciting or interesting enough to build a party around, especially one that would be remembered for decades to come.

I was genuinely at a loss, until one weekday night, while surfing through the four channels then available in Britain, I stumbled by chance across Talking Heads playing "Burning Down the House" live on some obscure television show. The performance was spellbinding. I had never watched anyone dance like David Byrne before. He whirled and jerked around the stage without any hint of self-consciousness, so comfortable, and almost liberated by his individuality. As he pivoted around, I marveled at the way his hair, which he had dyed a metallic silver, glinted and caught the eye. Suddenly, nothing in the world felt more important to me than being able to dye my hair a shiny color and similarly unlock my own sense of abandon and freedom.

I turned to my mother, who was dozing, curled up on the couch alongside me.

"I've decided. I'm going to have a punk party," I declared.

"Punk! How fun!" she said with as much validating enthusiasm as she could muster when drowsy and disoriented from caring for a new baby.

I agonized for a further week about whom to invite to this punk party. As time ran down, I defaulted to the members of the school chess team and debating society. After all, what could be more punk than that?

Half the party guest list was now cracked. The other half involved an anxiety that actually felt a thousandfold worse. Girls. Of whom I still knew none. Since my brother had hipped me to the reverse-spined books in my father's study, I had spent many a late-night hour obsessively mining them for information, laying the volumes out on the snooker table like a Second World War general poring over maps of his next battleground. Their mysteries had been a revelation but sentences such as "Hide-and-seek with the woman's pubic triangle is one of the oldest human games," or "Long gloves turn some people on—they suggest the old-style great lady" were as confounding as they were titillating. When I read those chapters, I was almost relieved not to have girls in my life at the College, a reality that meant I was freed from the burden of having to put some of those moves into practice, and undoubtedly failing.

The party situation changed that, and like a Secret Service agent willing to take a bullet for the president, my mum leapt into action. Every Monday night, she played a regular game of bridge with five women, none of whom were family, but all of whom I had to call "Auntie." My mum now shook this quintet down for addresses, rustling up daughters, nieces, and cousins, any warm bodies they knew who were female, Jewish, and vaguely age appropriate. Her constant updates as the invite list filled up with Marions, Victorias, and Amandas I had never met but that were now coming to celebrate my bar mitzvah only ratcheted up the sense of disquiet that churned within as the day approached. My life now revolved entirely around the event. The lessons with the rabbi had to be doubled up to minimize my crimes against Hebrew. Multiple early evenings were spent at "Prestige for Boys," the fancy tailors outside of Manchester that specialized in the bar mitzvah trade. I endured countless fittings for the two-tone three-piece suit I had selected for the festivities, not because I had developed a sudden taste for waistcoats, but because its pants were the least itchy of the dozens we tried on.

As life warped under the identity crisis of being told I was a colossus of adulthood one minute, and finding myself dumped back in double Latin class the next, I felt a genuine sense of calm when working on the speech that the bar mitzvah boy would deliver as the culmination of the party. I had always enjoyed writing and was grateful for the opportunity it gave me to express myself. It felt grounding to work in my native tongue and have a chance to say what I really wanted to say about family, friendship, and the responsibilities of becoming a man, with all that sweet, undivided attention upon me.

The day of the bar mitzvah itself was forgettable, a set of memories defined more by the feelings I have when I flick through the photographs of the day. Those feelings are mostly of mortification that my parents would allow me to go through the entire weekend with a pair of giant spectacles that were wonky and listed to the left. There was no communing with a higher power or experiencing the echoes of generations past. In the synagogue, I sat surrounded by the male members of my family, with my dad and my grandpa Sam flanking me. In an Orthodox congregation, the women are relegated to sit together upstairs. In the minutes before I was about to begin the recitation I had trained so hard for over the past eight months, I was smacked by a wave of stage-fright-level panic. I turned to my father and in a sickly whisper confided, "I don't remember anything, Dad. I have forgotten it all." To which he retorted, "Nonsense, Roger, just get up there, lad, and it will all come back to you." And he

A seminal moment in the history of punk: my bar mitzvah party.

was right. Even though my mind remained blank, something in my unconscious kicked in to deliver, maybe not the most tuneful, but a passable rendition of the day's proceedings.

Not totally humiliating myself felt like a borderline triumph, and by the time my punk party swung round, I was ready to unleash my inner Sid Vicious and rock and roll. Before my guests arrived, I feverishly cut up an old football jersey, wrapped some chains around my neck, and as the pièce de résistance, sprayed metallic blue hair dye and massaged it into my fringe. After attaching a couple of safety pins into my shirt to complete the rebel look, I stood in front of the mirror in the hallway outside of my bedroom and squinted, because I had decided to ditch the spectacles. A blue-haired wild character looked back at me, and for a moment I allowed myself to feel a bolt of self-satisfaction. "Now *that's* a man," I said to myself.

The doorbell went. My guests poured in all at once. The Liverpool College boys were startling to welcome because I had never seen most of them in civilian clothes before. The girls entered in ones and twos, a blur of garbage bag dresses, torn shirts, and triangle earrings, wordlessly handing over the gifts they were clutching as they walked past me on the doorstep. Almost all of their gifts turned out to be copies of Culture Club's "Karma Chameleon." I received eleven copies of that seven-inch that night, no doubt playing a single-handed role in propelling that release to the top of the charts.

The party took place in our living room, which my parents had emptied of furniture for the night. The DJ they had hired worked his turntables, but in truth, it was hard for him to get the party started. My parents insisted on keeping the lights on full beam, hovering by the door with my baby sister in their arms as a preemptive attempt to snuff out any sexual shenanigans.

They need not have worried. The girls and the boys sat limply around the perimeter of the room. Oil and water have been known to mix better. We college boys lacked the language to engage the girls or even talk about them among ourselves. We simply ignored them, and for the most part, ignored the music, too, getting up only once to pogo around halfheartedly when Men Without Hats' "Safety Dance" came on. Delighted to get any kind of a reaction, the DJ played that song three straight times. But for the rest of the night, we all sat in a ring, determined to kill out the clock until it was pickup time. I sat there surveying the sullen circle filled with my slumped classmates, and my mum's friends' friends, all of whom seemed silent and miserable. It was as if, inadvertently, the real theme of my bar mitzvah party was "Jewish room." So still and mute were my guests, that is what it felt like. Jewish room, but with music.

Twenty minutes before pickup, my mum and dad coaxed us into the dining room with the promise of cookies, chocolates, and assorted sweets. A large cake groaned at the far end of the table covered in dessert, and it was toward that that I headed to close the night by delivering my speech, the one I had crafted for weeks, workshopping the perfect balance of a barrage of opening jokes for my mates, before giving way to a conclusion filled with heartfelt meaning suitable for the occasion that would win over even the most cynical in attendance. After the trial by Hebrew in synagogue, this was the one moment of the weekend I felt truly capable of acing. When I unfolded my speech I felt a sense of delicious anticipation.

I looked down to the other end of the room where my mother stood, behind my ten-month-old sister, whom she had placed before her in a sitting position on the table, and prepared to wow her. I gave the two full pages of notebook paper that

These photos remain an agony for me to look at to this day. The girls so bored. We boys unable to talk to them. The empty dance floor. The boredom is palpable.

contained my speech one last scan and cleared my throat. My sister, with her adorable plump baby thighs protruding out of a blue sailor dress, chose that exact moment to break free of my mum's control, crawling across the table toward a box of After Eight chocolates. With mission accomplished, Amy proceeded to liberate one chocolate-coated mint from its wrapper after another and stuff it in her mouth, quickly coating her cheeks and chin in a thick smear of chocolate and dribble.

The bar mitzvah photographer was the first to notice her. He had been preparing for my speech, too, patiently framing up a climactic shot of me and the cake. Without ever taking the camera off his eye, he now swiveled away and moved stealthily toward the baby-chocolate carnage in the middle of the table, his motor drive whirring away as he fired off shot after shot of the enchanted two-toothed gurgling. The flash of his camera

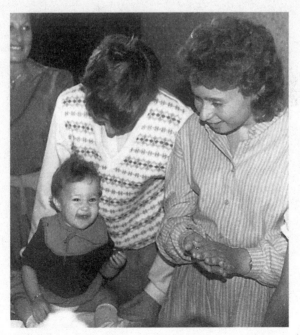

My sister steals the show.

shifted the focus of the room. Instantly, the crowd broke into cooing and laughter, as everyone delighted in the sight of this adorable baby doing adorable baby things. While the photographer crouched in front of my sister, zooming his lens to conjure the perfect shot, I stood alone at the other end of the table. Behind the cake, I tucked the speech back into my pocket, unread.

I became a man, upstaged by a baby.

CHAPTER NINE

The Pepsi Choice

I have rarely wanted to forget something more than my punk party. Yet I was unable to. It is a peculiar torture for it to take three weeks to wash the blue hair dye properly out of your bangs so that every time you look at yourself in the mirror you are reminded of the worst night of your life. I never wanted to go to a party again. That was exactly the opposite conclusion my parents drew out of my trauma. After my bar mitzvah, they began to fret endlessly about the lack of social connection I had to other young Liverpool Jews, almost all of whom attended the local Jewish school, King David, a shabby yet proud institution they had forsaken by electing to gift me a privileged Liverpool College education. Jamie's parents evidently lived with the same fear of assimilation, as they worked together behind the scenes to summon a pair of invitations to Jessica Goldfarb's bat mitzvah party.

Neither of us knew the bat mitzvah girl well, so it was obvious to all that this was a sympathy invitation. All we knew was she happened to be the daughter of one of the wealthiest Jewish families in Liverpool and that the party would be held at their home, which was a monstrously large new construction in the most picturesque part of the city. A mansion so sprawling, it was rumored to have its own squash court. I imagined her bat mitzvah would surpass the thrills of my punk party by benefit of location alone.

The whole event reeked of danger and my dominant emotion was fear when Jamie came to my house to pick me up ahead of the party. This fear deepened when I saw he was clad in a blue beret, red fingerless gloves, with a pair of plum leg warmers tucked into the top of his sneakers. "Have a singular style and let the ladies come to you," he said by way of explanation, sashaying past me as I opened my front door with my mouth hanging open.

Luckily enough, I happened to have a very singular style of my own. Every night when I went to bed, a pantheon of my current musical heroes—Adam Ant, Duran Duran, and Boy George—looked down at me approvingly from the posters that covered the walls of my bedroom. My greatest influence was John Taylor, Duran Duran's bass guitarist, who along with singer/heartthrob Simon Le Bon was on the cover of approximately three out of five teen magazines I consumed in 1982. I lapped up every interview I could find, mostly because Taylor insisted on repeating his life story, which was as inspirational to me as I imagine the Gospels were to a young Mother Teresa. This suave, stunning Michelangelo-sculpture-come-to-life claimed to have grown up as a shortsighted, bespectacled, Dungeons & Dragons–playing nerd who fell into music, and wised up to the fact that the way you looked trumped the way you sounded. And so, after mastering the art of slapping a mean, funk-driven bass guitar, he ditched the spectacles, bleached his hair, summoned a swarthy style from deep within, joined a band, and propelled himself into the dreams of every prepubescent girl in the free world.

When I read in one magazine that Taylor only wore linen clothing, I decided that I would do the same. This easy-to-crease flaxen fabric is supercool on a trailblazing pop star, not so much on a thirteen-year-old boy in the middle of winter, especially in a town where Sergio Tacchini sweatsuits were considered the height of fashion.

While Jamie lay on my bed in his leg warmers, blabbing away about all the girls we would make out with, I looked at myself in the mirror and buttoned up a white linen shirt, repeatedly attempting to pop the collar only to discover it was too flaccid and floppy to stay erect, a failure I attempted to mitigate against by squeezing more wet hair gel straight from the tube into my already-gel-soaked fringe.

My whole look still felt one bold fashion accessory away from being complete, so I charged back to my wardrobe and rustled through the back of the shoe section to retrieve an old arm sling. I had originally worn the medical support after suffering an arm sprain on the rugby field, and even though it retained a Deep Heat stink, I quickly flung it on over my linens, hoping it would make me seem mysteriously sympathetic when a gaggle of fawning girls asked me about it at the party. "Yeh. It was a last-gasp-save-the-day rugby tackle that won the game for the College. Sure, I broke my arm, but you don't really think about yourself when duty comes calling."

As my eyes flicked between my reflection and John Taylor, one of his own nuggets of wisdom returned to me. It was from a recent Q&A in Smash Hits magazine. Asked if he thought he was good-looking, he replied, "No, but I think I can fake it."

I had given my mother firm instructions to drop us off at the bottom of the Goldfarbs' driveway. Jamie and I found ourselves at the bottom of a long, tree-lined drive, which opened up to a circle filled with parked cars and a babbling fountain. Behind it loomed the house, a dauntingly immense silhouette broken up by colored lights pulsating out of dozens of windows synchronized to the echoing and intimidating sound of party. I instantly recognized the track that rang out in the darkness: the signature haunting guitar and pulsing keyboards of Flock of Seagulls' "I Ran (So Far Away)." The opening lines, "I walked along the avenue, I never thought I'd meet a girl like you," always felt rife with a sincere longing when I listened to them on my bedroom radio-cassette player at home. Now, hearing this song in this unfamiliar setting made it seem alien, even threatening.

We began to crunch our way up the gravel path, and I took internal stock of the sense of self-loathing and fear that held me in its clutches, attempting to alchemize it into confidence and likability as we approached the two vehicles at the top of the path, two identical black Jaguars with matching vanity license plates "GoldyDad1" and "GoldyMum1."

A castle-sized double front door was wide open so we crossed the threshold to the Goldfarb house unnoticed and without welcome. The ground floor was enormous, open-plan and stuffed with leather, Lucite, and all shades of gold. To enter was to leave Liverpool and be transported to a magical fantasy land akin to the opulent American soap opera sets I had seen on *Knots Landing* and *Dynasty*. There was no discernible form of human life around so we allowed ourselves a moment to breathe in the splendor of it all: the white shag pile carpet; the enormous glass sculpture of a naked woman holding an apple; and an oil painting on the wall of the entire Goldfarb clan: GoldyDad1 and GoldyMum1 in the middle of one of the leather couches, flanked by their beaming progeny, twin boys Guy and Murray. In front of them all lay the woman of the hour, kid sister Jessica, spread across the floor in front of the couch, one arm casually propping up her chin as she smiled innocently in a flowered skirt.

A change in tracks to Michael Jackson's "Beat It" was a reminder of the night's true purpose. We came to party. And that party was evidently up an enormous marble double staircase. We followed the music, each one of Jacko's pants and squeaks like a siren call.

We smelled the party before we saw it. A lick of dry ice misting up the top of the stairs, enveloping us in its sour musk of intrigue and excitement. The sight that greeted us was of a world gone mad. The room was as cavernous and open-plan as the one below, but it had temporarily been remade as a discotheque, replete with rented wooden dance floor, light show, and strobes. Leather couches lined the walls around the dance floor, which was packed with kids our age. Boys and girls. Talking to each other. Dancing together. Calmly. Casually. Naturally. This was going to be torture.

Without needing to speak, Jamie and I adopted an observational position at the side of the dance floor, alongside the DJ, who had set up his turntable on top of a light box that bore the legend "Frankie Mazeltov, Liverpool's Number One Name in Bar Mitzvah Soundz." A DJ, whom I presumed to be Frankie Mazeltov himself, was basking in the attention of a small knot of girls screaming song requests from all sides. To his left, an acne-ridden assistant with eyes glazed and long, thin, greasy hair listlessly fired bursts of dry ice from a large black box, using a pedal that lay at his feet. I followed the smoke's path back onto the center of the dance floor to watch the action unfurl as avidly as if it were a football match. The boys jockeyed to be the center of attention with their moves, despite the fact that many of the girls were more physically advanced and a head or two taller than them. A stab of jealousy struck me along with the realization that the comfort these kids felt with each other came because they all went to a coed school. What they were really learning in those King David classes was how to talk to the opposite sex.

In moments of rising panic such as this one, one of my father's classic adages came to mind. Not because his koan-like proclamations had ever proved true, but simply because he repeated them constantly. Like a Liverpudlian Obi-Wan I heard my father's voice in my head, "Be the protagonist in life, Roger! Take control!"

My legs complied, marching me over to the front of Frankie Mazeltov's flashing booth. The DJ himself looked down at me from his commanding position behind two turntables.

"All right, lad." He smiled without looking up as he busied himself cueing up the next record.

"Can you play 'Hurts So Good' by John Cougar Mellencamp?" I asked, reaching for a self-assured tone I did not feel.

"Some Melle Mel? Def," he replied before pursing his lips and swiveling his hips for effect as he added, "Rang-dang-diggidy-dang-a-dang." "Sound as a pound, that song, mate." With a dramatic flick of his hand on the fader, the DJ propelled the opening pulses of "Billie Jean" out into the world. I just stood there misunderstood, in silence, and with my confidence bleeding out until Frankie Mazeltov looked me up and down to see why I was still in his presence.

"Nice sling there, mate," he said, letting me know we were done. "What have you done to yourself, sad lad?"

A peel of squeals rang around as I slunk back to my watching brief alongside my only friend, just in time to witness one boy

Another night when I knew early on that it was not going to happen for me.

in the center of the dance floor bust out a moonwalk. "That's Mike Nagel!" Jamie shouted above the music. "He's some new kid who just moved from Dublin." I wanted to scoff at his sliding steps with every atom of my being, but even I had to admit Mike Nagel's moonwalk was passable. Jessica Goldfarb certainly thought so. Clad in a green Benetton rugby shirt and a pair of drainpipe jeans, she positioned herself at the center of the dance floor under a giant disco ball and waited for Mike Nagel to pivot and glide back toward her, upon which he spun round dramatically, bent one knee, and with eyebrow arched, mimed taking off an invisible hat and spinning it outward. Jessica threw her curly hair back and giggled, overcome with joy. The disco ball spinning overhead cloaked everything in its bewitching glow, forcing me to squint with astonishment, as for a second, I swear, I saw their hands touch.

By the time Melle Mel's "White Lines" crackled across the

dance floor, I had become painfully aware of the numbing bass from the DJ's speakers stack, which pounded at my body as if hell-bent on tenderizing my very being while Jamie and I stood by it for song after song. The two of us remained resoundingly invisible. Fortunately, Jamie kept himself busy by liberating can after can of Pepsi from a nearby side table groaning with sodas of every variety. My eyes, however, were glued to that dance floor. It was where I yearned to be.

"It's time for a group dance!" Frankie Mazeltov screamed into his mic. "This is . . . the Village People! You know what to do," he exclaimed while sliding up the fader to let the mirthful trumpets of "YMCA" announce themselves, the signal for every conversation in the room to come to a screeching halt as everybody charged to the center of the floor, obediently forming four neat lines and awaiting the chorus. That would be everybody apart from Jamie, me, and Frankie Mazeltov's assistant, who remained faithful to his dry ice assignment.

This was the moment in my life when I discovered there are few places in the world lonelier than a bar mitzvah group dance you are not part of. I watched on with envy as my fellow partygoers shuffled through the decreed moves, formatting letters with their bodies in dizzying synchronicity. Mike Nagel and Jessica Goldfarb were side by side, front row center. When the chorus kicked in and everyone made the letter *M*, he swung his hands together on top of his head with fingers touching, freeing a perfect kiss curl. As it swung to and fro across his brow, along with the beat, I was stung by an awareness of just how isolated I was in that moment. A woeful feeling of otherness. Different from the numbness that filled my school days, but perhaps more embarrassing because I felt both unseen and utterly exposed at the same time. I turned away only to make accidental eye contact with Creepy Dry Ice Guy. Though his eyeballs were cracked red, his sneer suggested even he could barely mask the pity he felt for me.

The group dance was the obvious prelude to the slow dance. The intense widespread ecstasy unleashed by the Village People instantly and seamlessly refocused into a chance for romancin' by the seductive satin-sheet saxophone of Wham's "Careless Whisper." Five minutes, four seconds of agony ensued again as I watched everyone on the dance floor break effortlessly from the straight lines they had been in and, like atoms reorganizing, pair off into boy-girl twosomes.

A dance floor that only seconds before had born scenes of collective cacophony was now light-dimmed ready for some serious business to ensue. Boys and girls swayed side to side, bodies so close together, despite the height differential that compelled some girls to stoop to rest their heads on their partner's shoulder. Mike Nagel and Jessica had obviously paired up. A white spotlight lazily patrolled the dance floor and when it landed on them, I could not help but stare as they danced cheek to cheek, him stoically staring off into space with jaw squared, her with eyes closed and a slight sweat dusting her temples. As she basked in the spotlight, I was overcome with the sense I had never glimpsed a more enchanting creature outside of movies, magazine covers, and television.

The song mercifully ended, only to be replaced by Foreigner's "I Want to Know What Love Is." But a number of the couples dispensed with Foreigner's thrall, electing instead to walk hastily hand in hand to a small room behind the bar. Curious to discover what could be going on, Jamie and I followed them through the doorway, stopping to grab our fifteenth soda each along the way to maintain the discreet distance that we knew from television cop shows was standard protocol to employ when trailing perps.

The room had no light and it took a moment for our eyes to adjust. When they did, we saw a couple more couches facing a large, boxy television screen mounted on a wall in front of a stationary exercise bike, around which, across the floor, were four or five of the couples making out. Right there before us, writhing in each other's arms, silently, bar the occasional groan.

Jamie and I shuffled mutely to the back of the room, taking care not to step on any human limbs that flailed around all over the carpet. The back wall turned out to be a balcony. The peculiar odor that greeted us as we reached it was of old sneakers, rubber, and dry sweat. The telltale sign we were in fact suspended over the Goldfarbs' much-coveted squash court. I turned my back to it and stared out at a room now filled with boys and girls our age brazenly making out before us, tongues lashing. The sight gripped me in a quiver full of contradictory emotions—awe, confusion, excitement, thrill, and disgust—caused both by the scenes I was witnessing, and what they made me realize about myself. There was no sense of "Ahh, we are doing this now, are we? Me next!" I was no more able to do *this* than if I had walked into a room full of kids who sprouted wings spontaneously and flew laps together around the ceiling. For a moment I felt angry at Liverpool College for leaving me so far behind my supposed peers, but that anger quickly turned inward.

I looked over at Jamie, who stood beside me, one leg warmer now up, the other sagging down around his ankle. Unusually for him, his ever-present grin was absent, replaced instead by a furrowed brow of confused sadness. I cracked open the can of Pepsi that was to hand and nodded at him to do the same, and he followed me as I extended my arm over the edge of the balcony, then turned it upside down so the sweet, sticky contents chugged straight out into the darkness and onto the squash court floor below. It was a random act of sugarcoated violence, an attempt to dull the pain born of defeat we both shared but could not articulate.

I do not remember how I made it home that night, but no sooner was I back than I raced up to the safe sanctuary of my bedroom, and rather than process what had happened, jumped straight into bed. With a practiced hand, I felt for the play button on the trusty radio-cassette player on my bedside table. When Mellencamp's "Hurts So Good" rang out, I lay back down and began to rock my head from side to side in time with the beat, singing along to transport myself away from the darkness of my bedroom, the bleakness of Liverpool, the confines of school, Mr. Stott, the judgment of GoldyMum1, and anyone more comfortable in their own skin. Snapping my head rhythmically backward and forward allowed me to fantasize that both the song and the backing band were mine. I was Roger "Cougar" Mellencamp. I was on *Top of the Pops* and the whole world tuned in to be mesmerized by my performance, especially the sexy girls in my imagination who looked like Jessica Goldfarb, the stars of *Dynasty*, and Dana Plato from *Diff'rent Strokes*.

BOOK TWO

THE HALF-LIGHT/ TRANSATLANTIC ROG

LIVERPOOL, ENGLAND, 1984–1986

"Happiness is as a butterfly which, when pursued,
is always beyond our grasp, but which if you
will sit down quietly, may alight upon you."

—Nathaniel Hawthorne

CHAPTER TEN

The King Takes America

LIVERPOOL, 1984

I adored spending time at Jamie's house. In stark contrast to the disciplined structure and rule-riddled culture that prevailed at the Bennetts', the Glassmans were laissez-faire parents. It was never quite clear to us what Jamie's dad did for a living, but whatever it was, he was clearly killing it. The Glassman house, a palatial mock Tudor in the countryside on the outskirts of Liverpool, was a land of plenty with its own tennis court, toy race car track, and a refrigerator stocked with more sodas than we could drink. Jamie's home life was one of bounty and freedom, and it was thrilling to pretend it was all mine for the taking when I visited.

One of our most sacred shared rituals was to watch *Entertainment USA*, a British television series in which Jonathan King, a minor DJ and creator of novelty albums, refashioned himself as a self-styled expert on all things American, exploring the story of one U.S. city after another on a weekly basis. To our eyes, this was broadcasting Xanadu. Think of an English Alexis de Tocqueville if De Tocqueville had been less obsessed with participatory democracy and was fascinated instead by Cabbage

Patch Kids and Pat Benatar's "Sex as a Weapon," and considered the sprawling bratwurst section of a supermarket in the Mall of America as equivalent to the Seventh Wonder of the World.

Each episode began in the same way—the show's brassy, spasmodic theme similar to those employed by the majority of 1980s pinball machines. The tune was accompanied by a visual feast: opening credits that unleashed a barrage of clichéd American iconography. Cheerleaders! Cowboys! Baseball players! Piles of cash! For Jamie and me, two kids who were fast falling for America's lore, these images alone were more arousing than those we had glimpsed in the porno mags that had begun to be shared around the schoolyard.

Then entered the King himself, a large man who elected to wear an even larger pair of glasses. With a deft sense of drama, he would reveal that week's location in his strange vocal style, slurring his words out of the corner of one side of his mouth, which, combined with the excitement of the city reveal and the frenzy of the theme music, made it sound like he was in the most exotic place in the world. "I'm in cowtown, Kansas City!" he would exclaim with pizzazz. Sometimes he would employ freewheeling editorializing: "Hello from Seattle, a town which is naturally law abiding and well behaved, where the people are conservative and muted in their emotions," or just go with a backhanded compliment: "Everyone told me this city was boring, but I am here and it is not. Welcome to Minneapolis–St. Paul!" Wherever he landed, King pinpointed his geographic placement with the declarative confidence of Neil Armstrong landing on the moon.

Indeed, from our perspective in the drab gray confines of Liverpool, the show might as well have been broadcast from the moon. For those thirty minutes, it felt like King was visiting an altogether different and far more alluring planet than the one we inhabited. He would plummet through the history, geography, and unique flavor of the city at breakneck speed. The glamour of Seattle's Space Needle, San Francisco's Golden Gate Bridge, or even the sperm whale skeleton he found in Maui eclipsed the overbearing grimness of our known world in the North West of England every time.

The urban tour was just the warm-up, however. The true glory of *Entertainment USA* was King's ability to introduce the trailer for whichever blockbuster movie was taking America by storm, or unleash the video for the latest smash hit to crash the *Billboard* charts. This is how we first laid eyes on such life-changing cultural jewels as *Back to the Future, The Goonies,* Wang Chung, and the Miami Sound Machine. The savvy King knew there was a distribution lag of up to six months between release dates in the United States and the United Kingdom, tantamount to an eternity in teenage time. Everything he showed us was a glimpse of the future. It was a bona fide crystal ball of cool.

To sit on Jamie's red leather couch on a damp, rainy night in Liverpool and encounter the saturated colors of Daryl Hall and John Oates's "Maneater" video for the first time felt transcendent, Hall dominant with his fulsome mane and predilection for flamboyant one-handed keyboard playing, the mysterious Oates working so hard to steal the eye with his permed mullet and caterpillar-lip mustache combo. I sat and calculated how long it might take to grow out my hair into similarly bouffant form or sprout the Oates-style stache. That was a feat too far out of reach.

The greatest thrill of watching this show was experiencing King's own giddy passion for the United States of America, which felt like an intense refraction of our own. His admiration ran so deep that he was able to interview global icons like Elton John or Dr. Ruth one minute, and then cut to an investigative report about America's biggest banyan tree or why Minnesotans like to dress their dogs up in three-piece suits, without any change in tone. The King's curiosity about every microfiber of the American culture enchanted us, from the A-list celebrities to the offbeat oddballs. For thirty minutes while feasting on this show, Jamie and I felt seen. All the way in Liverpool.

I watched and longed to stroll down the skywalks of Cincinnati or cruise the freeways of Tampa Bay in a white convertible Ford Mustang. After Jonathan King[*] explored Salt Lake City, Utah (which, out of the side of his mouth he consistently pronounced "Oot-awe"), spending half the show talking to members of the Mormon Church, and the other half at the local Raging Waters amusement park, both of which he made sound equally awesome, I sat back, wide-eyed, attempting to process all we had just witnessed. Turning to Jamie, all I could stammer was "Salt Lake City . . . looks . . . amazing." "I know," he said breathlessly. "We need to move there."

To be clear, Jamie and I both knew we were not the first teenagers to dream of leaving home. The yearning to live a different life is a rite of passage. But to us, Manchester, a fifty-minute train ride away, felt like a strange, foreign country. The economic opportunities of booming London were accessible only to the truly bold. King's America, though, presented an altogether different value proposition to anywhere on offer in Britain. A world of creative freedom, happiness, and the self-confidence

---

[*] A dark English postscript: In 2001 King was charged with molesting minors in the 1980s and was sentenced to seven years in prison. He served three years and is one of a number of British television stars from our youth who turned out to be sex offenders—google the evils of Jimmy Saville and Rolf Harris, two men who were the faces of children's television—a traumatic reality that has been shocking to confront.

to wear leather pants if you wanted to. Life lived in a fourth dimension.

Entertainment USA was front of mind, then, when my parents announced they would redecorate my room in the wake of my bar mitzvah. Part of becoming a man meant moving on from the Scooby Doo wallpaper that had been my childhood backdrop, complete with the Mystery Machine and Fred in his dashing red neckerchief. The choice of what to replace them with was an easy one to make.

A visit to the local hardware store, a magical paradise of Pantones, resulted in a dozen cans of semigloss in shades of Symphony Blue, Old Glory Red, and Chantilly Lace White. I had a vision of painting each wall in my bedroom a different color of the American flag. Our local handyman, George, was summoned for the task. He was the gent who fixed anything that my father was incapable of around the house, which meant everything beyond the complexity of lightbulb changing. I loved George. He was a man of few words. The cigarette he kept permanently tucked behind one ear was his preferred form of communication. Yet when it came to action, George was a Swiss Army knife in human form. As a kid, I always found it thrilling to be in his presence, watching him skinny and shirtless under his omnipresent blue work dungarees, hammering, drilling, and occasionally just jamming a screwdriver in and out of electrical panels with no apparent fear of the consequences.

George set up for work early one morning before I left for school. I returned that night to find him in his dungarees now splattered with the hues of Old Glory. "Done something special for you," he muttered, and then turned around to head back toward the stairs, which I understood was his signal for me to follow.

I reached my bedroom. George was standing proudly in the center with both arms raised, palms upward, toward my freshly painted walls, one now blue, one red, and one white. Yet it was on the fourth wall that George had crafted his masterpiece, using it as a canvas on which to unleash all the pent-up creativity he had repressed while roto-rooting drains or coaxing boilers back to life. An enormous rendering of the American Stars and Stripes now ran down the entire length of my room, with a clumsy yet heartfelt re-creation of the Manhattan skyline, and as the pièce de résistance, the Statue of Liberty herself, which proudly loomed over the desk where I did my homework.

If I wanted to nitpick, George's flag featured six-pointed stars instead of the traditional five, and his Lady Liberty was, for reasons unknown, gray instead of greenish in hue, but I was more than willing to chalk up these mistakes as creative flourishes. That night, I carefully cracked the curtains so the light from outside fell directly onto the face of the robed statue on my wall. I lay on my bed and stared at her expression. The goddess stared back, stoic and bold, a look that was both sincere and alluring. My single bed had never felt more comfortable.

George's masterpiece should have hung in the Louvre.

CHAPTER ELEVEN

Fat Knacker's Words of Wisdom

The Liverpool College staff room was like the Muppets' house band made real. The "masters," as we had to call them, were an eclectic mix of characters to be sure. Most of them lifers, some of whom had first set foot on school property in the prewar period when they themselves were pupils. Against that backdrop, the economics teacher, Mr. McNally, was as innovative as compact discs or car phones. Tom Waits in a world filled with Pat Boones.

The impression he made began with his size. He was a hulking Irish giant of enormous magnitude, the perfect ratio of height, girth, and beard, earning him the nickname "Fat Knacker" from we students. Knacker was a vibrant and passionate man, and his lessons were a mixture of intellectual challenge and personal conversation in which he delighted in engaging his charges in freewheeling discussion about the world, his travels across America as a student, pop culture, and the changing face of Britain. In short, he was unlike any other master in the building.

No matter what we discussed in class, Mr. McNally's tone

was always animated and impassioned. What mattered most, though, was the style of conversation. It was two-way, a subversive idea for the College, which was built on a strict master-pupil relationship. Fat Knacker treated us like men whose opinions mattered. He would stride into the classroom and gain our attention by standing up front with a signature smile and chuckle, a combination that was a radical statement in its own right. The very notion of a Liverpool College teacher feeling happiness was mind-blowing. "What do you want to talk about today, lads?" he would inquire to launch the class. "Let's talk about life, sir," screamed a voice from the back of the classroom one day. It was "Gripper" Stark, the toughest kid in our year. Even a boy who spent the majority of his schooling with his head against the desk asleep could not help but be enchanted by Fat Knacker.

McNally would then launch into whatever was on his mind: his thoughts on the ideal of love; the rise of the English south at the expense of the north; or the incomparable joy of seeing your favorite band live in concert, a topic that allowed him to relive one of the happiest moments of his youth—when, during the months he spent on a gap year working as some kind of fisherman on Cape Cod (or "the Cod," as he liked to call it), Joni Mitchell miraculously turned up at his local drinking establishment and ended the night launching into an impromptu show for the dozen or so regulars at the bar. "Round and round in the circle game, lads," he mused, almost lost for a moment in his own memories.

No matter which story Knacker told, all were winding roads that led to the same place: a challenge for us to be the best men we could be, which largely involved the ideas of "freethinking," "gaming the system," and "fulfilling our potential." These three

Mr. McNally patrols the College. He may have physically been in Liverpool, but his heart was definitely still on "the Cod."

building blocks were crucial in the foundation of Mr. McNally's core message, that we must all "believe we could do anything we wanted." McNally himself was aware just how breathtakingly revolutionary his own ideas were. Liverpool College was a school that prided itself on inculcating the traditional values of blind obedience as a cornerstone of its decades-long commitment of pumping out upstanding, if unremarkable middle-class citizens. Almost every Knacker class ended with a rumination from his formative time on "the Cod." "The United States is a place where people chase their own success, lads," he proclaimed, "as opposed to Britain, where we much prefer to revel in others' failures."

Around this time, computer studies found its way onto our school curriculum, and Mr. McNally requisitioned one of the four Commodore 64s the school purchased to set up an "Economics Data Resource Room" (which he insisted we pronounce in the American style "day-ta," as opposed to the English "dah-tah"). In reality the Data Resource Room was his own safe haven away from the rest of the teachers. During recess and lunch break, he could reliably be found playing John Cale albums on a cassette player while pounding away at the computer's keyboard with his meaty fingers, wowing us with his ability to program rudimentary graphics that would make the screen flash in shades of fuchsia and cyan. It also became a place for many of us to seek refuge, or to gain a hint of McNally's private wisdom on matters personal and pressing.

To speak with Mr. McNally was to be unburdened and enlightened, like confession without the rosaries and Hail Marys. I stumbled into the Data Resource Room on a rainy Monday afternoon after Old Boys Day—the annual midsummer Saturday in which the Liverpool College alumni who referred to themselves grandly as "Old Lerpoolians" returned to the school grounds. In reality, this meant that a self-selecting throng who still considered their college days to be the best of their life—a gaggle of middle-class accountants, car dealership owners, pharma salesmen, distillery regional managers, and the one semifamous old boy who fronted the local news' rugby broadcasts—descended upon the College to reunite, wallow in nostalgia, and compete against the current students at cricket and tennis.

I hated Old Boys Day, including the naive giddiness of the returnees as they marveled at the Head Boy's opening address of welcome, which was, for reasons unknown, partially in Latin, and the unironic bellowing out of school song as if no musical melody had ever sounded so sweet.

"Eia! Eia! Socii, Cantum iam Sollemnem
Tollite Collegio, Gloream perennem."

Went the first line. Which translates through to:

"Come my comrades, raise the song
Proudly tell the story, you to the School belong,
Of her Ancient Glory."

The Old Boys' collective passion for the education I was currently suffering through challenged me to my core. What could the point of existence be if these school days were, as they professed, life at its best?

I initially sought refuge away from the crowds by sneaking off to the bathroom with my Walkman. While washing my hands at the sink, a rasp of flatulence coming from the toilet stalls revealed I was not alone. I crept over toward the source of the sound and encountered the aforementioned rugby broadcaster. Due to his proximity to television cameras, this man had achieved iconic status amid our student body and was oft held up by our teachers as an example of where a Liverpool College education could lead. And there he was. The best future the school could promise, slumped on one of the crappers, pants half-mast around his ankles, scotch flask in hand in front of me.

Mr. McNally was in the corner of his Data Resource Room as I entered. He was polishing his coffeemaking machine, an elaborate Italian contraption of which he was very proud. He invited me to sit down and listened sympathetically as I unloaded the nihilistic feelings Old Boys Day had conjured.

The bell signaling the beginning of afternoon classes rang

out as I finished, but Mr. McNally ignored it. "It's not Old Boys Day that is upsetting you, Benj," he said, in his familiar style, using the warm nickname he'd chosen for me. "You just don't want their present to be your future." A commotion of footsteps and shouting penetrated the moment, but McNally went on, opening a drawer in his desk and rustling through its contents as he continued. "We Liverpudlians are sea people, Benj. We look outwards. We stare at the ocean, and we dream. More than anything, we know the world is bigger than our immediate surroundings. Don't be afraid, Benj. The only question you should ask yourself is, do you have the tenacity to make those dreams real?"

No adult had ever talked to me like this, with words at once so liberating and intoxicating. They were almost too rich with meaning. "The Cod, sir?" I offered quietly. "The Cod, Benj," he roared with his grin, thrusting the object he had finally retrieved from his desk draw into my hands. It was a cassette tape with a woman's face in mysterious close-up. "This is Joni Mitchell's album *Blue*, Benj. Listen to the track 'All I Want' and have no fear." With that he closed his eyes and mimed accompanying himself on an invisible acoustic guitar while intoning in his deep bass voice:

"I am on a lonely road and I am traveling
Looking for something, what can it be."

CHAPTER TWELVE

The Funky Chicken

Sunday nights in 1980s Britain were the loneliest nights of all. The nation still took its day of rest very seriously. Stores were closed. No professional sports were scheduled. Sundays felt like a vast, barren landscape that British television did little to enliven. Its meager offering of just three channels reinforced the somber mood, unleashing a battery of church broadcasts filled with hymn singing and pious sermonizing as well as the occasional moldy antiques road show. As anesthetizing as that mix was, it did little to divert the mind from the prospect of the looming return to school.

Imagine the thrill in 1982 when a maverick start-up network, imaginatively calling itself Channel 4, launched a weekly NFL highlight show on Sunday nights. Britain was suddenly introduced to a sporting spectacle we had no previous knowledge of in the form of an hour-long broadcast crushing highlights of all fourteen of the previous weekend's NFL games into a single hour.

And what a bombastic hour it was: a mélange of swollen blokes in pads and helmets, crashing into each other as an American broadcaster creamed himself over the "draw plays," "rushes," and "fumbles" that ensued. I watched episode one in openmouthed wonder, trying to piece together the terms and rules of this mysterious, chaotic ballet that unspooled before my eyes, exhilarated by the long bombs and hits as well as the gratuitous cutaways to big-haired cheerleaders lustily spilling out of leotards on the sidelines. All this action ran at nosebleed pace, mostly as montages set to the thumping pulsations of Bonnie Tyler's "Holding Out for a Hero."

The glamorous titillation and pizzazz that emanated from the NFL stood in polar opposition to the prevailing culture of English football, one gripped by a fever of hooliganism and rage. Few cities were more football crazed than Liverpool and my father and I would often drive to watch our beloved Everton Football Club play in a decaying stadium that felt mostly like a war zone. After parking on some densely packed side street, a swarm of seven- or eight-year-old local kids were guaranteed to descend upon the vehicle, shrieking "Mind us your car, mister?" which meant "Can I watch your car for you, sir?" which *really* meant "Give me fifty pence or else I will scrape the side of your car and snap your mirrors off."

After coughing up a coin to defuse their threat, we would walk cautiously toward the stadium, attempting to dodge phalanxes of hooligans crashing around the streets with violence front of mind. Just as dangerous were the horse-mounted policemen who chased them. It was so common to encounter the broken bodies of fellow supporters who had been savagely beaten and left to languish on the pavement that we would simply step over them.

Those NFL broadcasts introduced us to a style of fandom that was based on an altogether more enlightened way of being. The Cleveland Browns' "Dawg Pound" was a cheering section packed with grown men, many of whom had taken the time to handcraft enormous letter *D*'s and matching "Fences" to wave in the air when the other team was in possession of the football. The idea of sophisticated sports fans who could pull off and even appreciate such visual puns was flabbergasting to contemplate.

Even more so the New Orleans Saints fans, a long-suffering bunch who had been fated by geography to support a woeful team coached by a man in a cowboy hat whose first name was actually "Bum."* Bum's team lost. A lot. For English fans, the rational response to all that losing would be to knife a couple of opposing supporters to numb the pain. Instead, the Saints fans elected to embrace their hopeless team's incompetence by turning up to games with paper bags on their head and calling themselves "The 'Aints." The English sports fans I knew were angry, pent up, and tribal. Most followed their team because of the street-fighting opportunities presented. American fans showed me there could be another way, that attending sports could be about something more important: an excuse to drain light beers and consume vast quantities of sausage-based product.

That difference was just as stark on the field of play. Soccer stars of the day were not substantially dissimilar to the fans who worshipped them—an unglamorous bunch who huffed and puffed around a muddy field hell-bent on kicking something, be it ball or opponent, before retiring to the pub for a cigarette, beers, and a pie. NFL players, he-men like Lawrence Taylor and Lyle Alzado, were snarling slabs of muscle and pads. These were

---

* I was fascinated by Bum Phillips (1923–2013), and not just because of his first name, a family nickname that was the result of his sister's stuttering and being unable to say the word "brother." His whole look—blue jeans, cowboy boots, and trademark white Stetson—screamed Texas-archetype-American-original. The pulpit centerpiece at his funeral was an enormous oil derrick constructed out of red and white carnations topped off with sparkling light blue letters that spelled out: "Luv Ya Bum!"

startling athletes capable of superhuman feats. To my eyes, they were a testament to clean living and a single-minded dedication to your sport.[*]

Then there was the action itself. Goals in soccer were few and far between. When an English player finally scuffed the ball into the back of the net, tradition prescribed that he should briefly hug his teammates then lollop back to the mud-filled center circle. The first time I saw Billy "White Shoes" Johnson return a kickoff was a rapturous experience. The tiny Atlanta Falcon caught the ball, duked his way through midfield, and then accelerated toward the end zone, but that was just his amuse-bouche. Johnson was a player who lived less to score, more to celebrate, raising his arms in triumph while rhythmically thrusting his thighs in and out before dropping down into the splits in a giddy dance he coined "the Funky Chicken."

When Jamie and I first witnessed this display of bravado fused with showmanship, we would not have been more exhilarated if we had jammed our fingers directly into an electrical socket. The game became our everything. Jamie committed to the New York Giants of Bill Parcells, and I, because of the core belief I would have been born on the shores of Lake Michigan if only my refugee great-grandfather had stayed on the boat, de-

---

[*] Lawrence Taylor published a remarkable autobiography that later rocked my world. In *LT: Living on the Edge,* he wrote, "I did crack from the middle of the '85 season to the end," he said. "I'd stay out all night, get blasted on crack and then try to pick up as though nothing had happened the next day. . . . I knew that I was no longer going at 100 percent. But I also knew that my 75 percent was better than most other guys' 100 percent." Lyle Alzado admitted he took anabolic steroids in college in 1969 and never stopped. He died of brain cancer, aged forty-three, a cancer he believed was a result of his addiction. "It wasn't worth it," Alzado wrote. "If you're on steroids or human growth hormone, stop. I should have."

veloped an instant emotional connection to the Chicago Bears. And my timing could not have been better. The Bears were peaking, propelled by the free-flowing running of the legendary Walter Payton, the punk-rock tenacity of Ray-Ban-sporting quarterback Jim McMahon, and the limelight-stealing rookie lineman William Perry, a man so large he was nicknamed "the Refrigerator," taking to the field with an effusive passion and all the naive charm of an enormous, overgrown baby.

The more we sampled, the deeper into the gridiron wormhole we both tumbled. An English monthly magazine named *Touchdown* landed on newsstands to service the underground market of British NFL aficionados. Jamie and I subscribed quicker than Billy "White Shoes" Johnson returned kickoffs and would spend hours poring over team rosters, memorizing the players' positions, jersey numbers, and colleges they had been drafted from, reveling in the exotic sounds of "Alcorn State" and "Southern Methodist." The moment a new issue arrived, I would grab a pair of scissors and harvest the color photographs from the previous month's, carefully sticking them up on my bedroom wall. Walter Payton stiff-arming a would-be tackler, the Fridge catching a pass, and coach Mike Ditka chomping on a victory cigar in his signature Bears vest, now hung over my bed. I had even taken down a couple of Everton posters to make room.

A tiny classified ad in the back of *Touchdown* magazine introduced me to the existence of a "Tampa Bay Buccaneers UK Fan Club," an entirely unofficial gaggle of passionate fellow enthusiasts run by Phil, a random guy who was an insurance adjuster in Brighton. I signed up after learning that the fan club's main perk was that twice a season, Phil somehow procured an entire Buccaneers game broadcast on a VHS videotape which, crucially, had been converted so that it played on our British machines. That precious video was then circulated via mail to the fan club's twelve members in a kind of NFL-focused underground network.

When that tape first arrived through my mailbox, the glorious thud it made upon landing was matched only by the one I experienced in my heart. Finally, I had an entire three-and-a-half-hour game at my fingertips. Detroit Lions against the Tampa Bay Buccaneers, untouched by the heavy hands of Channel 4's highlight editors, who would have stripped the game down to the mere minutes of its exclamation-point plays. It felt as if Jamie and I had taken possession of the Holy Grail. As we partook of this visual feast for the first time it was an overpowering sensory experience. The colors. The sounds. The goose bumps on our flesh.

The second the video was slammed into the top-loading VHS player, we sat back and were transported to sporting nirvana. The experience of an entire game's ebbs and flow of play was soul-stirring, enabling us to witness moments we had never before been privy to. That coaching chess match fought out at the line of scrimmage. The trial and the errors. The two-yard runs. As great as the action was, the details of the broadcast package felt even more thrilling. A mundane twelve-yard flare pass was thrillingly accentuated by the commentator screaming "Holy Moly Guacamole!" as the ball briefly spun through the air and the yellow graphics package that accompanied the replay hypnotized the eye.

Above all, though, we were mesmerized by the barrage of commercials that interrupted the game, almost inadvertently trumping the action. The advertisements we watched on that NFL video were so different from those mundane trifles that cluttered English television. American actors with their perfect teeth, Day-Glo wardrobes, and aspirational joy, dizzily singing the praises of Chevy Nova Twin-Cams, space-age-looking Swatch sunglasses, and Cherry Coke.* It only took a single exposure to two old men named Bartles and Jaymes to make us practically ache for a new beverage called "the wine cooler."

We did not watch that Buccaneers video as much as we inhaled it. By game's end, its stunning smashmouth potency had fomented an electric energy deep within us, and we charged into Jamie's garden to run it off. The two of us English teens made believe we were actually in Detroit, flinging a rugby ball back and forth between each other, and trying to ape the moves we had just witnessed on television. In our imaginations, Frank Gifford was commentating, screaming "Holy Moly Guacamole" as last-second Hail Marys were flung and diving catches executed. Night descended, but we kept on, continuing to perform sack dances in the darkness and attempting the "Funky Chickens" until exhaustion kicked in.

That Tampa Bay Buccaneers tape was like eating an apple from the Tree of Knowledge. Now that we had accessed an entire game and knew the real deal clocked in over the course of several riveting hours, the heavily condensed Channel 4 highlight show was entirely insufficient. Desperate times called for desperate measures. English telephones were still considered to be the centerpiece of modern home technology, yet they remained money pits if used for anything but local calls. My father stud-

---

* There was one Ford commercial featuring maverick Washington running back John Riggins that was such an earworm that I can still remember the opening lines today, even though that video was only in my possession for a single weekend. "When it comes to trucks I'm a connoisseur from the size of the engine to the sound of the door. Because I've been know to treat things rough, you can't go wrong with a tough Ford truck." Hip-hop was in its early days, but Riggo was already all over it.

ied every monthly bill with the zeal of a forensic accountant and would go berserk if one of us had even dared phone nearby Manchester. Though only fifty miles away, that call would cost a long-distance small fortune.

That price paled in comparison to the tearing ache Jamie and I experienced on Any Given Sunday. So, whenever the Bears were scheduled to play, we would carefully calculate the six-hour time difference between Illinois and Liverpool and gather around the telephone Jamie's parents mistakenly trusted him to have in his bedroom. Yes, Jamie may have been a Giants devotee, but he was a sufficiently generous friend to cede to my fandom. With pulse pounding, I would watch him solemnly push the speakerphone button before dialing an entirely random 312-Chicago area code phone number. We would wait for the stranger to pick up at the other end and then launch right in, peppering them with questions about the Bears game they were inevitably watching. Who had possession? What down was it? How was the Bears' vaunted pass rush looking? The goal was to hook the unwitting Chicagoan and hope they could be persuaded to give us our own personal play-by-play.

It was astonishing just how many strangers could be tempted into conversation with two kids, losing themselves for up to half an hour, transfixed, perhaps, by our English accents. We would chat about who they were watching with, what they were drinking,* and whether they were fans of the television show *Cheers*, until our ever-more-invasive line of questioning wore them out. After thanking them profusely, we would slam the receiver down, laugh out loud, and go again. Another 312 number would be arbitrarily dialed, followed by a breathless wait as the

---

* Nine times out of ten it was Old Style, the favored beer of Chicagoans.

thrilling sound of the single peel of that American ringtone we were so familiar with from movies rang, live and directly into our ears. The two of us huddled together, anticipating the delicious moment when the call would click in, the next unwitting Bears fan answered "Hello . . . ," and we junior NFL anthropologists could begin anew.

CHAPTER THIRTEEN

Like a Rolling Stone

It became a sweet new sound to my young ears, the crisp thwack on the hallway carpet when the afternoon paper boy flung my copy of *Rolling Stone* through our mailbox. This delicious moment occurred once every two weeks, and I welcomed the magazine in its protective plastic with the same awe and mystery the biblical Israelites greeted the life-sustaining manna dispatched by God during their forty years of desert wandering.

That copy of *Rolling Stone*, a publication I had been introduced to by Mr. McNally during one of his ruminations of life back on "the Cod," had to be specially ordered and shipped over from the United States by my local news agent. The vagaries of the postal service meant that the issue I received was generally well out of date, but I didn't care. Its very presence was a sliver of New York City, Los Angeles, or even Indianapolis in my hands.

I was a magazine addict, a trait I inherited from my dad, who was a firm believer that any hobby or interest could be enhanced by a pertinent subscription as a symbol of knowledge and passion. This meant I blew four-fifths of my allowance at the newsstand. Music and fashion must-reads, *Smash Hits* and *The Face*, joined sports periodicals, *The Cricketer*, *Shoot!*, *Touchdown*, and *Fighter! Martial Arts*, as monthly reads. Yet the arrival of a new issue of *Rolling Stone* felt different. It was less a magazine, more a spiritual text. A publication that did not so much ask to be read. It demanded to be worshipped.

After scooping the freshly arrived periodical off the floor, I would rush up to my room. Upon closing the door and turning off the light, I would locate my desk by moving stealthily across the room in the darkness. There was a swivel-arm lamp stationed there that I would fumble, then flick on, to beam directly onto the magazine's cover.

Once seated, I would crack open the package and come face-to-face with the cover star, inevitably some striking, fresh-faced actor I had never heard of. *"Top Gun's* Tom Cruise!" or "Michael J. Fox fresh off *Back to the Future!"* accompanying headlines helpfully proclaimed, explaining movies that would not be released in Britain for months after they had opened in American theaters, or television shows like *Growing Pains* or *A Different World* that might never reach our shores.

After cracking the magazine's spine, I would flip to the center page, where a scratch-and-sniff insertion for Calvin Klein Obsession inevitably lurked. Shutting my eyes, I would inhale deeply, letting the synthetic fruity musk fill my lungs and wonder if that was how Debbie Gibson, Tiffany, or Dana Plato might smell.

I devoured the magazine from front to back in one sitting, beginning with every single letter to the editor ("Gina McDavid from Savannah, Georgia, writes, 'I crush so hard on Emilio Estevez though why did he change his last name? I would give up a lung to be related to that hunk, Charlie Sheen.'") through the titillating gossip contained on the "Random Notes" page ("Madonna and new beau Sean Penn were caught smooching at Whoopi Goldberg's party!!!"), into the features, then on to the record and movie reviews, before finally emerging through the back pages filled with tiny classified ads, each of which I scrutinized. I could spend hours just staring at the delicious maze of Pee-wee Herman fan clubs, Gumby T-shirts, and "I break for Bobby Ewing" bumper stickers on offer, attempting to absorb every microscopic detail.

Some of the material I encountered I simply did not understand. To read, or imbibe, *Rolling Stone* was akin to joining a riveting conversation in the middle, then trying to piece together exactly what was being discussed. It took months for me to glean a full appreciation for the concept of *Saturday Night Live,* which was often written about. Ensemble sketch shows did not exist in England at that time and so trying to decode the furious debate about whether the concept was stale and fallen behind the times was akin to trying to imagine a new color without being allowed to see it. The same went for Rodney Dangerfield and Huey Lewis, who to my eye seemed akin to the beer-filled older blokes who might sit near me at soccer matches, swearing their way through Everton games. But none of this mattered. Everyone else on those pages looked so damn cool, especially when compared to the motley assortment of those we considered stars in Britain, the majority of whom looked like their features had been chipped out of boiled potato.

This immersive exposure to American celebrity was only half the pleasure of *Rolling Stone.* The advertisements were a hypnotic enchantment in their own right, whole-page, full-color affairs trumpeting the merits of such exotic brands as Guess jeans, Swatch watches, Radio Shack amplifiers, and Tropical Blend Tanning Oil. The double-paged spreads contained such detail that I stared at them as if they were movies in their own right. Pontiac Fiero GTs speeding along switchback roads under cobalt skies in what looked like the Wild West. Michelob Ultra Dark beers being swigged by impossibly blond coeds throwing their heads back with laughter to display impeccably white teeth while taking a break from playing pickup football in the snow. A Honda commercial for the Rebel motor scooter featured Lou Reed[*] himself, in leather jacket with collars popped, legs akimbo, the Manhattan skyline in the background below the tagline "Don't Settle for Walking." I wanted that scooter very badly, just as I longed to fire up a Newport Kings Menthol, which promised to be "Alive with Pleasure" while posing an intriguing philosophical question to the reader: "After all, if smoking is not a pleasure why bother?"

The worldview, taste filter, and tone of the magazine, along with its eclectic nature, encompassing film, television, fashion, politics, and pop culture, meant that Rolling Stone provided a deeper understanding of America to me than everything I had embraced before. Plus, the interaction was a two-way affair. Immersing myself further in American culture, and a bewildering array of menthol cigarettes, enabled me to learn profound things about myself in the process—who I was and what I wanted in life: a pair of Ray-Bans to wear, a Bud Light to smash, and a game of coed football to play in, all while flirting constantly.

An interview with Molly Ringwald, "Golly, Miss Molly" from the March 28, 1985, issue, was particularly striking. The seventeen-year-old actress was fresh off *The Breakfast Club,* that pathfinding John Hughes movie that I had seen on four occa-

---

[*] I did want that scooter so badly. Now as I look at it today, Lou's bike resembles a clunky mobility scooter nonagenarians use to get around assisted living facilities across Florida. A radiator on wheels.

sions by the time I received the magazine. I loved the film not only because it was set in the northern suburbs of Chicago, which I had decided was my destined home, but because of the way it normalized teen neurosis, angst, and even rage, dishing all the best lines to the self-styled outsiders, which they mostly employed to mock authority.

The *Rolling Stone* profile made Molly seem even more relatable. She tousled her red hair, ate a plate of onion rings, and relived her career arc from its beginning on the outskirts of Sacramento, a truly sophisticated place in my imagination. The central thrust of the article was that despite her sudden fame, she remained down-to-earth. Just a "[f]reckle-faced girl from the Valley who hankers for McDonald's and Doritos . . . has a crush on Mel Gibson, worries about failing algebra, and wants to be taken seriously." All of which sounded just like me. Apart from the Mel Gibson part.

The more I read, the harder I fell. Molly "harbored aspirations to become a writer" and was drawn to guys who were "sincere and sensitive . . . intelligent, creative, and willing to listen." "I cannot *stand* guys who are so masculine," she opined. I read this statement at least two dozen times on first sight.

"*Rolling Stone* Ringwald" appeared to me as a Ginger Vision, the most soulful, sophisticated, sensitive human being on God's green earth. The capper was her admission that she was "touched by wit." Molly relayed a story about receiving such an "amusing letter from a teenage fan" that she was moved to answer, then jump into her "gun-metal Volkswagen convertible," and drive into the Valley to meet him in person at the See's Candy Store, where he worked. *Rolling Stone* actually published the fan letter and I was struck by a pang of relief when I realized how it was not really *that* witty* and was also stunned by the realization that Molly's heart was clearly hankering for a normal guy.

My grandmother often used an old Yiddish word, "Beshert." It roughly translates as "the single soul mate you are fated to meet and marry in life." As I reveled in those pages, I was certain that Molly and I were fated. She was my Beshert. I understood what Grandma Rita was talking about for the first time in my life.†

As I was so painfully aware, an ocean and 5,260 miles sadly separated me from Molly Ringwald. Believe me, I felt every one of them, especially after spending three emotionally exhausting nights composing a *properly* funny letter to Molly. It must never have arrived because she did not write back, a fact that reinforced the deeply frustrating aspect of my engagement with *Rolling Stone* magazine: how desperately hard it was to make the ideas contained on its pages real. I could not really expect Molly Ringwald to drive and surprise me in person. I also knew that as magnificent as the movies and television found in those pages sounded, there was nothing I could do to expedite their appearance on Liverpool's screens apart from exercising an uncharacteristic patience.

The one part of *Rolling Stone* that offered instant gratification was the music. Like many kids from Liverpool, bands, alongside football, were the primary ways I explored and made sense of

---

* Sample line: "Why don't we do lunch sometime or maybe dinner, or maybe breakfast, or maybe we could do, like a toothpick, or maybe we could just *do* it."

† A belief I maintained until she dropped off the Hollywood grid and moved to Paris at almost the exact time I ultimately moved to Chicago. A coincidental "ships passing in the night" moment I interpreted as the nail in our (non-) relationship coffin.

the world. I had fallen in love with vinyl when I was a nine-year-old who became hooked on late-night English indie radio, even though I was still too small to be seen from behind the raised counters common in the types of record stores that stocked the sounds I craved. It was a problem that at first necessitated my father accompanying me to Penny Lane Records, where he would astound the stereotypically mohawked store clerks by asking in his plummy middle-class English accent for the latest singles by such local bands as Lotus Eaters, Pale Fountains, or the Mighty Wah! I would stand by my dad's side, desperately trying to pretend we had nothing to do with each other until the moment I had to hand him my pocket money so he could complete the transaction.

So, music was a natural, accessible way for me to explore my burgeoning fascination with all things American. The fuzzy raw-guitar sound of bands like Hüsker Dü, the Replacements, or Stevie Ray Vaughan and Double Trouble were a stark contrast to the heavily produced synth-soaked British ear candy I had been reared on. The information flow I derived from the magazine's album reviews alone was perhaps *Rolling Stone*'s greatest gift to a boy whose self-identity, in major part, had always revolved around listening to music outside of the mainstream. Through its pages I was introduced to bands that only *I* knew about, something of utmost importance to many a teenager.

One of the most traumatic nights of my early teens was the evening Culture Club were revealed to have reached the number one spot on the charts with their breakthrough smash "Do You Really Want to Hurt Me," that teasing glam-fusion of reggae, soul, and Hebrew imagery. I had been one of the twelve people who had purchased their two previous singles, both flops. When I saw Boy George on British television in prime time crooning

"Give me time to realize my crime, Let me love and steal," the opening line of his new hit single, I was racked by a combination of jealousy and loss. The band were no longer my Culture Club; they belonged to the world. I craved obscure music that differentiated me from all my peers, and America gave me a seemingly infinite supply. Bands like the Windbreakers, the Long Ryders, and Los Lobos. And that's just a short list of the groups I discovered who were drawn toward the use of the definite article.

Rolling Stone only had to mention an artist and I would need to buy their music. I could read a John Cougar Mellencamp interview[*] on a Thursday in which he talked intriguingly about being a "wild man" with "a half pint of whiskey in [him]" to promote his album *Scarecrow*, have that album in my hands on Saturday, and by Monday night be on the school bus home, listening to the jangling guitars and crisp snare drum of "Minutes to Memories" on my Walkman. The song told the story of a life-changing late-night conversation between two passengers, one old, one young, on a Greyhound bus leaving Jamestown, Tennessee. As the chorus blasted through my headphones, I would look around the standing-room-only No. 68 bus, which smelled of stale fart and cigarette smoke and was packed with a combustible mix of kids from rival schools all aching for a fight. School was becoming harder, my body was changing in ways I had longed for but did not understand, and I was incredibly

---

[*] "Pink Houses" did not chart in the United Kingdom but I adored the single, though not for the reasons Mellencamp probably intended. The song's climax expresses concern about the masses who live uncritical lives in high-rises and vacation at the Gulf of Mexico, but the scathing social criticism was lost on me. When I listened to those lines from the perspective of my bedroom in 1980s Liverpool, I thought, "Yes, please. A vacation down in the Gulf of Mexico-o-o sounds AMAZING."

lonely. I would press my head against the window and make believe I was on that Greyhound bus to Nashville instead.

Because of my new identity as American music aficionado,
the act of swaggering down to Penny Lane Records on a Saturday afternoon to blow some bar mitzvah money on new sounds
became one of the most life-affirming of my week. The store
was dark, damp, and cramped. I would hand over a shopping
list of the albums I wanted, each of them cribbed from the back
of *Rolling Stone*. I spoke with authority and pride when I asked
one of the two highly stoned store clerks to special-order 'Til
Tuesday's "Voices Carry," Guadalcanal Diary's "Jamboree," or
Violent Femmes' "The Blind Leading the Naked."

The clerks would turn down the volume on whatever track
they were blasting (Television's *Marquee Moon* seemed to be
perpetually playing in the store), then slowly and methodically
note down my request, before handing over the batch of cassette
tapes that I had ordered the month before. I loved the feel and
sound of tearing the shrink-wrap plastic off those cassettes, all
containing real American sounds that had been imported, especially for me. The decision of which of these new acquisitions
would be the first to be slipped into my Walkman* was always
fraught. By the time I walked back out into the daylight of the
streets of Liverpool with fresh tunes pumping through my headphones, I was guaranteed to be tingling with pleasure, knowing
I was certainly one of the few people in Britain to have whatever
album I was listening to in my possession. That I had no one to

---

* My prized possession was the Walkman WM-22, which I had also purchased
  with my bar mitzvah money. It was a shiny red color, a shade I had never previously encountered in the world of electronics, most of which were still teak,
  wood, or oak in color. Designed to blend in. Not my Walkman. Just looking
  at it felt transgressive.

talk to about the music—like *Rolling Stone* itself—made the whole experience feel even more validating. I needed to be different to prove I was somebody, and with my headphones on, I could feel American for as long as those tapes played.

I had no doubt the track I was listening to—be it "And We Danced" by the Hooters or "Wrap It Up" by the Fabulous Thunderbirds—was the very one the Michelob Ultra Dark beer drinkers were listening to as they frolicked through their glorious, snowy pickup game, that Sean Penn was savoring as he made out with Madonna at Whoopi Goldberg's party, and most certainly of all, Molly Ringwald had blaring full-blast on her car-radio-cassette player in that gun-metal Volkswagen as she sped down the freeways of the Valley, roof down, on the way to surprise me.

"America" Playlist, circa 1986–1987

For two years the only music I rocked out to on my bedroom boom box were albums I had read about in the pages of *Rolling Stone* and ordered without ever hearing a single note. It is an eclectic mix, for sure, spanning many musical genres, from alternative rock to hip-hop to country and blues. To me, it all sounded like different branches of the same sound, a sound that went by the name "American."

"Wrap It Up"—The Fabulous Thunderbirds

"Little Wing"—Stevie Ray Vaughan

"Can't Ignore the Train"—10,000 Maniacs

"Cattle Prod"—Guadalcanal Diary

"Sweet Sweet Baby (I'm Falling)"—Lone Justice

"South Bronx"—Boogie Down Productions

"Gunslinger Man"—The Long Ryders

"Golden Ball and Chain"—Jason and the Scorchers

"I'll Be Back"—The Windbreakers

"Inner City Blues (Make Me Wanna Holler)"—Marvin Gaye

"Up in the Air"—Hüsker Dü

"Children of the Revolution"—Violent Femmes

"Walk in the Woods"—Peter Case

"Born Under Punches (The Heat Goes On)"—Talking Heads

"Alex Chilton"—The Replacements

"Paid in Full"—Eric B. and Rakim

"Minutes to Memories"—John Mellencamp

"I Heard It Through the Grapevine"—Creedence Clearwater Revival

"Battleship Chains"—The Georgia Satellites

"Living for the City"—Stevie Wonder

"Automatic"—The Go-Gos

"Mumbo Jumbo"—The Tailgators

"And We Danced"—The Hooters

"Honky Tonk Man"—Dwight Yoakam

CHAPTER FOURTEEN

Crockett's Theme

P ythagoras once said, 'Lust weakens both body and mind, lads," Mr. Lavin, our classics teacher, often spontaneously screeched as he patrolled the classroom during double Greek on Wednesday afternoons. I believed him, but always wondered why Pythagoras did not take the idea a step further and add "the will to live." That was close to the reality of my life. I was a fifteen-year-old gripped by deeply felt yet unfulfilled longings, emotions only matched by the panic that came from being wholly unfamiliar with the mechanics of kissing. What went on under the hood with tongues remained a mystery. The closest I had come was practicing making out with a Debbie Gibson wall poster.

As much as I yearned to separate myself from the rest of the world in my musical tastes, biologically I craved human physical connection. I spent more weekday nights than I would ever admit watching and rewinding the climactic scene of a pirated copy of *An Officer and a Gentleman,* breaking down and marveling at Richard Gere's three-step strategy:

1. Surprise the object of your affections at the factory where she works.

2. Declare your love.

3. Then clamp your mouth down onto your partner's, before carrying her or him out of that factory in your arms as the entire workforce breaks into spontaneous applause.

Gere made it all look so simple, yet lacking both a factory, and a potential target for my affections, I was unable to put his approach into practice. So, the more Jamie and I continued to dabble on the King David bar mitzvah circuit, the sharper the stabbing ache of desire I experienced became. We were not yet regulars, but we were no longer treated as invisible interlopers, which felt like progress. Eventually, the more forward girls saw us as fresh meat and competed to be the first to kiss us, or "cop off," in Liverpool vernacular.

I was woefully oblivious to the dynamic at play and was consequently astonished when on the way out of one of the discos, I was waylaid by a group of giggling girls. They were all clad identically in off-the-shoulder T-shirts thrown over leggings, with arms full of bangles jangling as they swooped down like a gaggle of Jewish Madonnas. One of them, Stacey Silverberg, was pushed forward. I had never spoken to her directly before, but I knew she was one of the girls who had copped off at Jessica Goldfarb's party. Up close I could see she had a sweet face, with slightly crumpled squashy features. Pixyish if a pixy had smelled something terrible. "Do you want to go out with me?" Stacey blurted, with all of her friends standing behind her as reinforcement. What could I say? "Yes," I stammered, which was clearly the right answer as Stacey stuck something in my hand and ran off laughing. It was a piece of crumpled-up paper on which her name was written in loopy girl cursive above her phone number and a heart.

These were seismic developments that urgently required unpacking the next night as I cracked snooker balls around the table with my brother. Talking Heads' "Born Under Punches" was on the turntable, its manic energy reinforcing the sense of confusion and panic I had been experiencing all day. I had rarely talked to a girl one-on-one, much less taken one on a date. I tried to affect a calm exterior as Nige broke down his analysis of exactly what I had gotten myself into, along with the expectations and the secret strategies for success.

"She clearly likes you or she wouldn't have asked," he said, assessing the situation while rising up onto his tiptoes, placing his butt on the edge of the snooker table, and swooping down with his cue to crack a confident, slow roller that dispatched the pink along the cushion and into the bottom corner. "We know she's a goer, right?" A goer was another Liverpool term used for anyone who liked to hook up or "cop off." "Yes," I said, feeling a stab of excitement with a chaser of fear. "Good. Here's what you do then," he said slowly, methodically, as he chalked his cue, as if building up the suspense. "Take her to the cinema. Dark room. Romantic."

"How do I know if she wants to kiss me?" I said, unable to prevent myself from blurting out my anxieties. "Here's your pro move," he said, drawing each word out so as to maximize the pleasure derived from doling out life advice. "While the cinema lights are up, keep things fresh and light. Keep conversation ticking," he said. "But the second that room goes dark and you are through the trailers, it's go time."

I nodded as if I understood *exactly* what he was saying while hoping for more details. Thankfully, Nigel was on a roll. His interest in the snooker game had melted away. His cue had been laid down, and he stood before me to mime the intricacies of his advice so there could be no misinterpretation. "The moment those lights go black is your cue to move your arm around the back of her seat. Slow is the key, here. Slow and steady wins the race," he said, miming a reach out with his left arm. "You can start the motion off with a yawn if it feels more comfortable, but the key is, once you have started, Do . . . Not . . . Stop!" he admonished. "There can be no going back. You have to keep moving that hand around her shoulder, but don't stop there."

"Why not?" I asked, enthralled, but a little too breathlessly, even for my own liking. "Where am I going?"

"Where do you think you are going?" Nige exploded. "To the tit. TO THE TIT, you idiot," he screamed, turning away with exasperation as if the answer was so obvious my question itself was stupid.

Silence. But I needed more. "What happens then?"

"What happens then? Touch the tit and she will know you want to cop off with her. It's the sign. It's just known. Have you not seen the drive-in movie scene in *Grease?*"

Monday night I called Stacey, using the phone in my parents' bedroom for privacy. I sat on the edge of my parents' bed with just the light of my father's bedside lamp. As I dialed the number Stacey had given me, the fear notched up with every digit. The conversation was quick, stiff, functional. Away from the dry ice, strobe lights, and copious sugary sodas of the bar mitzvah disco circuit, Stacey seemed less vampish and more compliant and coy. The call could not have lasted longer than about fifty-seven seconds, but it felt like an eternity as we sped through small talk to broaching a plan and drilling down into the details. Stacey had clearly put some next-level effort into the pre-call planning, as I only had to float the notion of a movie before she suggested we meet at the local Classic Cinema for the seven o'clock showing of *Woman in Red*. I instantly agreed and bailed out of the call, concerned that if I had stayed on much longer, Stacey would have been able to hear my heart pounding down the other end of the line. I sat on the bed and took some deep breaths, reassuring myself that the first hurdle had been overcome. It had all been excruciating but a tactical success.

The plan might have been decided upon, but the strategy still needed more work. For that purpose, I was blessed to have *Miami Vice* in my life, a television show I had become obsessed with from the moment it debuted on Tuesday nights on BBC One. Ostensibly it was about a pair of drug-cartel-busting undercover detectives in Metro Dade, but it felt like it had really been created for the sole purpose of acting as a how-to guide in the art of seduction for confused boys like me.

The show did not look like anything television had seen before, hooking viewers from the opening rattle of its credits. A tinny electric drum sequence akin to musical machine-gun fire gave way to a theme song propelled by revving guitar and pulsating synths. A dizzying montage jump cut accompanied it. Flamingos! Close-up bikini'd breasts! Jai alai action! A parrot! Rolls-Royces! Bad breakdancing! Women's buttocks! Speedboats! Glass-fronted buildings! More women's buttocks! It was a startling explosion of neon and pastel that made my throat constrict with anticipation.

This sequence spoke to me. Quite literally. Watching the flash and flesh in this apparent land of ten thousand boners,

I heard voices whisper, "Roger, you think you are alive. You are not alive. We have teal here. It is a color that has not even been invented in your country yet."

Over the course of each sixty-minute episode the detective duo could be relied upon to defang some of the most menacing drug-pushing threats to society. Yet *Miami Vice* was about detective work in the same way *Animal Farm* is about horses and cows. It was really a primer about machismo, sex, and attraction. There were two stars who were different models of virility and style. Don Johnson was the handsome yet haunted Sonny Crockett and Philip Michael Thomas was his laid-back partner, Ricardo Tubbs. Crocket was a raspy-voiced maverick narc who drove a Ferrari, kept a semiautomatic pistol permanently holstered on his person, and possessed a head of feathered hair that became blonder the more successful the show became. He lived on a boat with a pet alligator named Elvis, a setup that seemed so cool that when I had to fill out a form articulating my life goals ahead of a meeting with the College's careers officer, I wrote "to live on a boat and have a pet alligator named Elvis."

Tubbs was a stark contrast to his partner. A force of calm whereas Sonny was agitated. A streetwise New York City police officer who had washed up in Miami as an outsider, armed only with his charm, a customized sawed-off double-barrel shotgun, and a jawline that stole every scene. I killed off countless hours between episodes staring in the mirror inspecting my own chin, wondering what exercises I could do to chisel it, or whether that would happen naturally, a bit like chest hair.

The two men's* contrasting personalities were reflected in

---

* As sizzlingly cool as Crockett and Tubbs were, I also warmed toward another duo on the show, Zito and Switek, the backup team who did a lot of the their style. Tubbs was a natty dresser with a predilection for double-breasted suits and silk shirt combos. Crockett, though, was a pastel peacock, deep into his pinks and turquoises, favoring suits with T-shirts underneath, occasionally with his jacket sleeves rolled up, a style move that blew my mind. I tried to mimic this by folding the arms of my school blazer, but was apprehended by Mr. Stott and threatened with the cane before I had managed to walk so much as five paces.

Miami Vice was never constrained by such strict fashion rules. The show throbbed with energy as the duo strutted around thronging, ethnically vibrant beaches, art-deco bars, and suddenly deserted areas that were almost purpose-built for shoot-outs and drug deals, as if the city had zoning laws for criminal activities. Both cops and dealers had access to an infinite supply of Lamborghinis and Ferraris, vehicles waxed to such a gleam they could not help but reflect the city's skyscrapers in their hoods.

As much as I admired Crockett and Tubbs's police work, what most impressed me was that the duo were men who truly knew how to woo and court women. Repeatedly throughout the series, they only had to look at the objects of their affection to have them become hopelessly entranced. This happened both on-screen and in real life. I read an interview in *Rolling Stone* in which Don Johnson relayed a story about filming a scene with Philip Michael Thomas where they ran down a street, and some-

---

lesser surveillance and stakeout work. In stark contrast to the stars, they were asexual and a-pastel, preferring garish combos that tended toward Hawaiian shirts and chinos. Crockett liked to refer to them as "Girls," but I was always struck by the fact that however impotent they seemed, they also conveyed a sense of cool. In retrospect, they had slacker chill down pat before it was a thing.

thing suddenly started "falling around them." He went on to explain, "When they said 'Cut' I turned around and there were about 10,000 bras and panties covering the street. It turned out the ladies working in the offices were throwing their underwear at us." After reading that, I spent an enormous amount of time lying on my bed, wondering what it could possibly feel like to walk around with panties raining down all around you.[*]

Distilled to its essence, *Miami Vice* preached two life truths: "Charm, confidence, and good looks can get you through pretty much anything" and "Do not be afraid to be singular in matters of style. Find a look and commit to it," both of which I employed on the Saturday afternoon I began to prepare for my date with Stacey aka Destiny.

I puttered around my bedroom in my undies, the *Miami Vice* sound track booming out of my cassette player. As the darkness of the wet Liverpool night descended, I tried to calm my anxiety by thinking about the Tropical Life and listening to "Crockett's Theme." Yes, Crockett even had a personal sound track for his more reflective moods. For a moment, I tried to imagine if I

---

[*] Every *Miami Vice* interview was akin to a master class on the Rules of Attraction. Don Johnson told *Rolling Stone*, "I don't like one-night stands. I mean, I've been there, it's happened; but my experience is that you're left empty and unsatisfied. There has to be some poetry." I wrote that down in my diary for future reference. Philip Michael Thomas, though, was truly the gift that kept on giving in terms of deepening my understanding of human psychology. Among the human truths he revealed in the same interview, "I get thousands of letters. Most are very intelligent. I also get beaver shots and requests from chicks in the Army for a poster of me with my chest showing. Fat girls write, 'I've lost 30 pounds and I'm preparing for you. You're the handsomest man I've seen on earth, during your love scenes. I'm having sex with my husband, but think of you.' I take it all with a grain of salt, because even if I were the most sexual man in the world, there's no way I could fuck all the women who want to be fucked by me. The wildest stuff, though, is pubic hairs. Actual hairs. It's phenomenal."

lived in America, what "Rog's Theme" would sound like, before focusing on a far more time-sensitive question: How can I be dangerous and sexual like Crockett and Tubbs?

I hit the wardrobe hard for the next hour, trying on a pastel T-shirt under my bar mitzvah blazer, which was a gray flannel affair. Next up, a pair of khaki linen pants that had taken months of begging for me to persuade my mother to buy from Marks & Spencer (regrettably, not Versace), which was the best I could do in the circumstances. I jammed a pair of my mother's shoulder pads under the blazer and rolled up the sleeves as far as they would go. To complete the look, I had saved up three months' worth of pocket money to purchase a pair of red espadrilles at a women's shoe store in town. The rope sole felt dangerous as I slipped my sockless foot inside, but it also made me wonder how Don Johnson dealt with chafing. "Style hurts," I told myself. As a final touch, I sprayed a cloud of Old Spice into the air and walked backward and forward through the mist, a methodology Philip Michael Thomas himself recommended in an interview, and that was it. I was ready to live life in the fast lane.

The date went down like this. My mum dropped me off near the Classic Cinema. Stacey was already waiting outside. She looked amazing as I walked up to her. Her hair was parted deeply on the side and sprayed into a majestic waterfall that fell over the other eye. Despite the fact she had to keep her head tilted to ensure it all stayed in place, it looked truly awesome. Momentarily dizzied and unsure of the protocol, I played it safe, holding out my arm stiffly for a handshake as she approached rather than going in for the cheek peck.

"You look nice," I said, in a way I imagined Crockett would quip to a beautiful model at a bar, who may, or may not, be secretly working for a cartel hell-bent on killing him.

"You look . . . different," Stacey giggled while pirouetting around and heading toward the cinema door, a move that left me momentarily paralyzed in the cloud of her perfume.

Stacey was sweet and amenable as we bought our own tickets, then navigated the tricky first challenge of the concessions. I really wanted a Curly-Wurly but she asked for a Flake, which I purchased along with a large Turkish Delight, which I did not really like but hoped conveyed a certain sophistication. We took our seats. Conversation was stilted. Me asking "Are you all right?" Her giggling "yes" back while doing this thing where it made it look as if she was smiling with her eyes. I found follow-up questions hard and instead elected to study the side of the Turkish Delight ingredients until the movie trailers fired up and saved me.

Darkness set in the second the opening credits of *The Woman in Red* unfurled themselves. Time to put my brother's plan into action. I heard his voice echoing in my head, "There is no going back, Roger . . . no going back." On the screen, Gene Wilder's character became infatuated with Kelly LeBrock after he glimpsed her exposed satin g-string, which had been accidentally exposed when the dress she was wearing was blown up by hot air from a ventilation grate. This kind of scene would normally demand the totality of my attention. Not on this night. Instead, I feigned a dramatic yawn, flung both arms up into the air in the process, then allowed my left arm to slowly yet casually land on the back of Stacey's seat. I rested it there for a couple of minutes, trying to affect a blasé mood, despite the fact that the wooden edge of the headrest was cutting into the arm flesh I had exposed when rolling up my jacket sleeve.

I knew I had no choice but to forge ahead. The more Gene Wilder's desire for Kelly LeBrock grew, the closer my hand inched toward my own fleshy target. As my palm passed Stacey's shoulder blade, she leaned toward me. It was likely just an inch, but this felt like a great sign. A crucial one, too, as I was beginning to seize up.

I had just crossed somewhere around the lymph-node/armpit area when the mission became turbulent. By this point, my arm was in danger of severe cramping. I had no option but to pick up the pace. A fatal decision, as Stacey was having none of it. She intercepted my hand, flung it off, and looked at me in the darkness with eyes no longer smiling. A quickly hissed "Roger" was followed by my date storming out of the cinema, leaving me alone with my embarrassment, shame, and two-thirds of the bar of Turkish Delight. For a second, I wondered what Crockett would do. Would he run out and explain himself with a heartfelt declaration of emotions, turning the situation to his advantage in a scene set to "Own the Night" by Chaka Khan? I persuaded myself Crockett would stay put, with square jaw jutted, mostly because I was relieved that the ordeal was over, and relief can come from either success or just giving up, which is, in a way, what I had just done.

I dug in to watch the rest of the movie on my own, massaging the blood back into my arm, and feeling somewhat vindicated by my decision to stay as Kelly LeBrock inexplicably and gratuitously revealed her breasts and pubic mound in one of the final scenes. Yet, at movie's end, a deep sadness struck me as I staggered out into the Liverpool night, surrounded by dozens of happy couples in their matching Sergio Tacchini tracksuits who had enjoyed the film together. This sense of dejection deepened when I stepped into a deep pothole at the bus stop, sending a jet of muddy, leafy rainwater up my front, where it quickly soaked through the bottom of my linen pants and espadrilles.

I tried to walk home as if I were a drug kingpin who had narrowly escaped a cocaine deal gone pear-shaped on the Miami waterfront, but the night was incredibly cold, and my pants started to freeze, so I called my mum from a phone booth and was relieved when she agreed to pick me up. "Hello, love, did you have a nice time?" she said, oblivious to my pain as we pulled off. I had no choice but to "Crockett" it and shut down my emotions, turning the heating in her Ford Fiesta full blast in an effort to warm my chilled toes, numbed in the sodden espadrilles. As we sat in silence on the drive home I tried to make believe we were Crockett and Tubbs. "In the Air Tonight" was playing at full blast, and we were speeding along a Miami freeway as the streetlights of South Liverpool flickered overhead.

CHAPTER FIFTEEN

My American Twin

Despite my failed attempts at creating a romantic life, Mr. McNally remained a fount of wisdom. He could joyfully fritter away up to half an economics class on a jag about books that had been important to him on his journey. He alone had the confidence to stand before a classroom of two dozen teens cloaked in self-loathing and body odor and urge us to immerse ourselves in the ideas of writers like Kahlil Gibran ("Read *The Prophet*, lads, 'Think not you can direct the course of love, for love, if it finds you worthy, directs your course'") or *The Little Prince*'s Antoine de Saint-Exupéry. ("Eyes are blind. You have to look with the heart.") But the thirteenth-century Sufi poet Rumi was by far his favorite quote source. "The wound is the place where the Light enters you," he would exhort, or "What you seek is seeking you." Most of these nuggets were wasted on us, but I respected Fat Knacker so much, I would scribble each of his insights down in the back of my textbook. The serendipity of the latter line revealed itself in the summer of 1985.

By that time, the tenacity of our parents' desire to ingratiate us on the King David social circuit had ultimately worn down the heavy resistance to our presence. Our perseverance and repeat exposure after attending more than a dozen bar and bat mitzvah discos meant that over the long summer vacation we trotted out to Calderstones Park every day to hang out with the Jewish kids. We'd found our tribe. The designated meeting spot was at a disused playground in the heart of the park. Jamie and I tended to hang in a cluster with the boys around a rusting jungle gym, whiling away the day by talking about music and football, the two subjects we felt strong in. The main topic of the day, of course, was girls. We felt weak in this arena.

The girls mostly kept to themselves, whispering, gossiping, and giggling mysteriously near the swings. Occasionally, they would dispatch an envoy toward one of our crew, to float a trial balloon by suggesting one of her friends might "fancy" him. Awkward laughter and feigned confidence would then ensue.

One morning Jamie and I headed over to the spot. As we approached, it was immediately clear something had changed. The boys and girls were all mingled and the energy was high. As we drew closer the cause became apparent. In the middle of the cluster was a stranger holding court, a large, tan kid, with a thick bush of a flattop and a pair of sunglasses. I pulled one of the regulars aside when we reached the group.

"Who's that?" I inquired.

"It's some American kid," came the stunning reply.

If an alien life-form had beamed down from outer space in a throbbing flying saucer, I could not have been more gobsmacked in that moment. A. Genuine. Real. Live. American. More than that. A real live American who, it turned out, hailed from the same North Chicago suburbs that had so inspired Sir John Hughes and that Jamie and I had bombarded with cold calls on Chicago Bears game days. Seventeen-year-old Jeff Owen, from Northbrook, Illinois, was standing in our midst. He was a distant cousin of Kevin Bracey and was visiting for a week. Kevin was a quiet but sweet kid who lived on the fringes of our group. I realized I would have to ingratiate myself into Kevin's company and by extension Jeff's immediately.

I took a deep breath to steady myself and survey the scene. Jeff was a hairy, thickset boy. He might have been only a year older than us but his size and heavy stubble allowed him to pass for one of our dads. He was wearing a blue Champion sweatshirt and a pair of shiny black Umbro checkerboard soccer shorts, but it was his sunglasses that were captivating. I heard him explain to the girls that they were a brand called Vuarnet. The fawning that ensued was audible. We had only ever seen sunglasses in Britain on episodes of *Miami Vice,* because we had no sun. England was essentially a nation of mole men. I marveled at the way Jeff could express emotion like Don Johnson, by simply taking those shades on and off in different ways. Quickly to connote astonishment. Slowly to emit a sense of self-assurance and sophistication.

For all my dreaming about, longing for, and obsession with the United States, this was only the third actual, real-life American I had ever met. Back when I was twelve, my family had encountered two seventy-something New Jerseyans who happened to be driving around the same part of northern France during our vacations. Barb and Marty Weinberg were their names and we had dinner with them a few times. I would sit with them at restaurant tables laden down with carafes of wine, frog legs, and horse sausage in tiny French towns and be dazzled solely by the fire-engine red of Barb's hair, which was not a color I'd seen in nature, and Marty's seemingly inexhaustible collection of blue Izod polo shirts. The exclamation point detail they engraved in my mind was the casual revelation of the existence of "Cable

Television," with its hundreds of channels, a bounty I could not even conceive of.

Now, right in front of me, stood the first American I had ever met of my own generation. Jews around the world had a tradition of symbolically "twinning" their kids' bar mitzvahs to a fellow Jew who remained cruelly trapped behind the Soviet Union's Iron Curtain, as these teens lacked the religious freedom to celebrate. When my bar mitzvah rolled around, I inquired of my rabbi if there was a similar concept by which I could become some American celebrant's less-fortunate English twin. The idea was met with little understanding or reaction. But now behold! There was my American twin standing there in the flesh.

"What you seek is seeking you."

I plunged into the middle of the scrum, determined to elbow my way toward my mark, processing the perfect introduction that would instantly make me stand out from my peers. I thought about impressing him with a classic Sonny Crockett of *Miami Vice* line: "The secret to success, whether it's women or money, is knowing when to quit. I oughta know: I'm divorced and broke." Or testing him by dropping the classic *Trading Places* "Looking good, Billy Ray" to see if he could return fire with an appropriately enthusiastic "Feeling good, Louis!" This was an exchange that, for Jamie and me, was the equivalent of a Masonic handshake. Yet, the moment I forced my way to the front, and Jeff span round in my direction, the sight of my own face in the reflection of his Vuarnets unnerved me. The best I could muster was a mumbled "Hi, I'm Roger."

"Raju?" he said back to me with brow furrowed.

No, "Roooooooohhhhhhhh-geeeeer" I tried a second time, speaking slowly as if encountering a member of a previously uncontacted tribe in an Amazonian rain forest.

"Oh, Raah-jaaah . . . like Daltrey," he said, nodding with a sparkling enthusiasm that flooded me with relief. I extended my hand to seal the deal, but he dismissed the formal handshake, somehow sliding his fingers into my own, and clasping them for a brief second in a way that made the most satisfying snapping noise. The interaction was so kinetic, it took all the energy I could muster to smother the jolt of exhilaration I experienced, keep my exterior cool, and pass it off as no big deal.

After finding Jeff, I made sure to never let him go. For as long as he was in Liverpool, we were barely apart, as I shamelessly commandeered the week he had come to spend with his cousin. Every day that Jeff swaggered into the park trailing Kevin behind him was a chance for a different adventure. One morning he arrived clutching a glow-in-the-dark Frisbee, which we proceeded to chase around with a lemming-like frenzy. Jeff impressed us by unfurling a dizzying array of trick shots, raising the disc above his head and flinging it with a chopping motion as if it were an axe.

The next morning, he strolled in sporting a Chicago Bears jersey with an American football tucked under his arm, patiently teaching us how to hold it properly with just your ring finger and your pinky on the laces. In return, we exposed him to our cultural gifts, taking him to see the Everton Football Club. Jeff was not so interested in "the soccer" as he insisted on calling it, but was undeniably impressed by the fans' ability to siphon down vast quantities of lager and then brazenly empty their bladders by urinating through rolled-up programs in full public view, something his fresh eyes noticed that had always felt normal to me.

The week was a lightning-speed education. I unleashed the arsenal of questions I had stored from hours watching American television, listening to Mellencamp, and ingesting the pages of *Rolling Stone*. Did a Newport Menthol Light actually make your breath taste minty fresh? Had he ever met Bud Light's original party animal, Spuds Mackenzie? What did it feel like to experience the undulating weave of a Cosby sweater against your skin? Jeff calmly indulged each query, joyfully telling us stories of life lived large in the Chicago suburbs. We would stand in the park communing as the sun went down and darkness set in, totally enthralled as he patiently explained the different mechanics of dipping Skoal or Copenhagen chewing tobacco, and why Popov vodka was the brand to drink because it was both cheap and had the added benefit of coming in a plastic bottle that was practically unbreakable. All of these stories were fascinating to me in themselves. But, since they came out of Jeff's American mouth, which was attached to a bloke in a red satin Chicago Bulls Starter jacket, Jimmy'z shorts, with a pair of hairy, squat legs descending into the sweetest-looking Converse Fast Breaks, they felt like borderline gospel.

Jeff's final day in Britain rolled around, and Kevin and I agreed it had to be marked in befitting style. That American emporium of gastronomic nourishment and delight, McDonald's, had recently arrived in northern England with a fanfare that would have accompanied the opening of a new Disneyland. English cuisine was still so grim and stodgy that the swagger and brassy American confidence inherent in Mickey D's instantly made it one of the most hyped dining establishments in Britain. A slight technical challenge was that the closest franchise to Liverpool was in Southport, a sleepy holiday town an hour away. After a tiny amount of nagging, we persuaded Kevin's mother to drive us.

Although we arrived in midafternoon, after the lunch rush,

there was still a line snaking down the block. We were willing to line up patiently, as what is truly great is worth waiting for. It took more than forty minutes to reach the front counter, by which time we were so hungry, we ordered everything on the menu in triplicate, then proceeded to savor every mouthful of Big Mac as if it were Holy Communion. By the time I hit the Chicken McNuggets, I had to remind myself to chew slowly and savor every bite with intention. Then I burned my tongue on a scalding hot apple pie, and was thrilled by the pain. Two hours later, the three of us lay back in our booth in a food coma, beset by meat sweats. A tower of empty Styrofoam, cardboard, and dipping sauces lay in our wake. Jeff took off his precious Vuarnets and handed them to me. "I want you to have these," he said. Startled by his generosity, I slipped them on. The room turned black.

After Jeff returned to Chicago, I mourned. Life went on but I was hyperaware of just how plodding and dull it was. I still hung out with the King David kids in the park on a daily basis, but the chatter and the flirting now felt monotonous. It was as if I had accidentally fallen through a portal and was fleetingly exposed to a better future only to be dumped back into the dull, old present. Life was a silent movie after the invention of talkies.

After perhaps one too many nights wallowing in my room, sullenly playing and replaying James Taylor's "You've Got a Friend," it was my mother's suggestion that I harness my moping and write to Jeff. "'Tis better to have loved and lost an American, than never to have loved at all!" she chirped while waiting for the kettle to boil. I wrote and ripped up several drafts before mailing that first letter. I had enough self-awareness to realize my initial attempt might come across a little hot and heavy, as I used the word "love" to describe our friendship and compared his absence to a color that had been eradicated from the world. I was able to tone things down sufficiently by the third or fourth draft, playing it cool by offering my thoughts on the new *St. Elmo's Fire* sound track album ("John Parr Rulz!!!") and attempting to summarize the latest gossip from Calderstones Park in terms of who fancied whom.

Three weeks of numbness followed before Jeff responded via an overstuffed package, no less. The padded manilla envelope he had dispatched was jam-packed full of wonder—newspaper clippings from the sports pages containing the latest NFL preseason news, a sticker cryptically proclaiming "Indiana! The Crossroads of America," and most intriguing of all, a Chicago Bears painter hat. This curious flattop design thrilled me as I held it in my hands, even as my brother advised, "If you wear that outside on the streets of Liverpool you are asking to have your head beaten in."

Jeff's letter was written on yellow lined paper. In it he relived a selection of memories from our shared summer, talked about the new pair of Ray-Ban sunglasses he had just purchased, and interestingly enough, asked to be remembered to our park cohort Stacey Silverberg. I read and reread until it was memorized.

And so a great correspondence was born. With exquisite detail, Jeff would describe the experience of seeing Katrina and the Waves LIVE!!!! in concert; a pair of Avia sneakers he coveted at the mall; or how he missed Liverpool so much he had taken to wearing a cologne named English Leather for Men, which sounded so debonair. Crucially, his letters continued to be accompanied by a harvest of newspaper clippings and assorted paraphernalia, including copies of *Sports Illustrated* magazine, a cassette tape on which he had recorded a local sports radio call-in show in which Cubs fans predicted how the hitting of

Ron Cey and Ryne Sandberg would surely end their World Series curse, and a poster of the intimidating Bears offensive line in which the rippled players posed in shades and fedoras as the "Black-n-Blues Brothers."

I pored over each object like a CIA case officer analyzing raw intel. Each was a precious gem. Over time each object would be tacked up on the walls of my bedroom, alongside the painters cap, which hung proudly on a nail beside a carefully constructed Coke can collection I had begun to erect in a towering formation.

In return, I would dispatch programs and match reports from Everton's season, which was one of agonizing almosts. Propelled by the goals of poster-boy striker Gary Lineker, they came second in the league to archrivals Liverpool. At first, the letters I wrote to accompany them were a combination of two main streams of thought: profound Chicago Bears analysis and a retelling of the mundane details of Liverpool life. I would describe the experience of almost being beaten up by a pack of menacing eleven-year-olds who had tried to pick me off on the way home from the school bus or how a classmate had needed medical attention after a particularly savage thrashing on the buttocks from Mr. Stott went septic. Over time, though, I dug deeper, and the act of writing letters to Jeff allowed me to access emotions and unleash thoughts I could not express to anyone else—not friends, my parents, nor my brother. I would write in a stream of consciousness about my hopes, love, and dreams, and how I wanted to change my life. These feelings were so raw and unformed that to write them felt like finding a rhythm while swimming freestyle and turning your head out of the water for a delicious second to fill your lungs with air. I had never been this honest, not even with Jamie.

My bedroom walls resplendent with all the tchotchkes Jeff sent my way.
These walls were a manifestation of whom I yearned to be.

One of Jeff's packages included a special prize: a package of Bubblicious grape bubble gum, a flavor that English confectioners who seemed satisfied with offering only original and mint had yet to imagine. I rationed those five pieces as if world famine was coming, allowing myself to open just one square, which I then kept stuck on the corner of my desk. Every night I would recover it, pop it back in my mouth, and delight in chewing ecstatically while surveying the posters on my walls. Then I would slip on Jeff's Vuarnets and revel in the sensation of everything fading to black. The darkness enabled me to imagine a double life. An alter ego. American Rog. A kid who looked like me, but was clad in Ocean Pacific board shorts, an Airwalk T-shirt, and rocked a pair of Reebok Soldiers on his feet. I pictured him driving. Making out. Smiling. All the things I did not do in real life.

CHAPTER SIXTEEN

Super Bowl Shuffle

The establishment of a weekly transatlantic correspondence nourished and sustained me. This new ability to commune directly and personally with Chicago provided a safe haven from Liverpool College and made the school year fly by.

The spine of my alternate reality was the Chicago Bears' serendipitous season of wonder. The Bears had been a shambolic entity for the greater part of two decades, yet no sooner had I connected myself to their destiny than their fortunes changed.

Each smashmouth victory bound me closer to the city of Chicago and its fans, who reveled as their Bears took a wrecking ball to an inferiority complex built over decades. My emotional connection to the town my great-grandfather had set out for, but never reached, was enriched by Jeff's weekly dispatch from Northbrook, Illinois. His packages coughed up treasure after treasure that would quickly find a home on my bedroom walls. The crown jewel I affixed directly over my bed was a poster of William "Refrigerator" Perry leaning against an enormous fridge and making it tilt with one casual push. With his hefty girth, gap-toothed smile, and youthful bravado, Perry had established himself as the team's darling in his rookie season. An enormous defensive lineman who had become an offensive novelty act, the Refrigerator was the embodiment of the carnival that was the Bears' 1985 season. A team who embraced a hunger for dominance and lust for life in equal measure.

As long as the Bears were winning, I could handle the worst that Liverpool life had to throw at me. Even double periods of Latin or Wednesday's dreaded triple rugby were a breeze when I knew the Bears were living proof that suffering builds character, that goodwill and patience can triumph.

Yes, they suffered one defeat, in week 14, against the Miami Dolphins, but thankfully, that loss proved to be a wake-up call, both for the Bears and me. My team stampeded their way through the rest of the regular season. On the eve of the playoffs, a flat package arrived from Jeff. He had thoughtfully dispatched a copy of a seven-inch single recorded by some of my heroes under the name Chicago Bears Shufflin' Crew. It was dubbed "The Super Bowl Shuffle" and had become a *Billboard* hit and national sensation. I was used to English soccer teams going into the recording studio ahead of a big game to lay down a treacly traditional hymn or fan chant. This was next level, the first-ever rap track to be released by a sports team; it was six minutes and fifty-eight seconds of bombastic boasts, veiled threats of violence, and brazen hubris and I loved every single second as the Bears players promised to "Ring the bell" of those they faced, "bend" opposing quarterbacks, and generally predict Super Bowl glory. I was probably the only person in England to possess a copy of this song on vinyl, and I played it on repeat, a little part of me hoping I could soak up some of its swashbuckling confidence by osmosis.

My Bears proceeded to deliver, plowing their way through

the playoffs without conceding a single point. In Super Bowl XX, they would face the New England Patriots. This game was such a monumental match-up that British television stepped in to broadcast the brawl, which kicked off at ten in the evening Liverpool time, live in its entirety. Even though it was technically a school night, I stayed at Jamie's house. The two of us remained glued to the television in his bedroom until 3 A.M., taking turns to wear a giant orange and blue foam finger Jeff had sent over that proclaimed "Bears #1."

After considerable, shameless pestering on my part, my dad had folded and agreed to buy us both a single can of Budweiser to mark the occasion. Once the game kicked off, we ripped open the ring tab on Jamie's beer and began to share it, rationing sips throughout the first half as the Bears blew out a shell-shocked Patriots with their signature mix of furious joy. With the result quickly a fait accompli, I spent much of the third quarter staring at the can of Budweiser, becoming lost in its intricate red, white, and blue label. As the Bears hoisted the Vince Lombardi Trophy, Jamie and I hugged, toasting the beginning of the Chicago Bears dynasty I knew in my heart was inevitable.[*]

"Well played, Benj," he said generously.

"Thank you," I replied, reaching for a humble tone in victory, before shaking up my can of Budweiser with all of my might and ripping it open dramatically, unleashing a plume of lager that left us drenched and Jamie's bedroom ceiling stained.

---

[*] A mixture of arrogance and poor planning undermined the Bears' title defense. The team went 14-2 in the regular season but lost quarterback Jim McMahon to injury along the way. The offense was immobilized without him. When the Redskins ran roughshod over my heroes in their opening playoff game, I wept. The unstoppable dynasty lasted exactly one season.

It was 3 A.M. We had school in the morning, but I would not sleep. I lay in Jamie's guest bed, listening to his soft snoring, hugging my giant foam finger, now lager-soaked, imagining I was part of the Chicago Bears Shufflin' Crew and was thrust forward to ad lib my very own line.

"My name is Rog. I bring the doom
Could start a fight in an empty room."

CHAPTER SEVENTEEN

The Goers Go

The Bears' world championship took place 3,779 miles away from me. I had not lifted a single finger to contribute to their success. Yet its accomplishment gave me a strut in my step that I very much needed.

By now, even the most introverted King David boys had hooked up with a girl and become "goers."* That I had not created an intense self-awareness, a wound that pained me, not just at parties where everyone else but Jamie and me was copping off, but perpetually. The only time I had felt that so profoundly useless was when I was five or six and my parents forced me to go to a pool party even though I was the only kid who did not yet know how to swim. I spent an entire afternoon feeling a sense of inferiority and humiliation, marooned on a poolside bench alongside the birthday boy's senile wheelchair-bound grandmother, who gargled involuntarily as we watched everyone else splash deliriously, spin diving and cannonballing with shrieks of delight. This same shame now plagued my waking life in the everyday.

---

* Liverpool slang for someone who has hooked up with a member of the opposite sex.

The nadir was the Saturday night that Mike Nagel, the handsome paragon of virility of the King David crew, threw a house party. With his perfect bangs and well-stocked wardrobe, Mike was desirability personified. He had double cachet born of the fact that his elder brother briefly dated an it girl who ended up becoming a child bride of one of the Rolling Stones. Word also had it that Mike had recently been the recipient of a hand job from a university student at a fresher party, a rumor that, if true, radically escalated the stakes for all of us.

This breaking news made it a medical miracle Jamie and I were able to set out for this party in the first place, as we both were almost immobilized by both dread and hope. This sense was accentuated by just how far Mike's house was from the nearest bus stop. The Nagels lived in a sprawling new housing development that had risen overnight on what had previously been a contaminated wasteland. The two of us stumbled in the darkness and damp around the unfamiliar labyrinth, squinting at the numbers on one identical house after another.

It took us an eternity to find the Nagel home. Whitney Houston's "How Will I Know" was throbbing through the closed curtains of the front room. We rang the bell. Mike Nagel himself answered but strangely decided to keep the door on the latch as he did so. Two girls, Laura Blumenthal and Stacey Silverberg, hung off his shoulders, trying to pull him back into the fray.

"What do you want, lads?" he purred in his smooth Irish brogue, which, as Mike Nagel was well aware, gave a new arrival an air of exotic sophistication in a city filled with rough Scouse accents.

"We're here for the party," Jamie ventured with a thin smile, attempting to evidence a confidence we did not feel.

"Can't come in. This is a cop-off party," Mike replied with devastating finality.

"It's only for goers," added Laura Blumenthal with a laugh, as Mike slammed the door emphatically in our faces.

Jamie and I were left in the dark. We stood there shell-shocked in silence for what felt like an eternity. First of all, our hope was that Mike Nagel would come back and open the door with a laugh and tell us he was only kidding. Then, when it was clearly established that that was not going to happen, we just wallowed in a sense of excruciating embarrassment. Our shame was all the more searing because it made sense. If I was a girl, I would want to be alone with Mike Nagel, too. Why should he let us in?

Suddenly, Jamie snapped back into action, clasping his hands together and saying "Shall we go to town then?" Neither one of us had the strength to address the humiliation we had just shared as we began to traipse the long way back to the bus stop. Sometimes it is more convenient to cope with pain by pretending it didn't exist. As I had come to realize, sometimes you become numb because you are unable to feel anything at all, but at times like this one, you can become numb because you feel too much.

The bus did not come. The rain started to fall. We desperately needed a sense of movement. Any movement to put as much distance between us and the scene of our shame as quickly as possible, and thus we elected to shoulder the expense of jumping a cab and to make believe we both had wanted to go to the movies in the first place.

Titillatingly, Mickey Rourke and Kim Basinger's 9½ Weeks was one of the movies on offer at the theater. The sexually ex-

With Jamie. And girls. Who wanted nothing to do with us.

plicit erotic blockbuster's "sex-in-the-rainy-alleyway scene" was a national sensation. To be able to say you had watched the scene in which Kim Basinger masturbated in her workplace would have garnered us serious respect on the Liverpool College schoolyard, but *9½ Weeks* came with an 18 rating and we lived in fear of being asked for proof of age by the octogenarian cashier. Jamie and I both knew we could not take a second humiliating rejection in one night so were relieved to discover John Hughes's latest release, *Pretty in Pink*, was also playing at a theater nearby.

The movie proved undoubtedly to be one of the greatest creative achievements in cinematographic history. The intensity of the characters' feelings was set at hyperbolic levels that matched my own. Molly Ringwald's performance as Andie, the working-class outcast who remains true to herself while winning her man Blane, was nuanced, entrancing, and life-affirming. Yet watching Jon Cryer as her dweebish sidekick, Duckie, made me pale. Duckie was quirky, geeky, and filled with self-loathing. He believed all you needed to do to land a woman was to secretly pine for them. The similarities between his passive approach and mine were haunting. What fools we were to hope that a mixture of self-deprecation, support, and tenderness could lead anywhere but to be overlooked.

The second big life lesson in the film was delivered via Andrew McCarthy's preppy. He had the playbook to follow; he was a bloke who was calm, willing to admit mistakes, and confident enough to articulate his feelings directly. He won Molly's heart by packing an entire arsenal of emotions into twenty-three words—the mind-blowing "You said you couldn't be with someone who didn't believe in you. Well I believed in you. I just didn't believe in me." This would be my new offense for engaging the loins of the opposite sex or whatever it was that scientifically stirred beneath a girl's waistline.

I saw this film at a crucial juncture. My fifth form year[*] had come to an end, which meant it was time for Liverpool College's recent, crude coed experiment to extend to my grade. For the past few years, the College had taken to admitting small numbers of female students to each sixth form class. I had seen them. Heard about them. But as they were members of the upper classes, I had never actually interacted with one of these

---

[*] A rising junior in American terminology. English educations back then were narrow but deep. For the last two years of high school we all selected three subjects. From the age of sixteen on, I studied only English, history, and economics. Every other subject—the entire body of sciences—was flung aside. A system that made me, like thousands of others, incredibly sophisticated in some realms, and a naive dunce in others. My knowledge of biology and medicine remain at medieval levels.

specimens. Rumor had it that a dozen brave girls had now signed up to join us. And so, on the final day of the school year, there came an orientation. We were to meet our new classmates.

The setting was the school hall. The seventy or so boys in my year who intended to return for sixth form had already been cooped up for close to an hour as Mr. Stott stood onstage to provide a final overview of the new realities and ground rules in place to adjust to a female presence. "The girls are to be treated like normal lads," he explained, reaching for a tone of fairness and equity that had never been his strong suit. "Courting the opposite sex on school property is strictly forbidden," he added awkwardly before pausing for questions.

"What's courting, sir?" was the predictable opener designed to heighten Mr. Stott's obvious discomfort.

"You know exactly what that means, Stark," he snapped back in an effort to reclaim his authority.

Another kid piped up cheekily, "Will you cane the girls, sir?"

Stott did not have time to answer, as at that minute came a knock on the door. Madame Lamaire, the French teacher and the only female member of the senior staff, then walked in theatrically with a dozen girls following submissively behind.

"Boys, all rise," commanded Mr. Stott, as the girls were led up toward the stage alongside him.

The nine years I had spent at Liverpool College had been filled with noise—the devastating sound of derisive laughter in classrooms, grunts as rugby balls were kicked on the playing fields, the terror-filled snap of locker room towels being whipped at exposed buttocks. College boys were a raucous, rowdy, boisterous bunch. So when those girls entered the room, it was astonishing that the scrape of chairs being pushed back by seventy boys obediently springing to their feet was followed by absolute stunned silence, a stillness that only reinforced the life-changing nature of the moment. Our first glimpse of girls. Our Girls. The only sound audible was that of seventy respiratory systems delightedly overworking in synchronicity.

For their part, the girls kept their eyes to the floor, cruelly exposed as they climbed the stairs and ascended the stage before us. Most had dressed for the occasion as if they were attending church services or a bar mitzvah. There was an array of colors, fabrics, and limbs exposed in miniskirts, silk blouses, and high heels.

"Men, these are your new classmates," said Mr. Stott, extending both arms to either side while straining to repress his typical tendencies toward racism, homophobia, sexism, and pretty much any isms and/or phobias. "Please join me in giving them a Liverpool College welcome."

Like the rest of my class, I welcomed the girls by staring at them, with eyes wide open, slack-jawed. For their part, the girls did what came naturally when being ogled by seventy boys—packing together like a herd of sable antelopes trying to escape wild dogs tracking them on the African savanna.

In the middle of the cluster, a tall brunette with a head full of curls and rosy red cheeks stood out. In her hands, she grasped a thin leather briefcase as a prop to give her a sophisticated, worldly air, like a young lawyer off to court. A blonde with the straightest hair I had ever seen, dark skin, and a dimple stood beside her. She had the confidence to stare directly back at us and look like she was scrutinizing each boy with more judgment than we could ever cast her way. "That's Annabelle Starr," Jamie whispered, having done his due diligence. "She's an actress. Appeared in some local television commercials." Standing right by her was another, even blonder girl. Her large chest was accentuated by a low-cut wrap shirt she had elected to wear. "That's her friend, Sally Joyce. She's a real goer."

My eye, though, had been drawn to the far left of the stage. Leaving a gap between herself and the rest of the pack was a girl with red hair artfully flipped so a curl hung over one eye. Her long-dress, Doc Marten combat boots, and suede jacket suggested both mystery and thrift store leanings. A pair of large gold hoop earrings topped off the look, wavering as she looked around the room with a sense of defiance as she stood with hands in jacket pockets, her smirk suggesting she knew just how asinine the whole scene was. It was as if Molly Ringwald herself had descended from the Valley, having elected to quit the entertainment industry and complete her academic life at Liverpool College.

Could it be true? Had this girl really committed to spend two years living and breathing in the same classrooms as me at Liverpool College? As Stott began to explain the coining of the school motto, "Non solum ingenii verum etiam virtutis,"* I pondered how she might react if I dropped some Andrew McCarthy–esque lines on her. For a second it felt like our eyes locked. I was not 100 percent sure, but I experienced a pang of excitement and a blush of shame born of being caught staring, and instantly looked away.

The briefing ended when Stott ran out of energy and announced he needed a cigarette. The girls were abruptly ushered offstage by Madame Lamaire, who led them through a side exit, as Mr. Stott explained, "to attend their own orientation."

---

* Despite going to the school for eleven years and memorizing that motto in Latin, I just had to Google translate it to find out what it actually means. "Not Alone by Ability, but Also by Character."

"What's that about, sir, tampons or something . . ." Stark wise-cracked from the back of the room. Stott had reverted to his old self now that the newcomers had left us, and the dynamic was safely all male again.

"Shut up, you impudent fool, or you will be caned," he seethed, as he fumbled for the cigarette. "Cheer up, Stark," he said before inhaling deeply, "you only have to wait two months and you can see your girlfriends every day, lover boy." He then pivoted smartly to exit the stage, dismissing us with a curt "Have a meaningful summer holiday, gentlemen."

With those words, a huge roar went up. My classmates jostled their way out of the hall, loosening their ties, playfully slapping each other as they swapped observations about the girls, most of which revolved around Sally Joyce's knockers. My mind was on other matters. Summer vacation meant nine long school-free weeks now lay in front of us. Fifth form was typically the year all Jewish kids made their first ever visit to Israel, joining youth tours traveling around the country. Think farming on kibbutzim, touring Jerusalem, and making out with North London girls while floating in the Dead Sea.

Not me, though. In a recent letter, Jeff had pitched the notion of my flying to Chicago to spend the summer with him. I had only left Britain once in my lifetime and that was just to drive around France. As much as I obsessed about America, plane travel cost a small fortune, and America felt like it was on another planet. Nonetheless, I braved broaching the topic with my parents. My father in his legalistic way brusquely told me he and my mother would take the idea "under advisement." A week later he delivered judgment. If I could achieve grades at the ridiculously high level he set, which he admitted he felt was beyond my ability, he would purchase a plane ticket. The academic goal was lofty, but it was nothing when compared to the sheer depth of my yearning to go on this adventure. I worked my ass off, delivered the A's and sprinkling of B's my father had targeted, and an air ticket from London Heathrow to Chicago-O'Hare was purchased with my name on it.

"You have surpassed yourself, Roger," my father intoned with astonishment during a lengthy monologue in which he proudly presented me with a thick wallet filled with documentation from the local travel agent. As his lips moved, only one word kept going through my mind:

"America."

I was coming.

BOOK THREE

THE LIGHT/
AMERICAN ROG

CHICAGO, ILLINOIS, JULY–AUGUST 1986
LIVERPOOL, ENGLAND, 1986–1988

"What you seek is seeking you."

—*Rumi*

CHAPTER EIGHTEEN

Beef, Democracy, and Freedom

CHICAGO, ILLINOIS, JULY 1986

In times ancient and modern, remarkable people have undertaken epic journeys to unlock the secrets of life. Aeneas found truth in *The Aeneid* while wandering to Rome. *The Pilgrim's Progress* saw the heroic Christian climb from the City of Destruction to the Celestial City. In a remarkably similar vein, I boarded a Boeing 767 in the summer of 1986 and flew 3,937 miles from London to Chicago. I was on a quest to make real a dream that had long had me in its clutches, and to discover whether it was possible to be what you are not: an American who had never visited America.

The flight time was over seven and a half hours, more than enough time for the batteries in my Walkman to die. Even the sound of R.E.M.'s already-murky "Cant Get There From Here" churning away almost mournfully at three-quarters speed did nothing to diminish my excitement. The fourteen cans of Coke I had drunk down in flight combined with my surging adrenaline to provide a level of enthusiasm that could only be measured by the look of annoyance on the face of my seat mates. I had bought a pair of knockoff Ray-Bans at Heathrow Airport duty-free, and once we had flown over New England, I spent the last portion of the flight in the bathroom taking them on and off in the mirror, working on my emotional range.

We made landfall in midafternoon. You know that feeling of total meltdown that overpowers you when a sports team you love wins a game in the final seconds? That's the kind of euphoric rush that hit me as the plane taxied to a stop. I tried to play it cool, though, with the new shades positioned archly on the tip of my nose, Walkman proudly clipped onto my belt as I stepped over the threshold of the plane's exit and toward the shuttle bus that would take us to U.S. Immigration, also known as the United States of Roger Bennett's Dream Come True.

My first impression of Chicago was the heat, a singeing kind of blast I had only experienced when venturing too close to the pottery furnace in the school art room. The feverish fire that made it hard to breathe. For a second, I told myself it was from the plane's giant propellers. When I realized this was not the case, and this wet 93-degree heat was Chicago's standard, I panicked. My lungs were accustomed to the damp false hope of English summer. Was the oxygen I was sucking in sufficient to sustain life? I pushed the new faux-bans up on the back of my nose and steeled myself to find out.

After the lull of clearing passport control and dragging a cumbersome suitcase off the carousel, my energy levels were restored to manic by a hefty, holstered customs officers waving me through and proclaiming "Welcome to America" in a gravelly voice. I approached two sliding doors that led to the arrival hall and took a deep breath to center myself before taking my first steps out into the USA, the land that had fired my imagination, filled my dreams, and whose flag I had badly painted on my bedroom wall. Now I was actually here.

The doors purred open and I was met by an explosion of sound, a cacophony of welcomes, reunions, and unlicensed cab rides being hawked. More overwhelming than the noise were the sights. The neon logo of a Burger King kiosk made my heart throb. I shuffled forward, trying to take it all in while wondering what extraordinary fare a restaurant named "Dunkin' Donuts" might offer when I slammed into Jeff, who was hanging over the arrivals barrier with a scrawled "Hey Rog, Go Bears" sign. I hugged him with all my might, inhaling a potent whiff of citrus and musk in the process. "English Leather cologne, baby," Jeff said, grinning, before pivoting to the guy beside him. "This is my friend Andre," he said, pointing to a tall, laid-back gent with a molten mane of blond hair.

Andre smiled and picked up my suitcase as if it were as light as a backpack, and we headed toward the parking lot, where he flung it into the trunk of Jeff's two-tone gray car. "It's a Pontiac Phoenix," he said proudly. "It was my mom's, but they're my wheels now." I recognized the model from *Police Academy 3: Back in Training.* Then we were off, speeding onto the highway. I sat in the backseat, fighting waves of jet lag, determined to soak in every second of this month.

Out of my window, I caught sight of an American highway sign, in the distinctive green and yellow I had glimpsed in countless books and television shows, unfiltered for the first time with my own eyes. Speeding past were American automobiles, not only brazen in size, in comparison to their tiny, fuel-conscious British counterparts, but brilliantly colored, too. English cars come in black, brown, and dull. American wheels are fiery red, brazen blue, shimmery lime. This magical land I had coveted from afar was becoming more real with every passing mile.

"You hungry?" Jeff asked as he pulled off the highway and swerved into a parking space without ever really decelerating speed. "First stop in America gots to be some beef au jus," said Andre, emitting a genuine sense of pride as he pointed to a cowboy hat logo emblazoned with the word "Arby's." Minutes later, the three of us had squeezed ourselves into a booth, and I opened the wax paper wrapping that held my very first Hot French Dip. Lifting the steaming, thinly sliced roast beef delicacy to my lips, I took a bite, and as the gravy dripped down my chin and back down onto the table, I could have sworn it tasted of Beef, Democracy, and Freedom. I was ready to eat my fill.

Andre (left) and Jeff (middle). I owe a lot to both of them.

CHAPTER NINETEEN

Game Show Winner

Behold Northbrook, a jewel of Chicago's North Shore. This tiny suburban universe was built on affluence and comfort, just twenty-three miles northwest of the urban center. I had never set foot near its white-fenced single-family homes with stylishly manicured lawns, and yet it all felt so familiar. These malls, schools, and homes were the canvas upon which filmmaker John Hughes had painted his movie masterpieces. Because of *The Breakfast Club* I was overcome by a sense of déjà vu as I drove through the town's quaint downtown for the first time. Everywhere we went, it felt like I had been there before.

Jeff opened the door into his family's modern suburban home, and we walked into an open-plan den to which you only had to add Anthony Michael Hall and Kelly LeBrock to make a sequel to *Weird Science* come alive. I marveled at the bright colors, convenience, and casual luxury of it all, a stark contrast to the scuffed hardwoods, tatty carpets, and shabby family heirlooms that filled the average British home. Here there were couches that hugged you in their embrace. Shag carpets that were eager to massage your feet. A La-Z-Boy recliner in which I frittered away much of my first morning there, marveling in

Finally. In the Promised Land.

its engineering while repeatedly snapping the footrest backward and forward. Even the bathrooms had thick foam-padded toilet seats that you sank into as you went about your business. America. A land where extravagant comfort was the prerogative, even in nature's most primal moments.

Televisions were littered everywhere. After growing up in a home where the single set we owned had to be wheeled around the house, it was like a trip to Narnia to live in a place where each room had at least one. In the bathroom, there was a tiny waterproof screen attached to the wall below the showerhead, and a Sony Watchman had been set up by the toilet, enabling me to multitask: I could keep one eye on *Wheel of Fortune* while whacking off on that foam-seated throne.

Our days fell into an easy rhythm. As if following a child-care truth established by *The Goonies* and 73 percent of American sitcoms, Jeff lived a self-sufficient life, entirely shorn of parental oversight. His mum and dad, Bobbie and Buddy, were barely around. Having a guest living in the family's midst for weeks like this would never have been possible with my family, yet Jeff's parents achieved the feat by electing to relinquish all responsibility. Buddy Owen, a cheerful squat gent with a magnificent gray hair-helmet, was an executive in the rag trade and rarely home. His wife, Bobbie, also worked full-time as an occupational therapist. Every 1980s teen movie I had ever seen reinforced an unwritten rule that moms could never be cool. Smart and sassy, Bobbie undercut that single-handedly. Liverpool mothers tended to express their love for their family in the kitchen, one home-cooked meal at a time, yet Jeff's mom's hands never touched the oven. The only night we ate at home as a family, she commanded Buddy to fling a half dozen of the largest tomahawk steaks I had ever seen on the barbecue.

Jeff also had a younger sister, Barb, who looked like she had just taken a photograph of Jennifer Grey to her hairstylist and commanded them to make it so. Super snarky, she was too hip to have any interest in us and spent almost the entire summer holed up in her bedroom talking on the phone with the *Pretty in Pink* sound track playing on repeat. The guest bedroom I slept in was next door to hers and the Psychedelic Furs hummed through the wall at all hours of the day.

Barb's disdain and Buddy and Bobbie's absence meant I spent an enormous amount of time in the Owen home utterly alone. Jeff's days did not tend to begin until twelve thirty, a slacker schedule that did not align with my jet lag, but I quickly learned not to mind. Once my eyes had been exposed to the barrage of syndicated game shows that dominated American daytime television, I set an early alarm just so I did not miss a minute of their magic. My mornings were akin to that scene in *Splash* in which Daryl Hannah's wide-eyed mermaid teaches herself English by binge-watching *Bonanza* and Richard Simmons's infomercials. For me, *Wheel of Fortune*, *Jeopardy!*, *Family Feud*, and *Hollywood Squares* became a self-education in the tenets of American life. I savored them all, clicking from one to the other on the guest bedroom television with the remote control, never having to leave the comfort of my bed.

The feast of glitzy game shows with their dizzying, shared tropes had me in their thrall: the large woman being plucked out of the audience as a contestant and barely able to mask her excitement nor keep her ample flesh in her blouse as she scampered onto the stage ready to have her life changed. The piles of cash won and lost, then won again. The shiny new Chevy Corvette, luxury powerboat, or complete set of nonstick gourmet cookware wheeled on as the grand prize as the climax of every show. All these images reinforced the same message to me—America was a place where everyone had a shot.

That sense was reinforced by a summer-long promotion run by Coca-Cola in which they had ingeniously hidden a small fortune's worth of cash in specially engineered spring-loaded cans across the nation. Commercial after commercial would depict high-denomination banknotes popping out of some lucky bastard's drink. That prospect coated my life in a state of perpetual titillation, instilling a sense that whenever I opened a Coke, which I did between ten to fifteen times a day, a cool grand would appear.

MTV upped that ante. The network toggled between the videos for Peter Gabriel's "Sledgehammer" and Belinda Carlisle's "Mad About You" for my entire stay. Sandwiched in between, it ran a competition* in which one lucky sweepstake entrant could win an entire town in Texas for simply mailing in a postcard. This was a ludicrous concept, yet one that, after feasting on a binge diet of American daytime television and Coke, did not surprise me in the least. I entered this competition four times during my stay, cocksure of victory as I dropped my postcard into the mailbox on every occasion.

On my second morning, the realization hit me as I stood under the high-pressure showerhead, eyes fixed on that tiny plastic screen, watching some hopeful contestant taking a spin on *Press Your Luck*. After lapping up countless John Hughes creations, I had essentially walked through the screen into my own movie. Every one of Hughes's signature story lines was present: the vulnerable yet thoughtful kid grappling with teen angst, of which I had a surplus; capers ensuing with crushes, and please, God, even romance, to be sprinkled in; lived out against a backdrop of the jocks, geeks, rich kids, dweebs, babes, goofs, and wasters of Chicago's northern suburbs in which adult supervision did not

---

* I looked this up to make sure my memory was not warped with time and it is shockingly true. The network purchased a hundred-acre tract of land in the Texas Panhandle as the first prize for the winning postcard drawn in the competition. An article in the *Los Angeles Times* reported one winner would take "the acreage, stereo equipment, 1,000 compact discs, a satellite dish to keep up with MTV, which is not otherwise available there, enough candy and gum from contest co-sponsor Nabisco to supply a town, a Jeep and $100,000 cash." The residents of the nearby town of Shamrock were desperate to win to keep the land in local hands, but the winner, Mrs. Lowery of Jackson, Alabama, never took possession of the land nor did she ever watch MTV. She just liked entering competitions and learned about this one in a magazine that captures the optimistic zeitgeist of Reagan's America: *Contest News Letter*.

exist and everything felt possible. All that remained to be seen was whether I would turn out to be like Andrew McCarthy's or Judd Nelson's character? Or even Ally Sheedy's.

Later, Jeff emerged and knocked on my door at his traditional time, around midday. By then I had consumed between three and four hours of game show fare, which meant I had witnessed a dozen or more contestants arrive with nothing and leave carrying off piles of cash or luxe seven-piece kitchen knife sets at the very least. When Jeff mumbled it was time to pick Andre up and head over to "the Shore," his words triggered all my pent-up energy, like a manic Labradoodle desperate to be let off its leash. I was ready to embrace whatever was to come.

CHAPTER TWENTY

On Glencoe Beach

English beaches I was familiar with were different. The polluted ocean contained a higher percentage of chemicals than water, and an unfortunate, dead sheep carcass could often be spotted bobbing idly up and down to the rhythms of the tide. As a kid, I had spent countless family vacations cowering under umbrellas at the seaside in North Wales, eating ice cream cones and pretending we were having fun, even as the wind whipped the sand into our faces to reinforce our discomfort. Glencoe Beach, by comparison, was a shore-side paradise—a slither of coast crushed against Lake Michigan filled with bronzing teens, yellow Sony Sports Walkmans, and where the air smelled faintly of Hawaiian Tropic dark tanning oil.

Our first stop was always the Red Rooster, a beach shack that doled out slices of pizza that passed as breakfast. We would share a pie weighed down with pepperoni and sausage, chug a can or two of Orange Crush, and wait for Jeff's high school friends to emerge and assemble, an incredible gang of boys who were obsessed with muscle, abs, and lifting weights, and as a result comfortable without their shirts. They all wore magnificent green shiny shorts proclaiming "New Trier Athletics" just above the knee. I coveted those garments as much as their hairstyles, which flowed and flopped over their eyes at exactly the right moments. Above all, I yearned for their ability to transition between land and water so effortlessly, executing a series of simple yet vicious strokes that allowed them to slice confidently through the waves. My crude breaststroke could not hope to keep up with them.

The girls, forever bronzing, never went in the water. Occasionally they would walk to the lake's edge to cool off, but otherwise they seemed content to spend hours laid out on beach towels, chatting and listening to Mr. Mister on boom boxes, a tangle of oiled flesh, tanned limbs, and micro-bikinis. The novelty of my presence as an outsider equipped with a British accent broke down the barriers that had traditionally existed between myself and the opposite sex. In Liverpool, the die may have been cast. Glencoe Beach offered a fresh start, a chance for me to assert myself as the confident raconteur I longed to be.

I spent hours among those girls, lying back on a bath towel I had liberated from Jeff's guest bathroom, dazzling them with my wit and repartee and patiently answering every last question about the Who, *Monty Python,* and *The Young Ones,* English cultural relics that all seemed bigger here than they remained at home. I did all this while surreptitiously trying to steal glances of cleavage.

One girl stood out in particular: Casey, a pixie-haired sophomore at New Trier who had been born in England while her academic parents were teaching at Oxford. Though she had returned to the Midwest at nine, her Englishness still clung to her, expressing itself via the pair of well-worn paisley Liberty shorts and the music she listened to, which she communicated via an impressive concert shirt collection, rotating between the Cure and the Smiths on a daily basis.

Casey's experience in Britain equipped her with a dual perspective. It was as if she spoke two languages, empathetically understanding the grim, confining realities I grappled with in Liverpool while being able to translate hidden insights about the American life she lived and which I craved. "My mom always says that British people take most satisfaction from being less miserable, less poor, less far down the class system than those below them," she would muse, sitting cross-legged on her towel, "but in America, people look up, define their life goals, then work out how to go grab them." As Casey talked about her own future using words like "happiness," "ambition," and "optimism," she would toy with her sun-bleached bangs and stretch out her smooth, tanned legs. Lying beside her, I felt the soak of the sun on my own pale body. Britain was the darkness. I had found the light.

That light extended to Jeff and Andre, who spent most of the day clowning, flirting, flexing, or flinging a football theatrically while kicking up a sandstorm at the back of the beach. What shocked me about their friendships was how easy and supportive they all seemed. Liverpool College was survival of the fittest, a brutal world filled with savage put-downs, mental evisceration, and fistfights. *A Clockwork Orange* but worse. Glencoe Beach felt like *Fantasy Island*, an alternate universe of positive, casual affability. Why fight when there were so many better things to do? Late afternoon we would leave the beach and head back to Andre's. He lived in a modernist box of glass and steel set above the edge of a wooded ravine, where we could kill off the day dive bombing in his indoor swimming pool before sweating out the day's pepperoni intake in the sauna. We would sit, perspire, and gleefully shoot the shit as to whether the Grateful Dead or the Rolling Stones were a more consequential band.

Evenings were reserved for cruising around Chicagoland in Jeff's Pontiac, Andre flipping between radio stations in a perpetual hunt for Steve Winwood's "Higher Love," the song of the summer. Every night was a choose-your-own adventure. We visited the Hard Rock Cafe, which felt like the height of culinary sophistication. Even more exciting was the restaurant's gift shop, which I plundered for the coveted yellow-circled "Hard Rock Chicago" T-shirts with the frenzy of a pillaging Viking. I fell in love with baseball at Old Comiskey, enthralled by the way the scoreboard exploded every time the White Sox clobbered a home run, and by my recognition that the game's tactical nuance was a thrilling combination of chess and chewing tobacco. Yet most nights were about the food as we strove to hit all the culinary institutions of Chicago. We plowed through extravagantly filled plates of sweet ribs at Carson's, inhaled obscenely swollen deep-dish pizzas at Pequod's, and drained one strawberry malted milk shake after another at Ed Debevic's. At my behest, there were also multiple late-night return visits to a twenty-four-hour Arby's that had established a special place in my heart. Eating in Chicago, like life itself, felt like attempting to satisfy a hunger that was insatiable.

It was impossible to overstate the amount of crap I accumulated in the process. One afternoon, we headed downtown for a Cubs game in the Wrigley Field bleachers, attempting to pass ourselves off as regulars, by draining a slew of Old Style beers obtained with fake IDs, then heckling Mets outfielder Mookie Wilson along with the rest of the bleacher bums. After the game, we charged around the Loop, competing to see who could amass the most swag from the voluminous amount of promotional crap on offer in the stores, offices, and restaurants downtown. Within two hours, all three of us were weighed down by overflowing bags stuffed with Bears posters from local drugstores, menus from the legendary Billy Goat Tavern, cheap plastic sunglasses from a new wave radio station, and more.

Our plan had been to end the night by visiting the observation deck at the top of the Hancock Tower, but we were not the only tourists with the same notion. The line was long and as the wait dragged on, our Cubs-fueled beer buzz wound down, causing Jeff and Andre to lose interest in their treasure trove of tchotchkes. "Easy come, easy go," Andre explained with a tired laugh as he and Jeff tossed four bags in the garbage. Despite their urging, I could not follow their lead, clinging to my haul as we entered the elevator, which whisked us skyward. The T-shirts, visors, and stickers were still in hand when I reached the ninety-sixth floor and encountered the ethereal sight of Chicago spreading out below. I stared out at the illuminated grid of freeways, neighborhoods, and cross streets, and it seemed to ripple and pulsate with a sense of power, prosperity, and progress. I gripped the bags tightly. They did not seem disposable. Everything I collected on my trip felt like little pieces of myself.

Casey listened as I processed this epiphany with her on the beach the next day. "You sound like some character in a fairy tale who has to undertake a crazy, dangerous journey through an enchanted forest and leaves a trail of bread crumbs to mark the path so they can find their way back," she giggled. "All that crap you are collecting—those are your bread crumbs." This insight instantly made me self-conscious of the Arby's baseball cap that sat wedged on my head. I adjusted it and tried to ignore the fact that Casey's analysis made me feel like a naive child in the woods. "Come on," she said as she sprang to her feet. "I am going to take you to a place that will rock your world even more than the Hancock."

CHAPTER TWENTY-ONE

Don't You . . . Forget About Me

We pulled away from the beach in Casey's car, a Volkswagen Golf convertible that she propelled at a rapid clip through the maze of identical tree-lined suburban streets. With every gear change my anticipation grew, but it leapt into overdrive as she pulled into the large empty parking lot of a school campus. After charging into an open spot, Casey pointed to the main building that loomed ahead. "Welcome to New Trier High School," she said, knowing full well that those were six words guaranteed to blow my mind. New Trier. Casey's school. But also the real-life setting for the original *Breakfast Club*. A constant muse for John Hughes. Parts of *Sixteen Candles* had been shot here, which meant Molly Ringwald's feet had almost certainly walked these very same hallways.

The scale of the place was enormous. To my English eyes, New Trier felt more akin to a university than a school. Casey guided me around the modern, clean lines of the empty campus. Though school was out, one of the front doors was unlocked, and we were able to stroll around its deserted hallways freely.

Everything was how I imagined it would be. The linoleum corridors were lined with lockers and bulletin boards were pockmarked with wrestling team updates, band practice calendars, and flyers for pep rallies past. An intimidating gym with polished floor, championship banners, and empty bleachers was still heavy with expectation. Classrooms smelled of chalk dust, loose-leaf paper, and hair spray.

I stood in the corridor and attempted to absorb the tiny details of its aesthetic beauty into my memory: the bright strip lights that ran along the ceiling; the texture of the heavy white-painted walls. Liverpool College's musty, wooden school desks replete with built-in inkwells could not compete with this place. At any moment it felt like Ally Sheedy, Judd Nelson, and Emilio Estevez could liberate themselves from their detention, charge down the hallway, and retrieve some weed from John Bender's locker.

Casey was right. To come face-to-face with a row of lockers was as awe-inspiring a moment as the one atop the Hancock. An American School Locker, the silent metallic supporting costar of so many movies, so many sitcoms, so many moments I had experienced via my television screen was now standing right in front of me. I approached the double tier and ran my fingers over its ventilation slats with a touch of reverence and wonder, gripping a door latch by the handle and yanking it back and forward. I lost myself as I repeatedly swung it open and closed, the crisp crack of its locking mechanism making the most gratifying sound.

Casey stood patiently behind me, silently giving room for this first encounter between man and sheet metal. Then she stepped in and grabbed the door from my grip, preventing me from slamming it shut for what would have been the fifty-seventh time. "Hold on," she said calmly but firmly while opening the door wide open and looking inside. The locker was empty apart from a piece of shiny green fabric balled up toward the corner of the bottom shelf. Casey crouched, reached in, and grabbed her prize. She opened the fabric wide in her hands to reveal a shiny green pair of New Trier athletic shorts. She looked at the waistband with a smile, holding up a name tag that read "Steinberg," then ripped it off using just her teeth.

"These are yours now," she said, holding the shorts out with faux-solemn ceremony, which acknowledged an awareness of just how badly I had craved a pair. "I need you to know that everything you have seen here . . . both these lockers . . . and these feelings you are having . . . they're all real."

She handed over the shorts like a teen Zen master. "When you go back to England, there will be good times, and we both know there will be bad." I stared down at the garment now in my possession, mostly so I did not have to look Casey in the eye, which I knew would make me cry. "Take these shorts out then," she said, "and know there is a whole world filled with opportunity. When you feel trapped, remember, this place is there for you." I did not cry. But I did not *not* cry. A single tear fell and soaked into the green polyester fabric I clung to in my hands below.

CHAPTER TWENTY-TWO

Midnight with the Fridge

There is no such thing as having it all. And though we packed so many moments of discovery, joy, and beach-filled wonder into my Chicago experience, there was one serious blemish that stained much of my stay. In a horror of cruel coincidence, I flew to the United States at the very time the Super Bowl champion Chicago Bears had elected to decamp and play their first ever game in London, England.

The American Bowl that pitched the Bears against the Dallas Cowboys at Wembley Stadium, the home of English soccer, was a bold move by the NFL to beta-test growing European interest in the razzle-dazzle of their game. Part of the draw of Chicago was my desire to place myself in the proximity of Walter Payton, Refrigerator Perry, and their team of heroes. I had flown over with the hope of seeing a preseason game in person, or failing that, to catch a glimpse of their training camp in action, only to discover there was once again an entire Atlantic Ocean separating me and my Chicago Bears. We had merely swapped places.

Every morning, I had to open up the sports pages of the *Chicago Tribune* and be subjected to a deluge of photographs of my sporting heroes being fawned over by English people who could never love the Bears in the way I loved them. One day they were at Buckingham Palace. The next they were mugging it up with English policemen who had lent them their distinctive pointy helmets. Perhaps most galling of all were the shots of Phil Collins and his son hanging out with Walter Payton during training. I detested Phil Bloody Collins in that moment. Seeing him smugly yukking it up with the greatest Bear of all time felt as if the gods were personally taunting me. I was where the Bears should be. They were in a place where I was normally trapped and hated. Worst of all, they seemed to be having the time of their lives.

The game was on a Sunday afternoon, Chicago time. I anger-watched it at Andre's house. He had some kind of home television projector that involved the largest television screen I had ever encountered. "Doesn't it make you feel like you are actually at the game?" Jeff asked chipperly. Thankfully, it did not, because that would have made us feel soggy, wet, and damp. It did, of course, rain torrentially for much of the game. Both offenses bogged down in the mud and I derived a bile-filled sense of schadenfreude every time the cameras cut to the crowd scenes featuring 86,000 English fans sodden and shivering under makeshift ponchos. Those emotions were replaced by crippling waves of jealously as 316-pound Refrigerator Perry delivered the party piece most had come to witness, plunging into the end zone from the one-yard line. Six or seven Cowboys defensive backs impotently bounced off him on the play, which put an exclamation point on the Bears' 17–9 lead.

I sat and seethed as the game clock wound down and the English fans saluted the players by unleashing a selection of football chants. As the sound of thousands of joyful English voices resounded around Wembley, the broadcaster let slip that the Bears would be turning round and flying directly back to

Chicago O'Hare right after the game. This made me sit up like a purebred bloodhound detecting a scent.

"What did the commentator just say?" I asked of no one in particular.

"The broadcaster?" said Jeff. "Something about the Bears coming back tonight."

"We have to go meet them," I declared.

Andre was always so easygoing and up for anything.

"Sure, sure," he responded. "Why not?"

The real game was on.

Cut to midnight, an hour at which my parents would never have dreamed of letting me out of the house under any circumstances. They were thousands of miles away and powerless to stop us from rendezvousing, somewhat woozily, and jumping into Jeff's car, each of us clad in every last piece of Bears merch we owned. Basic math suggested the earliest the team could arrive would be sometime around 2 A.M. So, after a brief stop at Arby's to kill time, we set out for O'Hare, found the airport's international arrival terminal, and dug in to wait. The vast welcome area was totally deserted. The only other human beings there apart from us were the janitorial staff and a two-person camera crew from NBC's local affiliate who had been dispatched to cover the Bears' return. We entertained ourselves by faking crowd scenes in which they shot our tiny group in extreme close-up to make it look like a massive number of fans had turned out to welcome home their triumphant heroes.

Just after 4 A.M., the Bears groggily deplaned. Coach Mike Ditka was the first to emerge from customs, chomping on his signature cigar, which he waved in my face as I approached, bellowing, "These men are your heroes, leave them alone." This kind of logic was totally lost on a starstruck fifteen-year-old desperately suppressing an erection the second I spied the silhouettes of the fatigued, lumbering giants behind him. Aware it was a lost cause, Ditka stumbled off, shaking his head. "You kids should be in bed," he barked. "Go to sleep! Go to sleep!"

Armed with a state-of-the-art 35-millimeter Ricoh camera that had been one of the choicest gifts I had received for my bar mitzvah, I swooped among the players, desperate to find my favorites and force them to pose for photographs. Offensive guard Kurt Becker was the first I recognized. I asked the six-foot-five Illinoisan if he would mind taking a photograph with me. "Fuck off" was his instant reply, so I quickly moved to Plan B, firing off my flash in his face.

Matt Suhey, the great blocking fullback, was more accommodating, posing for a photograph like a dandy in his head-to-toe Adidas tracksuit. Then I spied Walter Payton ambling toward me, and my nipples started to tingle. The man who would ultimately amass 16,726 career rushing yards, who was well on his way to a Hall of Fame career, and more meaningfully to me, whose poster hung above my bed alongside Debbie Gibson and Danny DeVito, was now standing directly in front of me.

I summoned the courage to tap Payton on the shoulder as he waited for his driver. The running back spun round and smiled, holding out his hand and introducing himself in his soft high-pitched voice, "Hi, I'm Walter." My tongue was suddenly so thick in my mouth, I could not formulate words, but seeing my camera and being a true pro, Walter knew the drill. Living up to his nickname, "Sweetness," he beckoned over an elderly airport porter to take a quick snap, and patiently draped his arm around my shoulder in standard athlete-hero pose.

The porter spent an age lining up the shot, but then lowered the camera before it had so much as a single flash, a look of

Walter Payton scurries away. That I never got a photo with him remains a top-ten regret to this day.

concern across his face. "It won't let me take anything," he muttered while staring at the camera lens with confusion. Realizing the shutter lock was on, I charged toward him with a suddenly debilitating panic, frantically pushing buttons and willing my camera back to life.

Walter and I posed again. The porter raised both the camera (and my hopes) before lowering it once again without a shutter sound. Walter had understandably had enough. "I'm sorry, I gotta go," he softly squeaked, ambling off with his driver and trunks toward a waiting limo. The porter handed me back my camera and shuffled off in silence, leaving me momentarily alone, with only the screech of the revolving door in his wake.

There was a sudden crash behind me. I spun around to see the enormous hulking presence of the Fridge lolloping toward me. The NBC camera crew was covering his every step as a small posse of similarly ginormous, swollen men followed behind him,

William "Refrigerator" Perry arrives back at O'Hare Airport. Unbeknownst to him, he is about to change my life.

each appearing to carry a piece of his luggage. Unlike the other Bears, who were mostly fatigued and ill-tempered, the Fridge exuded an approachable affability that I tested by speed-walking toward him. My initiative was rewarded as the defensive lineman wrapped an enormous arm around my shoulder and let me trot alongside him as he ambled toward the exit, bringing his face so close to mine that the famous gap between his teeth seemed chasm-like. "Live your dreams, kid. Be yourself," he muttered in my ear with every step. "Everything is possible. If you want it. Do it. Like I did."[*] And then he leaned in, took a pen from his pocket—it looked like a toothpick in his enormous hands—scribbled his signature on a piece of paper, and handed

---

[*] At the time this advice seemed so personal, individually aimed only at me and life-changing. Now that I have spent a career working in sports, I recognize the Fridge's words as an amalgam of pretty much every quasi-inspirational cliche all athletes toss in the direction of any young kid they encounter.

it to me. Then he, too, was gone through the spinning revolving door. I acted quickly to record William "Refrigerator" Perry's precious golden nuggets of life wisdom, taking to one knee and scribbling them down across the top of the copy of *USA Today* I had bought at the airport to kill time.

On the freeway back from O'Hare to Northbrook at 5 A.M., Jeff and Andre were in the front seat of the car, desperately attempting to process the out-of-body experience we had all just shared by repeatedly screaming "Oh my God" and high-fiving each other with gusto. I sat alone in the back, staring at Perry's autograph illuminated by the flickering freeway lights. He had fully embraced his persona and signed his name as "The Fridge 72." As I scrutinized each curve of his slanted handwriting, I repeated the message he had whispered to me like a mantra. "Live your dreams . . . Be yourself . . . Everything is possible" were his words. "Do it," I told myself. "There is nothing wrong with dreaming. So, be a man of action. Give me a higher love. It's that higher love I keep thinking of."

CHAPTER TWENTY-THREE

The End Is the Beginning

The Fridge telling me anything in life is possible had roughly the same effect as God talking to Moses on Mount Sinai. William Perry was an athletic giant among men, a defensive lineman who could run the ball on offense, catch touchdown passes, and even 360-degree dunk a basketball. So, his words filled me with an unusual cocktail of optimism, positivity, and energy. As my last night in the United States approached, it would be a stretch to suggest I felt dangerous. But I felt borderline capable, which for me, was progress.

My first challenge was packing. When you are young, your relationship to time has two points of reference. It either feels infinite or it's over. When I arrived in Chicago, the summer month looming ahead seemed endless. Suddenly it was the final day and I found myself bereft, frantically packing in the guest bedroom. Picture me on the floor, alongside a wide-open brown leather suitcase into which all of my belongings had easily fit when I had flown over. Now I was trying to stuff inside all of my clothing as well as the collection of precious treasures I had painstakingly scavenged during my stay: the posters, menus, baseball caps, plastic soda cups, fridge magnets, and other me-

mentoes, all of which lay scattered across the carpet around me like confetti.

Jeff's dad popped his head into the room to survey the scene as I struggled to slam my case closed. My helplessness caused him to scoff, "As they say in Texas, 'Boy, you are trying to pour ten gallons of cow shit into a five-gallon barrel.'" With that, the notion of having to leave some things behind struck pain in my gut. Then the Fridge's words of wisdom came back to me, "Everything is possible," and within an hour every last article had been jammed into my suitcase, which stood proudly upright in my room, practically mummified with the application of three entire rolls of duct tape.

I sat down alongside the bag and took a moment to process my endless Chicago summer. It hit me that I had watched my last daytime game show; eaten my last breakfast hovering over the visual feast that is the *Chicago Tribune* sports section; savored my last visit to the culinary Elysium that is Arby's for a roast beef sandwich. I had one night left. "Fridge Rules" commanded I make it count.

How we would spend that night was a topic of heated discussion among the New Trier kids at the beach all afternoon. For roughly an hour, it seemed like we were all headed to watch Mr. Mister play a massive local outdoor amphitheater in a far-flung suburb. I was immensely relieved when that idea was canned in favor of meeting up at a carnival that had pitched its tents in a nearby Glencoe park. It was an overpowering scene. The crackling excitement of a crowd on a hot summer's night lining up for rides. The smell of fried food and donuts hanging in a cloud over the flashing lights of the fairground as Kenny Loggins's "Danger Zone" blared from a low-rent speaker system.

One of Jeff's crew got his hand on a twenty-four pack of

Budweiser, which we cheerfully drained in the parking lot. I was now buzzed but agitated. Casey had promised she would meet us but had not yet materialized. Her absence gnawed at me, but I tried to play it cool as we chugged the Buds, reaching for a casual tone as I asked everyone I encountered if they had seen her.

I tried to channel my growing anxiety by throwing myself into the rides, first with a round on the bumper cars. I then survived a rattling trip around a deathtrap of a tiny, old, wooden roller coaster, before risking a quick reunion with a supersized corn dog I had wolfed down by jumping aboard the Tilt-A-Ride. After four minutes of being flung around at all angles, I woozily staggered out of the still-spinning car, amid a crush of fellow thrill-seekers eager to ride again, to find Casey there to meet me, standing on her own, to the left of the exit, and laughing at my tentative, pathetic efforts to regain my sea legs.

She was wearing a dark gray paisley peasant dress that looked familiar to me because it evoked the one worn by Molly Ringwald in the kissing scene of *Pretty in Pink*. My realization of that connection meant that even though the two of us had spent the entire summer talking, for once I did not know what to say. Dizziness prevailed—from the rides, from excitement, from sadness, from fear.

Casey took control of the situation. "Wanna blast some shit?" she said, pointing over to the nearby shooting gallery. As we strolled toward it, I was hyperaware of the carnival lights flashing, and the Glencoe heat, and the fact that the throbbing keyboard energy of Van Halen's "Why Can't This Be Love" pounded through the sound system, with Sammy Hagar beginning to unleash his vocal range.

I forked over a dollar to the very stoned long-on-the-side-yet-bald-on-top hippie who operated the game and waited for

Casey to select her air rifle of choice and shoot her best shot. With a growing sense of awe, I then watched as she sniped three targets dead center without so much as having to stop chewing her gum.

"I got SEAL Team Two–level skills, huh?" she said with a wink, cracking open her weapon for effect, then directing the hippie guy toward the prize she wanted him to hook down from the dozens of sagging plush toys hanging from the gallery's roof. "I got you a Bears bear," she said, shoving a saggy orange and blue creature into my hands, then grabbing me by the shirt collar, pulling me flush against her body, and pressing her lips against mine. Her tongue tasted of mint chewing gum, cotton candy, and lip balm.

I put my hand in the small of her back, a move I had seen before in countless movies. The warmth of her skin radiating through the fabric triggered an out-of-body experience. I felt as if I were floating past the top of the shooting gallery, drifting into the sky above the fairgrounds and looking down at this wonder. I was finally making out with a real-life woman and not practicing on my Debbie Gibson wall poster.

That sensation made me realize this moment right now would forever be enshrined in my memory along with all the other important firsts, including "the first football game I attended" (April 1, 1978, age seven, with my dad on a freezing day; coincidentally also the first time I tasted scotch, which my old man poured down my throat from his flask at halftime) and "my first live concert" (May 27, 1984, Orchestral Manoeuvres in the Dark's Junk Culture Tour at the Liverpool Empire; age thirteen, also, the night I smoked my first cigarette). I was reminded of a Philip Larkin quote Mr. McNally would often yell in class:

"On me your voice falls as they say love should, Like an enormous yes."

A line that had never made proper sense to me until this moment.

I was not so much a blind man who suddenly could see; more a boy freed of a good deal of the stress, self-doubt, and anxiety that had plagued me. The fear there was something wrong with me rolled away. The lingering dread that I was unkissable. That I would die alone.

I pulled away to look at Casey face-to-face, attempting to deliver the Don Johnson side grin.

"You will be back here in Chicago, Roger Bennett," she said.

"How do you know?"

"Because you are just an American trapped in a Liverpudlian's body."

The way I felt right then, I could have flown home and back again without a plane.

CHAPTER TWENTY-FOUR

New Rog in Town

Here are the four most sacred things I brought back with me from Chicago:

1. A "Hard Rock Cafe Chicago" T-shirt

I was now a strong believer in the life truth that it is possible to divide humanity into two kinds of people: people who were worldly enough to go to Hard Rock Cafes and people who were not. The white Fruit of the Loom shirt I purchased at the restaurant chain's gift shop, with its distinctive golden circular logo, made it clear which category I fit into.

This matter was more than just a marker of exclusivity and cool. There was a sophistication to the garment because it also proclaimed exactly where in the world you had traveled. And while a ton of Liverpool kids were able to boast "Hard Rock London" shirts, no one had so much as glimpsed the "Hard Rock Chicago" version. Those were the words emblazoned on it, but the shirt actually said, "I have been there, and you have not." Over the course of the next eighteen months, if a special occasion required me to make a dazzling first impression, there was a good chance I would be busting out that article of clothing. Like

Buzz Aldrin wearing a NASA lapel pin on his return from the moon, that shirt proved I had journeyed somewhere the rest of my world had only visited in their dreams.

2. Party-Sized Packet of Double Stuf Oreos

I had developed a low-level addiction to Oreos in Chicago, guzzling down the chocolate cookies with sweet crème filling as if they were sponsors providing the "Official Snack of My Entire Vacation Experience." Andre gifted me a carton on the eve of my departure, presenting the enormous party-sized fifty-two-cookie Double Stuf packet with tears in his eyes before engulfing me in a bear hug. The relief I experienced when I unpacked my luggage and discovered they had not been crushed to smithereens bordered on ecstasy. Andre's intuitive brilliance was to equip me with a near infinite supply of an American foodstuff that tasted stale even when fresh. Every night, ritually, I would shut the kitchen door, turn off the light, and consume my self-imposed ration of half an Oreo in the dark, letting it act like a synthetic Proust's Madeleine, a foodstuff capable of emotionally transporting me back to the beach, New Trier bleachers, and fairgrounds of Chicago's northern suburbs. Even after the remnants of my party pack turned fusty, they still tasted of memory and laughter.

3. Run-DMC's "Raising Hell" on Cassette Tape

Run-DMC's "Walk This Way" had been in heavy rotation all summer long on MTV, a track that fused the rock of Aerosmith with the emerging genre of hip-hop like pineapple on pizza, feta and watermelon salad, or Holocaust comedies that should not work together but do. The way Run and DMC switched off on the lyrics was infectious, and the remarkable thing about this album, which turned me on to hip-hop, was that the smash hit was the worst track. From the opening cut, "Peter Piper" with its Mardi Gras bells, the album emotionally ensnared you in its brassy boasts and beatboxing. This was an art form I tried to emulate on my own, which mostly meant spitting on my bedroom mirror.

Upon my return from Chicago, I rarely felt more alive than when walking around Liverpool listening to this album on my Walkman, embraced in the wit and wisdom encoded in the lyrics. Even more than the music, I revered Run's and DMC's personas. Clad in synchronized tracksuits, Kangol hats, and Adidas shell toes, they were unabashedly loud, confident, and playful. So many of the bands I had listened to before them—the Smiths, R.E.M., and 10,000 Maniacs—were the music of passive, wistful longing. Run-DMC was loaded with swagger, bravado, and innuendo—they were a musical reflection of the new Rog I aspired to be.

4. A Pair of Black Chuck Taylor High-Tops

I had coveted a pair of Converse Chuck Taylors the second I walked out of the movie theater having watched *Back to the Future*. It was impossible to shake the mental image of that delicious black pair that featured in close-ups whenever Marty McFly executed a skateboard stunt scene. I immediately undertook a prolonged hunt for the canvas sneaker, which like Ray-Bans and Levi's 501 jeans screamed "American design classic." Small problem: Chuck Taylors were not distributed in the United Kingdom, a fact that only made me want them more.

A prolonged bout of telephonic detective work enabled me to track down a single pair in a random sports store in a northern London suburb. A four-hour train trip plus fifty-minute bus ride was necessary to reach this sneaker mecca, which was actually a musty shop with limited offerings. Indeed, they only had one pair of Chucks, which had clearly been on the shop floor for some time as they were dust-covered and missing two eyelets. The good news was, they were on sale. Bad news, though: they were size 7 and I was 9. A small hurdle. I snapped them up and spent a year stumbling around Liverpool with my toes scrunched up, blistering the skin on my feet into callouses while reminding myself that there is suffering in art. It was an inexplicable relief to pick up a pair of high-tops that actually fit me in a bountiful American mall. Black ones, too, identical to Michael J. Fox's. When I looked down at my feet, I felt as protected as Dorothy in her ruby slippers while navigating Oz.

All of these treasures made it safely back with me to Liverpool, along with the New Trier shorts; a Nerf mini-basketball hoop on which I could while away whole evenings practicing dunking, tongue out à la Michael Jordan; two dozen random sports teams pennants;* and photographs of myself with Casey, with Jeff, with Andre, and with the Chicago Bears, all of which I taped above my bed. More than objects, they were like support dogs easing me through the transition from heaven—the United States—back to "hell." Home.

---

* I panic-bought these on my last day, much to the consternation of the confused pimply store clerk who could not understand why I was choosing so many rival teams: pennants for the Chicago White Sox and the Chicago Cubs, Kansas Jayhawks and the K-State Wildcats, Chicago Bulls and Detroit Pistons. To me, it was not so much the individual teams that were the point. It was the collective effect. I tacked them up on my wall in enormous banks. When I touched them, it felt like I was living in the fifty-first state.

On the long flight back from Chicago, I was braced for darkness. We had studied Dante's *Inferno* in Mr. Stott's English class, and instead of watching the in-flight movie, I sat and fretted about the prospect of having to live out Francesca's claim that "[t]here is no greater sorrow than to be mindful of the happy time in misery."

Yet, counter to my fears, it was not depressing to be home. Yes, I had traded in a bold world in which stories like Reagan's Star Wars program, Wall Street's unstoppable ascent, and Macintosh Plus home computing filled the front page of the newspapers. Worse, I had returned to my grim northern English existence of cities in decay, class warfare, the Irish Troubles, and industrial decline. This was a jarring transition akin to a movie shot in shimmering, glorious Technicolor snapping back into the gloom of black-and-white. But what I had seen and experienced in Chicago could never be taken away from me. My greatest fear had been that the Liverpool reality was my only possibility. Now I knew there were other ways of being. I had glimpsed America and its central promise that rather than just being passively depressed by the future, you could actively shape it. After being exposed to that different world, the one I was currently trapped in could not contain me.

The release of the John Hughes juggernaut *Ferris Bueller's Day Off* was a timely, life-affirming experience. The first time I watched the film, I savored it as if it was a documentary of the freedom I had experienced all summer long on those very same suburban streets. Glenbrook North High School, the "Save Ferris Water Tower" in Northbrook, and even Glencoe Beach make appearances. The climactic trip to the city was the mirror of mine, with stops to watch the Cubs from the Wrigley Park bleachers and savor the Impressionist collection at the Art In-

Michael Jordan poster and Nerf basketball net on the back of the door. Pennants all over the wall. When I lay on my bed, it felt like I had never left Chicago.

stitute of Chicago. I sobbed through the parade scene in which Ferris sang "Twist and Shout" accompanied by the throng of a dancing crowd. A mix of races, ethnicities, and generations sharing a collective jubilation bordering on rapture. Cosmic unity achieved via the power of a rather badly lip-synced song.

When I returned to the movie theater for a second viewing, I realized I had been a Cameron overwhelmed by life. I was now an aspirational Ferris, committed to adventure and sharing joy. And so I strutted around Liverpool as if I had never returned from Chicago, clad in the armor of my Hard Rock Cafe T-shirt, faux Ray-Bans, and black high-top Chuck Taylor's. I was invincible. That was the uniform I was wearing in the city center as I killed a late afternoon with Jamie at the end of summer break. I was hell-bent on buying Van Halen's *5150* LP at the local HMV.

Jamie had tagged along in the hope we could make a fly-by at the Lobster Pot chip shop for a quick steak and kidney pie.

In our rush to fend off my friend's hunger pains, we charged from record store to chippy, and clattered right into a passing girl. As I slammed into her, I pulled the plastic bag containing my new vinyl acquisition out of the way, protecting it by reflex. I looked down to apologize, only to realize it was the same girl I had spent an hour staring at during the last day of school. The one with the intriguingly flicked red hair and Doc Martens. The moment of recognition was mutual.

"I know *you*," she said with the shock from our collision turning into a coy grin.

"I'm Lisa-Marie O'Riordan."

"I'm Roger. Roger Bennett."

"See you in a week, Roger Bennett," she said while looking me up and down. To my delight, her eyes lingered for a second on my Hard Rock Cafe T-shirt.

"See you in a week then," I said as she turned away, leaving me in the grip of an unfamiliar feeling.

For the first time in my life, I could not wait to go to school.

CHAPTER TWENTY-FIVE

The Transformation of Titty Thomson

I strode through the gates of Liverpool College that first morning experiencing an unprecedented surge of anticipation as I swung my new school bag proudly over my shoulder to ensure its large, fake FILA logo could gain maximal exposure. I had no idea of just how much my life was about to change until I yanked open the Sixth Form Common Room door and was met by a thick backdraft of Old Spice. In that second, I realized that everything I had known about school had been turned on its head.

I should note, the very notion of a Sixth Form Common Room was both a privilege and a brave new world. In the entirety of my previous ten years, school breaks, come rain or snow, meant being forced out onto the schoolyard to play football or huddle together for warmth, no matter the clime. But for the last two years of school, sixth formers* were deemed sufficiently responsible to merit our own private space or "common room." This was a large area with a design aesthetic that could

---

* The English equivalent of junior and senior years in high school.

My sixth form class. I am front row middle. None of the Rugger Buggers or the girls who went out with them bothered to turn up for the photograph.

be best described as "budget airline airport lounge." There were scattered armchairs, a couch, a wall of lockers, and, perhaps most exotically of all, a working kettle that enabled us to make our own cups of tea. This perk felt like the height of luxurious sophistication and one that had forced me to spend much of the last night before school agonizing over which mug to bring to make the right first impression. I settled for a Chicago Blackhawks cup I had snared at the Hancock Tower gift shop that I thought conveyed just the right combination of worldliness and virility.

The night before that first day of term, I had experienced a hellish stress dream in which, en masse, the girls decided not to show up for the school year. It was with some relief and excitement that they were all present and correct then, clustered

in a group in the center of the room. The girls had commandeered the sofa area and were attempting to affect an air of being engrossed in casual conversation all while emitting a whiff
of terror-filled anxiety that was only natural considering that a
throng of boys surrounded them like a clan of spotted hyenas,
seventy of my peers reciprocally pretending to be unfazed by the
presence of the female newcomers in their midst as they fiddled
with their school bags and lockers, while simultaneously ogling
the girls on the sly. The only one I looked at was Lisa-Marie,
who was sitting calmly next to the other girls, listening but not
talking.

The girls were not the only new element. My male classmates
had also transformed. We boys were now men. Hairstyles had
never before been a thing. Yet, on the evidence of the dazzling
array of freshly trimmed crop cuts, quiffs, and flattops now littered around the common room, barbers across Liverpool must
have had a boom summer. Even Trevor Weekes, the president of
Liverpool College Dungeon & Dragons Club, had discovered the
magical properties of wet-look hair gel.

A widespread awareness of fashion had also emerged out of
nowhere—no small feat within the walls of Liverpool College,
where a strict, traditional uniform code had long been in effect:
black blazer proudly bearing the College's shield, gray slacks,
black sweater, crisp white shirt set off by a red-and-black-striped
school tie. Yet, with subversive elegance, all the boys had spent
the summer customizing within those constraints, creating en-
sembles in which black Lacoste or Fred Perry sweaters sat above
pairs of gray Levi's slacks. A silent consensus had seemingly
been forged to knot the ties supertight, cutting right into the
wafer-thin collars of an oxford shirt. Doc Martens were now de
rigueur for the feet.

If the musky air quality of the common room was any guide, all of this Liverpool College chic had been topped off by slapping on enough cologne to fill a deepwater aquifer. Bottles of Brut, Old Spice, and Drakkar Noir had clearly been opened and emptied. Yet the earthy, citrus scent of manliness that now hovered in a cloud was not the starkest transformation. In an effort to sound more mature, boys were openly addressing each other by their first names, in defiant violation of a centuries-long custom that emphasized the dehumanizing use of surnames only. A bedrock tradition so enshrined that I had even referred to my closest friends as "Pye," "Lyons," or "Needham-Jones." We were now "Terry," "Paul," and "Wayne."

My world was upside down.

The apogee of that astonishingly bewildering first morning came when "Titty" Thomson, who had previously been our late-flowering class weakling, strolled into the common room. The last day of the previous school year, he had been a pudgy eunuch with puffy breast-like nipples (hence the cruelty of his nickname). He stood there before us a man transformed, a ripple-muscled, stubbled Adonis. As I would later discover in the school changing rooms, he now had two circular scars where his man-breasts had been, steroid-aided six-pack abs, a forest of chest hair, and a sudden ability to break school records at the shot put. When this radically remade Titty suggested "Call me Phil now, lads," we did.

Yet there was too much going on for me to dwell on Titty Thomson's startling transformation. Let history note, Gripper Stark, the hardest boy in our class, and his sidekick Stevie Tuffnell were the first lads in my lower sixth's year to cross the gender barrier. The two lads, who by their own admission had only stayed on at the College to keep playing rugby, swooped into the circle of girls and made talking to them look almost effortless, engaging the outgoing beauty Annabelle Starr and the eager, buxom Sally Joyce in conversation. I looked on knowing that in that moment, nothing would ever be the same again. School no longer felt like school.

All the girls had now risen from the couch and were engaging my classmates in conversation. Hands were being run through hair as laughter filled the common room. There was a collective sense that after suffering years of famine we were all poised to feast. Every one of those boys in the room was a virgin. It was clearly not going to stay that way for long.

CHAPTER TWENTY-SIX

Leveling Up

It turns out, our teachers were no more adept at talking to the opposite sex than we were. Most were College lifers who had spent decades in an all-boys milieu barking out orders to terrified pupils who obeyed them blindly for fear of the consequences if they did not.

As we soon discovered, it is impossible to discipline what you cannot cane. The tutors were forbidden from beating the girls, a prohibition that stripped them of their authority. My female classmates intuitively understood the shift in power and played it to their advantage. In the early weeks they delighted in tormenting the faculty, expertly assessing each teacher's vulnerabilities like a dojo of Aikido black belts redirecting their opponents' own power and using it to defeat them. All Sally Joyce had to do was walk into the classroom and aim the coquettish compliment "I like your socks, sir" at one of the feebler teachers like Mr. Weakstone and he'd be thrown off an entire lesson plan.

The truly fearsome faculty members could also be defanged by quietly questioning their commands. Mr. Stott began his class in signature fashion, with a dose of overt racism, ordering one of the terrified Asian kids to read out loud from the novel we were studying so he could be quickly humiliated. "Gupta. Rudyard Kipling's *The Man Who Would Be King*, page seventy-three. Proceed, lad!" But before the terrified kid could so much as open his mouth, Annabelle Starr interceded and calmly asked, "Why do you only ask Gupta, Banjaree, or Niryana to read first, sir?"

We all quivered as Annabelle's startling question hung in the air. Mr. Stott's jaw stiffened as he instinctively leapt up from behind his desk to dispense justice in the form of a thrashing that would make an example of the insolent little shit who had so openly defied him. He had only managed a single step before registering that it was a girl who had thus challenged him.

Stott had no choice but to try to explain his actions, something he had precious little experience doing in the course of his fifty-plus-years career. "I asked Gupta to read because . . . I am interested in his opinions, Starr," he stammered with a sudden lack of confidence. With lips pursed so tightly that the veins throbbed in the side of his head, an uncharacteristically bewildered Stott fired up a Benson & Hedges and muttered that we should read silently to ourselves.

How could we possibly be expected to read silently when LIVING, BREATHING, TALKING GIRLS WERE OUR CLASS-MATES? Chaucer's *Canterbury Tales*, Keynesian macroeconomic systems, or the rise of European nationalism in 1848 paled in the face of the tension we were experiencing in and out of lessons. The entire class was swamped by the sense of possibility and knowledge that a single smile, quip, or interaction could change the direction of our lives.

With the teacher's authority neutered, everything was suddenly up for grabs as we engaged with the girls. Yes, girls had been enrolled at the school for four years, but these were *our* girls. In our classes. A group we were actually able to speak to all day, every day. Or, more accurately, learn how to speak to.

"You have to work your way into it," a fervent Jamie explained to me one day after rugby practice. "I've trained by focusing on the least attractive ones first to build my confidence before I try and hit my stride with the prettier ones," he said, swinging his games bag gleefully. "It's like Donkey Kong. Everyone will find their level. You got to aim for just above average."

Indeed, it was scientifically fascinating how everyone did indeed find their level. The more advanced boys—essentially the leading lights of the school's First Rugby Fifteen—started to go out to the pubs and nightclubs of Liverpool with Annabelle Starr and Sally Joyce on a weekly basis. These lads were physical specimens, a group that had given themselves the name Rugger Buggers, Gripper Stark and Stevie Tuffnell along with James Kay and Tony Ives. These were men who were all six feet plus, had to shave every morning, and carried themselves with a strut that comes with owning copious amounts of chest hair. With their bodies gripped by strange, primitive urges they barely understood, all these blokes knew was that everything felt better when they dressed like a member of Kajagoogoo every Saturday and headed out for a night on the town.

Compared to them, I was still smooth of cheek, a relative boy who spent my weekends in a secure bubble with the King David kids, far, far away from the in crowd. Besides, there was only one new girl I was focused on: Lisa-Marie. We shared no classes because I studied humanities, and she was in the sciences track, so I lived for the lunch hour. During that time we would find each other and chat, celebrating how our interests overlapped almost entirely: indie music, fashion, football, and an unshakable belief that John Cusack was the Greatest Actor of All Time.

Lisa-Marie would delight in brewing up a pot from a cannis-

Lunch in the school dining hall. Second from the right.

ter of passion fruit tea bags she kept in her locker for the two of us to share in a quiet nook in the corner of the common room. There we could sit alone and talk intimately. Every so often I would inhale a stealthy whiff of her Body Shop scent, which she later told me was called "White Musk."

"Where did the name Lisa-Marie come from?" I would ask.

"From my dad. He named me after Elvis Presley's daughter," she said in her thick Scouse accent. "Why are you called Roger?"

I thought about trying to explain the historical complexities of my mum's desire for her kids to have names that did not sound Jewish in any way whatsoever, but thought it wiser to deflect the subject back to her favorite topic: the Smiths, that Manchester powerhouse whose despondency and literary self-pity had by this time garnered them a cultlike following throughout the north of England.

I liked the Smiths plenty, mostly for their emotional range and the way the band were willing to ricochet between feeling worthless and deciding to take over the world within a rhyming couplet. But Lisa-Marie was obsessed and scrawled their lyrics all over her schoolbooks in Wite-Out. The only thing she liked to do more than listen to *The Queen Is Dead* was talk about it, framing endless debates in which I was more than happy to engage. We whiled away countless lunch hours agonizing over whether it was better to live miserably or die romantically, or engaging in the big questions as if they were matters of theology: Was singer Morrissey or guitarist Johnny Marr the One True Godhead? Was Morrisey actually in love with Marr? Had I noticed that Morrisey always tried to dominate band photographs, but Marr always found a way to steal the spotlight by smoking a cigarette or wearing sunglasses off to the side?

Two weeks in, Lisa-Marie gifted me a tub of Brylcreem and encouraged me to start styling a high quiff à la Morrisey. I was distressed to discover that no amount of back-combing could prevent my tight curls from undermining these efforts, but I still reciprocated by staying up all night to make a mixtape on which I hoped to impress her by sharing my favorite American bands of the moment. Hüsker Dü's "Makes No Sense at All" set the opening tone. Stevie Ray Vaughan reinforced that with "Change It." I taped, then erased, then retaped and erased the Replacements' "Kiss Me on the Bus," fearing it might be misconstrued as coming on too strong, only to be shocked and delighted when Lisa-Marie countered two days later with a mixtape of her own that included the Talking Heads' "Creatures of Love," Prince's "Dirty Mind," and the Ramones' "Baby I Love."

All of this was so incredibly titillating. Yes, I may have recently kissed a woman for the first time, but this was next level.

Me on the right in a portrait drawn by one of the girls while we were cutting class.

The possibility of a relationship. What Mr. Weakstone, our medieval lit teacher, once described as "courtly love" and what Mr. McNally, with tongue in cheek, called "wooing a lady." An art I was bluffing my way through, gleefully, but with trepidation, day by day. It was an intricate game, for which a savior arrived in my hour of need. His name was Mr. Bruce Willis.

With fortunate timing, the television sensation *Moonlighting* had just made its debut, catapulting Willis from obscurity to superstardom overnight. The show was a high-concept detective drama/rom-com hybrid in which Cybill Shepherd's former supermodel Madelyn Hayes solved crimes and slowly fell in love with Willis's David Addison, a down-on-his-luck gumshoe. The plots were often ridiculous, but on-screen, Willis was riveting. His Addison was far from the perfect bloke. His hair was thinning. Clad in cheap sludge-colored suits, his life mantra was

"Live fast, die young, leave clean underpants." Yet the joy of the show lay in Addison's repartee and self-deprecating bravado, and the signature quirkiness and fast-talking rhythmic patter with which he approached life. "Trouble's my middle name," he would say in a moment of challenge. "I laugh at trouble. I tickle trouble on the chin."

His love of wordplay, alliterations, and puns lay in stark contrast to the prevailing stereotypes of stoic manliness—your Clint Eastwoods, James Deans, and Steve McQueens, heroes who let their achingly good looks do the talking. Willis would not shut up. His mouth was permanently set on "fire hose," and not in a Woody Allen angst-and-neurosis-filled kind of way. He pioneered a new model of "cool-guy chatty." Like Duckie in *Pretty in Pink* if Duckie actually landed the girl of his dreams.

Watching this character on a weekly basis was akin to taking a master class in charisma. Don Johnson never felt comfortable. His chiseled cheekbones were unobtainable. But Willis worked for me. I had learned on the beach in Chicago that was something I excelled at. Now I could reinforce those skills by practicing the artful eyebrow raise or one-sided grins he uncorked to express a range of emotions: affection, irresistibility, or remorse.

The man even played a mean harmonica. *Moonlighting*'s writers appeared to conjure gratuitous story lines just so he could unfurl a slow, mournful rendition of "Blue Moon" on his harp that melted Cybill Shepherd's heart in a way words never could. Of course, I immediately went out and purchased my own harmonica, which I did not know how to play but would carry in the inside pocket of my school blazer, occasionally pulling it out to blast random notes that I liked to believe were similarly soulful and irresistible to all women.

So, it was Bruce Willis I channeled during the lunch break

when Lisa-Marie turned to me and said, "Come out with us Saturday night, Roger Bennett. . . . It's Annabelle's birthday. We're going clubbin' in town."

It was immediately clear to me that "us" meant Lisa-Marie, Annabelle Starr, Sally Joyce, and all the Rugger Buggers. I was gripped with an instant, debilitating sense of tingling excitement and fight-or-flight-caliber panic. But then the Willis mantra "Live fast, die young, leave clean underpants" prevailed.

Lisa-Marie's invitation needed a response, and I attempted to feign a confident one with the aid of a David Addison line, "Do birds fly? Do ducks duck?," which I tried to deliver casually, though the back half of his quote became trapped in my throat by a gulp of panic, forcing me to grasp for that harmonica stashed in my blazer pocket. I pulled it out and while looking at Lisa-Marie with one eyebrow raised archly, blew a single, long, rasping note.

CHAPTER TWENTY-SEVEN

Bigmouth Strikes

At times of peak duress when I desperately needed life counsel, I always turned to my brother, Nigel. To me, he was akin to an oracle of Delphi. Before blowing a wad of my savings account on the neon-yellow Rollerblades I had craved since my return from Chicago, I sought his last-minute approval, only to be curtly instructed: "Don't do that. Americans might think they are cool but in Liverpool, everyone will despise you if you take to the streets wearing them." It was advice I followed, no matter how emotionally devastating it was to hear. The night before my sixth form year had started and I was thunderstruck at the prospect of having to impress girls long term, he advised: "When you join a new group, keep your mouth shut, let the wankers reveal themselves first, get a feel for the room, then make your move."

So, after Lisa-Marie freaked me the fuck out by inviting me to go clubbing on a Saturday night, it was my brother I needed once again. Even though he was in his first year at Reading University, I tracked him down via the pay phone at his hall of residence to gain his insight.

"Number one. You are definitely going to go," Nige said, with the sound of doors slamming and laughter echoing around him. "Rule number two: No matter what you end up doing on Saturday night, whatever pub or club you end up at, and whatever time you finally make it home, when Mum and Dad ask you on Sunday how your night went, for God sakes, just tell them that you went to the movies, it was fine; that you got home early and had a good time."

Even down the phone line, I could tell my brother, Nige, was clearly distracted by whatever university hijinks were going on around him and that I was not receiving his A-game, attention-wise. Perhaps in order to dislocate himself from the call, he tersely moved to action steps. "Look, go into my bedroom. Third drawer down on the left of my desk. Everything you need, you'll find in there."

For a second, I was rocked by how quickly I had been dispensed with in my hour of need. That feeling changed the instant I slid open the prescribed drawer to discover a flask-sized bottle of Bell's scotch resting beside a small, crisp, official-looking document. I picked it up. "British Rail Senior Citizen Railcard" was emblazoned across the top, under which my grandfather's name (Samuel L. Polak), date of birth (September 6, 1913), and occupation (kosher butcher) had been written in neat script. What a genius my brother was. He knew I would need ID in case I was carded on the way into the pub. I glanced back at the card, did the math, and realized it would be a tough ask to pass myself off as a seventy-three-year-old. After pocketing the card and the bottle, I knew it would be better than nothing.

Saturday rolled round. The prospect of a massive night out filled my belly with fear, especially since Friday afternoon, when Gripper had pulled me aside by the lockers and slightly reluctantly informed me it had come to his attention I would be joining them at the weekend, and that the invitation was strictly for one, ending with a slightly menacing "Glassman won't get in where we are going." Thus I was deprived of the calming presence of an enthusiastic, if deeply ineffective, wingman. My first trip to the Wild West of Liverpool's pub and club land was a journey into the unknown. That it would be made in the company of Liverpool College's alpha males was almost more unnerving than the possibility of hooking up with the girl on whom I harbored an enormous crush.

I looked at myself in the mirror before I left the house. After an afternoon spent ringing through wardrobe permutations, I had settled upon a pair of Black Levi 501 jeans, my black Chuck Taylors, and a white T-shirt, topped off with a tan corduroy jacket that I wore only because it had an inside pouch where I could stash the half bottle of Bell's blended whisky my brother had given me. It now felt like confidence in my pocket.

With the concealed scotch and the Old Aged Pensioners Railcard as my sword and shield, I left the house and prepared to meet up with some of the Rugger Buggers, hyperaware that in comparison to them, I would look like a twelve-year-old tagging along with his older brothers, a realization I attempted to address by smothering myself with one more layer of unnecessary aftershave.

I had arranged to meet up with Gripper Stark and James Kay, who lived close to me, so the three of us could take a taxi into town together. They were not begrudging company but were not exactly welcoming, either. James Kay was decent enough. He was a suave lad who glided effortlessly through everything—schoolwork, rugby, talking to women—because he had been blessed with early puberty and had the good looks and confidence of a kid who had seemed eighteen since he was eleven.

Gripper was feared throughout the College as the "Cock of

the School," an honorific title awarded to the best fighter on the schoolyard. He had earned this status the previous winter when squaring up against the reigning cock, Prowser, a muscular, quick-tempered Goliath. The fight went down in the locker room after rugby. Prowser had two years and about a foot and a half on his opponent. But as he closed in on Gripper, with fists reared, his supposed victim coolly picked an old, discarded cricket bat from the floor and used it to bludgeon his astonished opponent as ferociously as if he were chopping down a tremendous redwood.

I had been on the receiving end of Gripper's fists myself once as a seven-year-old. He knocked two of my front teeth out with a single punch after I accidentally bumped into him during recess. I spent the next three months doing damage control by telling everyone it was no big deal because they had been super loose anyway. That memory flickered through my mind as Gripper and Kay now sat opposite me in the back of a black cab speeding through Liverpool's streets.

By the time the cab spat us out at our destination, an old mock Tudor pub named Rigby's, I was cold-sweat-gripped by fear. This was moment-of-truth time. If the bouncers on the door asked for an ID, my evening would be over before it had begun. To be turned away or "knocked back," as the humiliating act was more colloquially known, would be devastating.

If the doormen had checked carefully, they would have discovered they were admitting a seventy-three-year-old retired kosher butcher named Samuel Polak, but to my immense relief, they simply sized up the enormity of my companions and nodded, as I slid in, undetected, on their blind side. A wall of noise greeted me along with the heat of a packed bar, which caused my spectacles to fog up almost immediately. Even with the blurred vision, the air of menace was palpable. I was aware we had entered the bowels of a room in which a single accidental elbow causing someone to spill their ale could trigger a mass bar fight. Years of listening to my brother's stories about Saturday nights spent out in Liverpool city center had made this possibility abundantly clear; what a terrifying vortex it could be. A global leader in random acts of violence per acre. A place in which evenings could end up in one of two ways: "copping off" with a heavily perfumed stranger, or having the shit kicked out of you late at night by a random drunk in a packed chip shop who was angrier than you that he had not gotten to third base. My brother's last advice on the telephone had been words of caution: "Remember this: Getting in is mostly not a problem; getting out alive often is."

James and Gripper carried themselves with the brazen confidence born of experience, commandeering a corner nook and getting the beers (three pints of Guinness). We stood around a high-top table as they sparked up ciggies to kill time waiting for the rest of the boys to appear, by generally looking around and attempting to project an air of menace. One by one they turned up: Tony Ives, a six-foot-six mammoth who had left the College at sixteen to join his family's building trade; Baz Long, another hefty unit I did not know well but had regularly seen on the rugby field driving back an entire opposing scrum single-handedly; and Joseph Nwanko, a wiry beanpole of a boy who as the son of the local Nigerian consul was one of the only black kids in my grade and remained supercool, despite having to answer to the obvious and unfortunate nickname "Wankstain." "Wank" for short.

There was a lot of "draining pints," and a little bit of conversation, much of which centered on Gripper's recent suspension from school for stealing the music department's pride and joy: its one and only synthesizer. I nodded along and tried not to look aghast as Gripper relived his crime and the story of how he was busted. The synth was kept in the same rehearsal room as his personal drum kit, to which he was the only person apart from the music teacher to have a key. Although Gripper had thrown a brick through the window to simulate a robbery, he'd made the mistake of throwing that brick from the inside of the room out. A rookie error.

By this time, the nook was tight with all the rugby boys crushed around it, our table covered in empty glasses, and the entire bar was a hot, smoke-filled throng of noise. Pub protocol was a mystery to me. Tony Ives barely moved. Baz Long spent most of this time perfecting the smoke rings he sent floating lazily above our heads. James and Gripper did most of the talking. A pressure to participate in the conversation and justify my presence welled up inside of me, but I was also at a loss for the right thing to say. My companions were fighters, not lovers, so it was abundantly evident this was not Bruce Willis line-dropping territory. I felt the contours of the flask of Bell's press against my side and yanked that confidence in a bottle out of my pocket, taking a swig, before passing it round.

"Nice one," said a surprised Gripper. Even the laconic Tony Ives nodded approvingly as he took a slug from the bottle.

Four Guinnesses down was the hour it felt right to move on to the club and meet the girls. Our destination was the State Ballroom, a dance club so legendary that Frankie Goes to Hollywood had chosen to shoot their video for "Relax" there.

Fueled by more of my brother's stories, the State was lodged in my imagination as a mystical place, up there with the likes of Shangri-La, Valhalla, and El Dorado. Beered up, I practically floated my way toward it on the short walk through the city center's rain-slicked streets. Sandwiched in between the swaggering Tony Ives and James Kay I vacillated between feeling out of my depth—a kid who still had a Debbie Gibson poster on his bedroom wall, for crying out loud—and, with that flask of scotch banging around in my jacket pocket and me about to enter a bona fide holy of holies, older than I had ever before.

We arrived at the front of the State. I kept close to James and Tony and, with head down, crossed the threshold, manually overriding my nervous system, which maniacally signaled that this was not a place for me.

The State was a setting of immense juxtaposition. The music pounded, the energy felt debaucherous, and once we had passed the coat check, there was exposed flesh everywhere. The venue itself had originally opened in the 1930s as a genteel tearoom and retained its ornate splendor even after its modern reincarnation as a nightclub. Banks of spotlights carved their way over an exquisite mosaic-tiled dance floor, offering occasional glimpses of delicate wall carvings and lavishly paneled ceilings. Banquettes skirted the walls, and we laid claim to one as we waited for the girls to arrive.

The DJ was establishing himself by spinning some Echo and the Bunnymen to set the mood. Baz Long set off for the bar and returned having successfully procured a clutch of Buds. As I took my first swig, a fellow clubgoer cruised by in front of us and my eyes could not help but focus in on his defining feature, his gigantic nose. Unfortunately, the man attached to that nose was as hyperaware as he was self-conscious. He intuited the staring, stopped, and pivoted toward me, emanating a sneer of violent intent as in thick Scouse tones he leered, "You lookin' at me or chewin' a brick? Either way youze gonna lose yer' teeth, mate."

I stood there paralyzed by fear as the lad pulled back his fist to dispense Scouse street justice, only for a giant hand to intercept the punch as it hurtled toward my face. This was no miracle. Tony Ives had stepped in to take charge of matters, calmly looming over the toucan-nosed assailant and delivering two stinging slaps to the side of his face, while growling, "Stroll on mate, stroll on," the single most emasculating command a man could hear as it called his bluff to fight or fuck off.

Toucan Boy hastily assessed his odds before sagely scurrying off into the swarming crowd behind the bar. Tony, my savior, shook his head from side to side, laughed, and clinked his Bud bottle against mine, an affectionate gesture that made me feel invincible. "Nobody can touch us," he said to me, and for one moment I was invigorated by a completely unfamiliar sense of omnipotence. The feeling was cruelly, quickly crushed by a pang of anxiety that incapacitated me as Lisa-Marie turned up with Sally and Annabelle and a posse of girls on the other side of the club working their way toward us.

Lisa-Marie was wearing a brown suede jacket with fringed tassels that made her look fantastic. I had no idea how to engage with her. "Club-going Rog" was a new persona that was still half-formed. I had only just worked out how to hang with the Rugger Buggers. Yes, I lived to chat with Lisa-Marie at school, but that was one-on-one in the comparatively sedate surroundings of the College Common Room with a cup of tea in hand and no one watching.

Gripper took control of the group. He bought a round of drinks, unilaterally deciding it was time for us all to move on to the ciders, the club's specialty, which they served up super strong. I sneaked an occasional glance at Lisa-Marie while positioning myself as far away from her as possible, using the combined girth of Tony Ives and Baz Long as a shield.

The club was filling up and the DJ continued to build the energy. The bar area held many familiar faces. Even some of the Jewish kids were there. It was Mike Nagel's older brother's birthday and Mike came over to say hello, giving Lisa-Marie the once-over for longer than I cared, which was rage-inducing enough for me to freeze him out by acting too drunk to recognize him. I was standing at the time by Nwanko, who was proper hard, and I tried to look tough by association. It was a bit of a ridiculous move on my part, but now that I was with this new crew, I made an executive decision to brush off the King David kids. It was a decision I had no option but to see through once I had committed to it. Mike Nagel stood there awkwardly as I left him hanging while taking theatrical swigs from my flask until he shrugged and walked off.

A burst of dry ice snaked out from somewhere close to the DJ booth. Lasers snapped backward and forward across the room. When the opening guitar riff of "Bigmouth Strikes Again" sizzled over the sound system, its impact was instant. The room exploded as if a fan had applied a taper to a flare at a football match. The transformation was as astounding as it was thrilling to me. All this time I had listened to the Smiths song at home, completely oblivious to the fact it had come to serve as some kind of clubland signal to charge the dance floor. Bodies collided from all sides of the room, ours among them. Groups of girls formed, dancing dizzily around discarded handbags as the boys circled them, sizing up opportunities.

I had absolutely no idea of club dance floor etiquette and so elected to play it safe by unleashing a series of moves I had seen

Morrisey make on television then imitated for hours in my bed-room, airplaning my arms around and letting my body follow. The dry ice became thick like a fog in a fairy-tale forest. Faces fleetingly appeared out of its mist like woodland creatures. Grip-per popping and body-locking with Nwanko. James Kay careen-ing around, his face soaked in sweat on the dance floor just as it was on the College playing fields. Tony Ives moving slowly with his eyes closed and a bottle of lager in both hands.

The whole world seemed to be on that dance floor. I recog-nized one of the girls who worked behind the counter at our local dry cleaners'. She boogied into view, beaming before she lost her balance, tumbled over, and disappeared. For a second the smoke cleared, and Jonno Smith, the slightly creepy assistant coach from my local tennis club, nodded back at me knowingly. I was surrounded by joy and unself-consciousness on all sides, bodies freed in motion with no judgment as to dance moves, ignoring the crunching of the occasional broken beer glass underfoot.

The opening notes of "Bizarre Love Triangle" then pumped out, sending a full-throated cheer around the dance floor. Heads bobbed in affirmation. Beams of light sliced through the smoke. Limbs flashed and flailed along to the pummeling drumbeat. Just as lead singer Bernard Sumner opened his mouth to mur-mur the opening desire-filled lines, "Every time I think of you, I feel shot right through with a bolt of blue," Lisa-Marie appeared out of the fog, close enough for the suede fringes of her jacket to flicker against me like caressing fingers. New Order's cascading synth break kicked in and we lunged toward each other, mouths locking. Lisa-Marie kept dancing as we kissed, gyrating against me, with a hunger different from any first kiss I was familiar with: the slow-burn affection on display when Bruce Willis and Cybill Shepherd smooched, or the relief-filled tenderness I had experienced when locking lips with Casey back in Chicago. The physical sensation of Lisa-Marie grinding against me combined with the music and alcohol to create an unfathomable sense of release. For a moment, it felt as if the entire floor of the State Ballroom had been ripped from its foundations. The two of us were spinning off toward the stars, leaving the loneliness that had confined me to fall away and mix with the dry ice as a trail of vapor in our wake.

CHAPTER TWENTY-EIGHT

Liverpool College
Breaking Crew

A Caligula-style transformation had gripped my classmates. The motivators that had once driven us—intellectual enlightenment, a place at Oxford or Cambridge, or heroic sporting glory—suddenly paled into insignificance amid the debaucherous opportunities presented by the pubs and clubs of Liverpool. As Baz Long liked to exclaim when cheersing a round of pints at Rigby's, "These beers won't drink themselves." Plus . . . girls.

Early hip-hop in the guise of the Beastie Boys provided the perfect sound track. Their brash 1986 *Licensed to Ill* album informed our worldview: drink, partying, and sexual antics were all that mattered. The more destructive our behavior the better. A small cassette player that was plugged into the corner of the Liverpool College common room constantly blared out "The New Style" or "Rhymin' and Stealin'." Francis Swift and Nicola MacKenzie could more often than not be found making out alongside it. No matter the time of day, the two would shamelessly grind against each other as if they were thrill-seekers in a darkened corner of a club, as opposed to pupils at a private school cutting classes in Latin, Greek, and ancient history.

Because of their rasping New York accents, what the Beastie Boys actually had to say often meant little to our Scouse ears, but the brassy attitude of their delivery did. A cycle of depravity had gripped us in its thrall as we lived for weekends filled with city center boozers, sweat-soaked make-out sessions at the State Ballroom, and more often than not, James Kay crashing at my house, which meant him sitting up with his head over my garbage can puking away. All of this made me spend the night wide awake, not because of his heaving, but due to the pride I felt that the captain of the school rugby team was spending the night in my bedroom and filling up my garbage can with his vomit.

This anarchical spirit was reinforced by the headmaster's ill-advised decision to award Annabelle Starr absolute power as director of the annual school play. Taking matters into her able hands, Annabelle immediately revolutionized the long-standing winter tradition by declaring the entire production would be student-only.

Our whole grade eagerly vied for roles. The more naturally outgoing won coveted parts in the play itself, but there was truly something for everyone. The science dweebs stepped up to run lighting and special effects. Band geeks rose up to form the orchestra. Jamie lent his financial savvy to the box office. Even the grade's two Goths, Needham-Jones and Stavros, pitched in to do makeup.

The play Annabelle ultimately selected was *Our Day Out*, a minor work written by Willy Russell, a legendary local playwright. The narrative, about a class of remedial Liverpool schoolkids whose lives are transformed by a simple trip to the countryside, was a fitting choice. Its themes of liberation and reinvention were an echo of those we experienced in staging the production. Rehearsals meant that for two glorious months, our entire grade had a collective excuse not to autopilot back home after school and were instead left to our own devices in a wholly unsupervised space. Ostensibly we were running through lines and mastering our stagecraft, but in reality, we were embarking on a voyage of self-discovery in a place that existed outside of our teachers' oversight and parental control.

The anarchy of rehearsals took place at the same time we were studying the Middle Ages in history class. The parallels between the whole experience and the Children's Crusade were so uncanny, I decided to write a research paper on them. I was fascinated by this thirteenth-century campaign in which thirty thousand kids had been sufficiently inspired by the preaching of a twelve-year-old to set out to capture the Holy Land with him. An "infantocracy" was fleetingly created, granted, one that ended with almost all of its participants dying of hunger, drowning at sea, or cruelly being sold as slaves. In a way, *Our Day Out* was also an infantocracy—one that also began with lofty intentions before similarly going pear-shaped.

Daylight hours spent in class became a simple act of killing time until the final bell rang. That sweet sound commanded my entire grade to shake off our ennui and come to life, assembling in the school's theater so rehearsals could begin. In truth, there was a modicum of actual rehearsing. Annabelle worked tirelessly to breathe life into her creative vision, but there could only be a few of us onstage at any one time. The real action came when you were not blocking out a scene and could hang out in the wings, talking, flirting, or lolling around the stage door sucking on cigarettes. Couples old, new, and experimental could perpetually be found groping each other in the dark behind the scenery. This was a gloriously liberating time propelled by a frenetic drumbeat of gossip about crushes, hookups, and fallouts. Everything felt possible, with relationships crystallizing and falling apart in the life span of a mayfly. The entire grade lived out our nights in a state of near-permanent arousal before retiring to Rose of Mossley, the closest pub to the College that would serve us beers while turning a blind eye to the fact we were all wearing school uniforms.

Lisa-Marie and I were now very much an item. *Our Day Out* was a petri dish for our relationship. Her natural enthusiasm for life had equipped her with the acting chops necessary to land a leading role. I had originally missed out on a part because the audition was held on Rosh Hashana, Jewish New Year, a day on which I was absent from school. With Lisa-Marie's encouragement, Annabelle generously agreed to allow me to write my own mini-scenes at the end of every act, where I came onstage in my Hard Rock Cafe T-shirt and a Cubs hat, telling improv jokes in an American accent. My character was billed as "Chicago Tourist Guy," naturally.

My life, which had largely revolved around the safe, reliable anchors of home, school, Everton Football Club, and watching John Hughes movies with Jamie Glassman, now had a new pillar. Lisa-Marie O'Riordan. Dating, or "going out" as it was known in Liverpool, meant that the sacred conversations we already shared in the common room were now augmented by the titillating act of mutual gift-giving. Lisa-Marie's opening gambit was to present me with a cassette tape of Patti Smith's *Horses*, accompanied by a note written in painstakingly neat calligraphy that commanded me to listen to "Gloria" every night before I went to sleep, an order I followed at least twice.

I countered with a bar of Milka chocolate I had clumsily gift-wrapped myself in a copy of the local Liverpool *Echo*. Milka was a hard-to-find and ridiculously expensive German brand of chocolate that I had read somewhere was Morrisey's favorite. Lisa-Marie's response was so gratifying that I quickly followed up with a VHS copy of Jamie's and my favorite chestnut, *Diner*, accompanied by a letter in which I earnestly explained how I longed to develop the physical confidence of Mickey Rourke's Boogie, the mental acumen of Kevin Bacon's Fenwick, and the musical taste of Daniel Stern's Shrevie.

Lisa-Marie upped the stakes by leaving a blue corduroy blazer, a wondrous thrift-store find, in my locker. I pulled it on and a well-worn copy of Rilke's *Letters to a Young Poet* fell out of its inside pocket. When I saw Lisa-Marie had folded over a page and drawn a heart in pink highlighter pen around a quote— "Perhaps it will turn out that you are called to be an artist. Then take that destiny upon yourself and bear it, its burden and its greatness"—my heart thumped louder than the Beastie Boys' drum machine on "Fight for Your Right."

The nightly post-rehearsal walk between the College and beers at the Rose of Mossley involved crossing a secluded raised footbridge that ran over train tracks connecting Liverpool and London. Lisa-Marie liked to lag behind the rest of the group, so we were alone when reaching the top of this dank, high-walled path. We would then drop our bags and initiate a frantic making-out against the graffitied wall, both of us stabbing away at each other's mouths, she with a licorice-tasting tongue. The chill of Liverpool's winter could not dent our passion. Lisa-Marie delighted in unbuttoning her own shirt and forcing my hands onto her exposed breasts. The prospect was always so thrilling, yet the reality was undermined somewhat by my needling anxiety that some unsuspecting pensioners out walking their dog could chance upon us at any second.

For those nightly fifteen minutes it felt like I was living life on the edge. I was a dangerous new Rog. This made me walk taller and gave me all the confidence I needed to reinforce my relationships with the Rugger Boys. Free periods I once diligently dedicated to grinding away at my studies now felt better exiting the school property and heading to the local park with Gripper, Tuff, and Baz Long, Gripper always leading the pack. Tuff was filled with a spikey energy, always looking for objects to smash, graffiti, or commit a minor act of vandalism upon. Baz was just happy with any opportunity to puff away on a Marlboro Red. We would hang out in the rain under the cover of an abandoned bandstand, sharing swigs from a bottle of Merrydown cider and I would watch them chain-smoke cigarettes. We'd talk. Mostly about cider and cigarettes, then slowly meander back to school, slightly buzzed and feeling borderline immortal.

I had become such a fixture in this inner circle of alphas that Gripper invited me over on a Saturday afternoon to hang with the boys at his home, an invitation that came swift on the heels of news that I owned a VHS copy of *Let's Bust a Move* coming to light. This was an instructional break-dancing video I had purchased at Chicago's Deerfield Mall, because the cover had "I guarantee, you will soon be the best breaker in the schoolyard" emblazoned across it.

Our grade's obsession with the Beastie Boys had been turned up to eleven. "Fight for Your Right" was now faintly audible in every part of the United Kingdom. That raunchy coming-of-age sound track had pushed hip-hop into the mainstream, transforming it from cult club sound to pop radio fare. It's safe to say,

With James Kay (center). Whenever we were out on the town, I always looked like a much younger brother.

the song's message—"we will do whatever we want, whenever we want, and you can't stop us"—was generational catnip, tapping straight into the adolescent mind-set by conjuring poetry that was universally relatable. What boy under the age of eighteen could not relate to, as the B-Boys put it, mom throwing away their best porno mag?

One afternoon at the bandstand, Gripper declared it was time for us to form our own Beastie Boys–style collective. "Lads, we are now 'the Liverpool College Breaking Crew,'" he said with a tone of grandeur as if he had just glimpsed the future. This proclamation meant that we actually were required to break-dance. Hence the need for my videotape, the ownership of which had already elevated me to the status of one of Liverpool's fore-most breakers.

Having watched the hour-long masterpiece several times in my lounge, I did have some "skills." *Let's Bust a Move* consisted of a trio of dancers who took turns to unfurl a dizzying array of waves, moonwalks, and running men over the sound of stock B-Boy beats as an instructional narrator attempted to teach the art of popping, backspins, and hand glides in a soothing voice-over that gave the whole video a slightly soft-core quality. Since returning from Chicago, I was proud to be able to execute a passable six-step. If I was being honest, mine was more a five-step. But the only thing that mattered to me was that that was five steps ahead of most everyone else in town.

On Saturday afternoon, I knocked on the door of the Stark family semidetached. Having never met Gripper's parents, I was relieved that it was Gripper himself who answered the door, dramatically pointing toward a box-fresh pair of shell-toes that I immediately recognized as Run-DMC's much-hyped limited-edition collaboration with Adidas.

"Nice trainers," I said.

"Yeh. They have no laces," he answered proudly.

"That's cool," I replied, not really knowing what else to say.

"Prison rules . . . you know, to ensure inmates have nothing to hang themselves with."

"Yeh. I knew that," I lied.

By this time, we were in the hallway, which resembled the vast majority of English middle-class hallways I had ever been in. It was a tight space with a father's briefcase, umbrella, and galoshes neatly set by the front door within touching distance of a staircase that pressed against a back wall smothered in family photographs.

Off to the right there was an open door that Gripper tried to charge past even as a fairly menacing male voice emerged, bellowing "Who's that, Barnaby?" I momentarily recoiled in shock hearing someone refer to Gripper by his given name, then snuck a glance inside as Gripper ushered me past and glimpsed a physically large man standing menacingly over a seated woman who, I guessed by stealing a look at the family portraits, was Gripper's mum. "It's no one, Dad!" Gripper screamed back as he rushed in the opposite direction through the door behind us, pushing me through, then slamming it shut. I then found myself in the Gripper family room, an infinite sea of beige. Wankstain, Baz Long, and James Kay were standing awkwardly in front of the family's entertainment center.

"Have you got the goods?" James Kay asked with an eagerness whose tone momentarily confused me, making me feel I was expected to have brought contraband, like an eighth of weed or a porno magazine.

"The video," he clarified.

With relief, I felt the contours of *Let's Bust a Move* inside the same pocket of my corduroy jacket where I now routinely stashed a half bottle of scotch on Saturday nights. Gripper took the tape from me and carried it over to his video recorder reverently. As he did so, an undulating moaning came floating from across the hallway. Faintly first, then louder, until it was a low, rhythmic screaming, impossible to ignore. As Gripper bent over to insert the tape into his front-loading video player, Wank whispered to me, "It's Gripper's dad. He fucks his mum around this time every Saturday afternoon."

Gripper seemed to ignore the noise, so we all pretended to do likewise as he wielded his television's remote control to turn the volume up to maximum, just in time for the screen to burst into life with a sight that had become so familiar to me: a modest soundstage on which a couple of balled-up pieces of newspaper had been scattered to simulate a menacing urban environment. "If you take it slow and get it right, you'll be the hottest thing along the turf tonight," the VO crooned in promise. The effect this had on the Rugger Buggers was borderline hypnotic. "Poppin' is just sharp, jerky moves . . . the more you look like a machine, the better," the video narrator continued in his deep baritone mumble as they began to shuffle along on the sheepskin rug, mimicking the dancers on-screen, who controlled their bodies with a suave self-confidence as they performed "the Glide" and the narrator crooned, "The trick to gliding is to look and feel like you're walking on air."

After thirty minutes, group confidence had grown, smothering all remnants of self-consciousness, aided perhaps by the bottle of vodka that Gripper liberated from his parents' drinks cabinet. James Kay flicked through the neat stack of vinyl leaning against the hi-fi, holding a twelve-inch copy of Grandmaster Flash's pioneering smash "The Message" up above his head like a football trophy, then flinging the disc onto the turntable and dropping the needle.

"Liverpool College Breakdancing Crew, unite!" Gripper roared as the single's lyric-less B-side, "Melle Mel's Groove," erupted from the mounted speakers. We had no choice but to obey the track's rhythmic beats, hand claps, and spacey sonic sounds that now filled the room. Each of us shuffled into a line, tentatively at first, then finding the rhythm, uprocking side to side along to the track's underlying conga beat, ignoring the fact that break-dancing slides are exponentially harder to execute on lush suburban pile carpeting.

Wankstain started to lay down a beatboxing accompaniment and Gripper jumped in front to lay down the first rhyme.

"The name is Gripper.
And did I mention.
You will see me nightly
. . . In detention."

Baz Long then replaced him. With vodka bottle in hand, from which he had personally drained at least a third of the contents.

"The name is Baz.
And I'm the man
And next door, I can hear Gripper's dad
fucking Gripper's mam."

That kind of comment would normally warrant the immediate application of Gripper's fist to the teeth of the mouth that uttered it. But Liverpool College breaking crew rules were in effect. Anything could be said for the sake of the rhyme. Social anxiety still propelled me to try to change the subject, so I stepped in immediately. I had been desperately trying to get a "King Rog Rock" nickname to catch on, even though I knew at Liverpool College it was borderline illegal to try to give yourself a nickname. That never stopped me trying.

"I'm King Rog Rock
The one thing faster
Than Stott can cane
And he is the cane master . . ."

By this time our steps were coordinated, exaggerated, and joyful. As the music continued to boom, I looked down the line and saw Wank, lost in the hi-hat and snare beats he was laying down with his hands pressed against his lips. Gripper bounced and wormed wildly. James Kay attempted a corkscrew, bending his body in ways that made him seem possessed. Even Baz was power-stepping while simultaneously tackling the dregs of the vodka bottle. For a fleeting moment we were all free, uninhibited, and ecstatic, chanting in unison:

"We are the boys, the boys from the college.
We are the ones, the ones with knowledge."

We sang the lines, over and over to the accompaniment of Melle Mel's beats. Synths and drum fills originally crafted in the South Bronx were now making all of us feel so alive in South Liverpool, as we danced and howled like mad men barking at the moon, that even Gripper's parents' lovemaking was inaudible.

"You wake up late for school, man, you don't wanna go."

CHAPTER TWENTY-NINE

The Big Show

My world was now all about Sex, Drugs, and Rock and Roll. Without any of the first two. On the Saturday afternoon of *Our Day Out*'s final performance, I sat on the top deck of the No. 68 bus headed to school, willing each stop to be empty solely for my own benefit so I could reach my destination all the quicker and soak up every single moment of the pre-show backstage atmosphere.

I was living my dream life; hanging with the cool crowd; in a relationship with a girlfriend who was the star of a play in which I had a monopoly on the funniest lines. And perhaps best of all, after the performance, the whole grade was planning to celebrate our collective achievement by getting wrecked at the post-show-party-to-end-all-parties that Annabelle Starr was throwing at her house. Life, it felt, could not get any better.

This bolt of unassailable smugness was eviscerated the instant I set foot inside the stage door and found half the woodwind section of the play's orchestra staring at a message that had been spray painted on the backside of the scenery. "Roger Bennett is going to get laid tonite" had been written in graffiti so fresh the letters were still dripping. I was taken aback, to say the least. Once two years earlier, during geography class, Dunwood, a loner who sadly suffered from epilepsy, had experienced a fit and landed a punch on my chin with such force in the process that I lost my breath. That is how I felt in this moment. I did not even notice Lisa-Marie sidling up to me until she reached out and touched my cheek with the hand that was not grasping the spray paint can, a smile beaming on her face, clearly proud of her artwork.

My reaction was instantaneous and involuntary. I touched the sides of my neck with both hands and stroked the place where I imagined swollen glands would be and whispered "Not feeling very well" in a fake croak that attempted to project the notion of a sore throat. With lips pursed to simulate disappointment, I added, "Might . . . not . . . be able . . . to make tonight's party." While I had absolutely no fear about bounding onto the stage in front of a sold-out audience, the thought of being alone and totally nude with Lisa-Marie gave me performance anxiety. I had only just become confident at making out. The idea of sex felt like big-wave surfing for someone who had just learned to swim.

Lisa-Marie was having none of it. Ignoring the scandalized band members clutching their clarinets and oboes, she acted as if we were alone, reaching out a hand toward my crotch and patting it affectionately, chuckling, then heading off to makeup. I was left standing there, sagging under the weight of my own panic and confusion.

That night's performance proved to be an astonishing moment in Liverpool College's theatrical history. The house was packed. Each scene built on the last, delivering just the emotional crescendo the playwright had intended. My cameos landed perfectly. I knew as I delivered them that my jokes did not exactly make sense but I also realized that if I delivered them with Bruce Willis energy, they would kill.

Onstage, trying so hard to steal the show.

The response from the sold-out audience was intoxicating. A prolonged standing ovation thundered down during the curtain call, as Annabelle Starr took center stage to accept the acclaim she rightly deserved. She bowed deeply twice, pointing back toward the rest of the cast with feigned humility, then waved up the orchestra and the tech crews, commanding them to join us on the stage. Jamie and his box-office team took a moment to make it up from the front of the house. Even the two goths from the makeup unit were coaxed onto the stage, where they reluctantly sidled into the shadows at the back.

Together, we stepped forward to take one final bow. My entire class bonded in triumph, the Rugger Buggers, science nerds, art room kids, Dungeons & Dragons geeks, altar boys, computer freaks, "Pakis," Jews, and "Chinks." I felt fully aware of my own power. Even when I looked down the call line and saw Lisa-Marie in the center, miming grabbing my crotch with her hand, I did not falter.

I was still buzzing after the show as I changed into my party getup, flinging on my blue thrift-store blazer over the Hard Rock Cafe T-shirt and blue Levi 501's in the school locker rooms. That deep-heat and sweat-stenched hell-gate was different tonight. As I slathered my hair with Brylcreem in the changing room mirror, it was as if I were in a five-star hotel, suiting up to attend the Oscars.

Lisa-Marie met me outside the locker room. She was wearing her fringe-tasseled suede coat. We rode together to the party with the lads, squeezing into the backseat of the Citroën Dyane that Baz Long had borrowed from his mum, swigging a shared bottle of Merrydown cider on the way. After parking, we strolled up the Starr family driveway. We had all heard a lot about this house. Both of Annabelle's parents were architects and James

Kay, who was the only one of us who had been round before, had advised us the inside felt like being on the bridge of the USS *Enterprise.*

The house was indeed sci-fi, a tower of metal and glass. The front door was wide open. The first thing we encountered upon stepping inside was a giant fir tree springing up straight from the middle of the ground-floor hallway through the roof, as if it had been pried from an enchanted forest and replanted inside the glass shaft that now encased it. The tree set the tone for this magical playhouse in which every room joined at funky, mad-hatter-like angles. The walls were littered with unconventional design elements such as light switches that sat waist high, armed with palm-controlled dimmers. Like a slice of Los Angeles had landed in Liverpool, this was next-level cool.

Fairy lights had been flung up everywhere, which only added to the fairy-tale energy. Janet Jackson's "Control" blasted through tiny yet powerful speakers built into every room, all of which started to fill with anticipation as my entire grade arrived. The Jewish kids even crashed, a fact I first noticed because my nemesis Mike Nagel and his girlfriend, Jessica Goldfarb, had a very dramatic, and very public, argument that led to her storming out of the party in front of everyone.

I shuffled away from that awkwardness in general and Mike Nagel in particular, a human being who made me feel like Old Rog, reminding me of parties I could not enter. Lisa-Marie and I headed into the kitchen. Everything was sharp-angled, white, chrome, and gleaming. Annabelle was there by herself, having changed into a deep purple velvet dress that barely reached the top of her thighs. A pair of fairy wings sprouted out of her back. She was smoking a joint and leaning against an onyx countertop bar weighed down with half-gallon handles of Bailey's Irish

Cream, Malibu Rum, Buckfast, and every other liquor one could imagine. Crates of Grolsch beers towered behind, with their distinctive hinged-bottle caps screaming that good times were on their way.

"What can I get you, darlings," Annabelle slurred before fixing Lisa-Marie a Southern Comfort and 7-Up, and then me a Brass Monkey, which I only requested because it was a cocktail name-checked in a Beastie Boys song, not because I knew what it was. Luckily, Annabelle pretended she did. The three of us clinked glasses. "Monkey tastes def when you pour it on ice," Lisa-Marie chirped excitedly. "Come on, y'all, it's time to get nice," I replied by rote as we headed off to explore.

Truly great parties are like white-knuckle roller coasters that build anticipation by slowly crawling up an initial ascent before crashing down into a delirious free fall. One minute, we wannabe-revelers were on our best behavior, savoring each other, toasting our collective achievement, and even feeling slightly inhibited by the awe-inspiring architecture. The next, Public Enemy's "Yo! Bum Rush the Show" exploded onto the sound system, igniting a collective awareness that two months of total freedom were about to come to an abrupt end, and all hell kicked off.

Suddenly boys were walking round shirtless. Bottles were smashed. Furniture broken. Someone decided to redecorate the dining room by pinning pages from a hard-core porn mag on previously pristine walls. There was a crash in the living room as Baz Long urinated flush against the wall, standing on tiptoes in an effort to ensure his arc reached as high up as possible before keeling over and bringing down a batik wall hanging along with him.

We barely had time to process this before word spread that

one of the girls was being was being carted off in an ambulance. Everyone then spilled outside to discover the Starrs' driveway was now awash in the blue strobe light of an emergency vehicle, in front of which two stone-faced paramedics were indeed attempting to lift a flailing Sammy Howell onto a gurney. "She professed her love to Cosmo Bullens, who told her he only had eyes for Annabelle Starr," the always-in-the-know Gripper whispered, "so she downed an entire bottle of Malibu and has got to have her stomach pumped." This matter-of-fact commentary was soon pierced by Sammy screaming "Cosmo-oooohhhhhhh! I fucken' love you!" while her strapped-down body was jammed into the back of the ambulance. In the wake, Lisa-Marie mused, "Love is hard. Love between one person and another: That is perhaps the hardest thing it is laid on us to do."

"What?" I replied, nonplussed.

"Rilke. *Letters to a Young Poet,*" Lisa snapped, with a slight note of irritation.

I was saved by a cry of "Gerra load of dis in 'ere lads" screamed from somewhere deep within the house, causing us all to stampede back inside, ricocheting toward where the voice had come from. The kitchen was now filled with a crowd of astounded onlookers staring at a heavily inebriated Tuff, who had climbed up onto one of the kitchen's previously spotless white countertops. After initially fighting for balance as if he were an able seaman on deck during a storm, my friend proceeded to unbutton and lower his jeans, open the Starrs' state-of-the-art Panasonic microwave oven, and jam his ass inside.

"He isn't, is he?" a disgusted Lisa-Marie muttered in a way that made her nose wrinkle adorably as we both struggled to gain a better view from the back of the room. A rude rasp of flatulence quickly followed by the unmistakable explosive follow-through and diabolical splatter answered Lisa-Marie's question quite clearly. He most certainly was.

It was a scene that was repulsive and impossible to take your eyes off in equal measure. Utterly lost in his task, Tuff now pivoted his hips, turning to face the microwave, as he slammed the door shut with an elan that momentarily caused him to lose his balance, only to recover, scrutinize the power levels, and then with a creative flourish that only served to reinforce the horror of the moment, jab the button marked "reheat."

Kids closest to the front were the first to start retching, yet I could not look away. A calm-headed Lisa-Marie saved me, grabbing my wrist and leading us back into the hallway to escape the depravity. For a moment, we stood alone alongside the slender trunk of the fir tree, exchanging looks of bewildered amusement. Then Lisa-Marie sprang back into action. "Come 'ere," she whispered, taking my hand once more and dragging me toward the staircase that wrapped round and round the tree like Jack's beanstalk leading the way to a giant's castle.

Instead of a castle, the stairs led to the relative serenity of the Starrs' bedrooms. Lisa-Marie silently but fearlessly took charge, opening the door to the first. The room had been painted a dark purple, and the only light came from a Chinese lantern in the corner. Once my eyes had adjusted to the darkness, my first impulse was to marvel at the Starrs' interior design yet again. They had made ingenious use of a narrow space by suspending a bunk bed from metal rods extending from the ceiling and tucking a chest of drawers underneath. Murmuring and groaning emerging from the bed itself and a pair of fairy wings hanging off the side suggested this was Annabelle's bedroom and she and Cosmo were approaching ecstasy up there.

Someone had put Prince's "Purple Rain" on a cassette player

by the desk. In the far corner behind it was a pair of trousers that had been discarded on the floor. I guessed they belonged to Tony Ives, as the silhouette of the massive, pantsless bloke could be seen grinding away against a girl on a small couch against the far wall.

Judging from the state of her floor, Annabelle Starr was no neat freak. Hairbrushes, cassette boxes, and at least two bras fought amid other scattered flotsam and jetsam for space on the carpet. As Prince sang about weekend lovers, Lisa-Marie pushed me backward down to the ground. My butt landed on a telephone receiver, which hurt like hell, but I tried to laugh it off and nudged the phone aside. Prince was now approaching spiritual fulfillment, lost in the thrall of his own power ballad. Lisa-Marie stood over me, taking off her treasured suede jacket. The fringes flailed wildly as she chucked it off to the side. Then she undid the buttons to her white shirt, hiked up the long skirt she was wearing, and slowly descended, lowering herself directly onto my crotch.

Prince continued to croon as we kissed. Lisa-Marie executed her signature move of grabbing my hands and placing them on her breasts, arching her back and continuing to pulverize my fly. By the time she reached down to unbutton my pants, I was so swollen, I was less afraid and more just relieved to be free. There was a muffled girl's cry and a deep groan from over by the couch area, which forced Lisa-Marie to stop for a moment and look over her shoulder. She then turned to face me, her eyes bright, lip-syncing along with the Purple One, and began to readjust matters beneath her own skirt.

My brother had anticipated this day when he was last home from university a full six months before, gifting me a condom that he'd instructed me to keep in my wallet at all times. It was this condom I retrieved now, biting off the edge of its wrapper, then praying I had the oily contraption pointed in the right direction as I prepared to roll it on my shaft in the style he had shown me using a banana borrowed from my mother's fruit bowl.

The immense sense of achievement I experienced as it did so was immediately surpassed by the feeling that followed as Lisa-Marie thrust downward. The song had become all guitar outro now. I looked up at her face, her eyes closed, hands on my chest as she began to glide up and down on top of me. This was it, I told myself. This is happening. We are doing this. THIS IS SEX. THIS IS WHAT SEX FEELS LIKE. The immediate thought I had was of Brough Sandhurst, a kid in my brother's year who once had a lapse in judgment to confide to his teammates on the back of the rugby bus that he could only masturbate by thrusting his dick into half an orange, a revelation that had earned him the nickname "Jaffa" from that day on. The way Lisa-Marie's vagina was gripping my shaft now, I gained a true appreciation for what Sandhurst had been trying to get at.

We were approximately twenty seconds in when Lisa-Marie picked up the pace and started to bob up and down like an advanced aerobics instructor executing a set of jumping jacks mid-class. The change of speed threw me. There was too much stimulation. Too much feeling. Too many uncharted emotions. I had read enough readers' letters in porno mags to know the bloke was meant to go all night like Don Johnson. I had not even broken the minute mark yet and was already about to blow. Panic kicked in. Undertaking a desperate effort to regain a modicum of control, I tried to shift my mind as far from my crotch area as possible, laser focused on Beastie Boys lyrics instead. My tactic failed, as I was rendered with temporary memory loss.

"They got a committee to get me off the block"

WHAT THE FUCK IS THE NEXT LINE

"King   Ad   Rock . . . Something . . . something . . . something . . ."

THIS IS NOT WORKING

"Whiffle   Ball   Bats . . . White   Castle . . . something . . . Brooklyn . . ."

LISA-MARIE IS RIDING ME IN A FRENZY LIKE ANIMAL IN THE MUPPETS DURING A DRUM FILL

DON JOHNSON. DON JOHNSON. DON JOHNSON

I CAN'T HANG ON ANY LONGER. I CAN'T HANG ON ANY LONGER . . . I CAN'T . . .

Krakatoa and Vesuvius exploded less than I did. I was instantly overcome by an immense wave of relief that I strove to mask for fear of even being perceived as a virgin.

"How many girls have you made love to?" Lisa-Marie asked soothingly.

"Five," I said straining for a deep tone that could impart a "studly ain't no big deal" air of confidence.

"I thought so," she lied convincingly. "That was tremendous."

I took off the condom, now sperm-filled, and jettisoned it into the mouth of some half-empty can of Coke that had been discarded on the floor. We lay together panting softly, still exposed, Lisa-Marie making no move to button up the front of her shirt, even as a crack of light burst through the door while it opened and closed. It was Mike Nagel walking in alone. He let his eyes adjust, then recoiled as he saw Lisa-Marie and me lying there postcoitus. He leaned against the desk, attempting to affect a casual air, but for a second, I saw him wince.

For the first time ever, I had something Mike Nagel desired

but could not get. "What do you want, Nagel?" I said, loving the role reversal that had suddenly given me the upper hand. "Nothing," he said unconvincingly. "Just a drink." He reached over and grabbed the half-empty Coke from the floor, tossed his head back, and took a sip.

I felt a surging sense of satisfaction that in many ways even outstripped the pleasure I had just shared with Lisa-Marie.

CHAPTER THIRTY

The Wake-up Bell

Like eighteenth-century Europe in the midst of the French Revolution's Jacobin era, this was the best of times, it was the worst of times. While my life flourished socially, and sexually, my relationship with my parents deteriorated into a cold war. The cratering of my grades was the opening shot, and things went further downhill fast. My parents detested the company I was keeping. Even my mum, a contender for the world's least judgmental person, constantly wondered out loud as she puttered around the kitchen as to why I no longer spent time with Jamie.

For his part, my dad began to cross-examine me with intense vigor in an attempt to extract the specifics of my evening's plans before I left the house every Saturday night. He had made it clear that for reasons of common decency, when getting picked up by friends, he expected those aforementioned friends to be brought inside the house for a formal hello. This was fine in the old days when it was mainly just Jamie picking me up to walk down to the local cinema. The worst that could happen then was my father making my mate feel uncomfortable by grilling him menacingly about his progress as a left back on the school's field hockey team. But there was no way I was letting my dad anywhere near Gripper, Tuff, Wankstain, and the Rugger Buggers with his invasive line of questioning.

For the first couple of Saturday nights, when the lads came to pick me up, I would charge toward the door to intercept them as if they bore the imminent threat of a grenade tumbling into a foxhole. After screaming the quickest of goodbyes, I would then exit the vicinity.

Imagine my horror then, roughly four months in, when the doorbell went off and I executed my customary sprint toward the front door, only to be cut off by my father, who had been hiding in the empty dining room and swooped in at that very second. I stared at my father with mortification and dread as Gripper, Tuff, Wank, Baz Long, and Tony Ives blinked back at us in confusion from the darkness beyond our doorstep. My father took control of the situation, affecting his plummiest tone as he commanded, "Roger, aren't you going to introduce me." In a desperate act of self-preservation, I shut down. The whole scene was like the biblical story of Korach and his followers, who mutinied against Moses, causing God to open the ground beneath their feet, swallowing them alive. I was so filled with shame, that is exactly what I desired at that moment. For the hallway floor to open and devour me. Nothing more, nothing less.

I had no such luck as God let me down. And worse, my father filled in the deity's absence by stepping forward and starchily introducing *himself* to each of the lads. This formal gesture transformed the posse I had spent years aching to impress by stripping away their bravado and self-confidence. "Barnaby Stark, sir," Gripper said, stepping forward with arm extended for a well-mannered handshake. He instantly lost the working-class Scouse accent we all faked as he did so, sounding like a sweet lad, as opposed to a savage who had won every fight he had ever entered. "Joseph Nwanko, sir," Wankstain enunciated carefully, adopting the tone of a student who longed to study biochemistry at Oxford or Cambridge university and not a bloke who aspired to be the greatest beatboxer in the North West of England. "Barry Long, sir," Baz said, with a wounded tone that reflected that of a boy in need of guidance, not a young man who lived with his mum, had never met his dad, and whose sole life goal was to drain a bottle of vodka, with or without orange juice, and then get his rocks off.

"Your dad's a fag," Gripper concluded as we silently and sullenly took a cab into town for a night that never really recovered from my father's unexpected intervention. The boys, as if shamed by revealing themselves for what they truly were—simple, vulnerable, slightly lost middle-class kids—remained introspective and subdued. The pre-club warm-up beers did not taste as good. Lisa-Marie and the girls never materialized at the State, so when Wank got knocked back by the bouncers, it ripped the stuffing right out of the evening. We called it a night at around 1 A.M., preferring to grab a doner kebab at the Lobster Pot.

Liverpool chip shops late on a Saturday night are packed, and as merciless as the *Cobra Kai* dojo. Everyone is drunk, and when you factor in that the only people willing to line up for thirty minutes just to get a doner and chips are those without a realistic chance of getting laid, then you can understand the odds for violent conflagration are very high. The boys passed round a packet of Marlboro Reds to kill some time and we lined up in the queue, which snaked back on itself in the narrow confines of the shop.

To my horror, a local scallywag with one or two many pints in him was chatting loudly with his girl and accidentally elbowed Gripper from behind. It was an innocent mistake, but one with brutal consequences. On a good day, Gripper's anger levels were at "simmering." Tonight, a combination of my dad's formality, the girls' absence, and Wank's knockback meant he was aching for an outlet for his fury. The unwitting boy had no idea what was about to go down. One minute he was loudly reliving an incident from that afternoon's Liverpool match, the next he was on the receiving end of two savage uppercuts from Gripper, who kept unloading punches even as his unwitting target fell to the floor and his girlfriend screamed in horror.

As sickening as the act was, the audience in the chip shop was barely moved. They had waited a long time for their kebabs and were not going to let a random act of violence prevent them from the satisfying exclamation point that a packet of warm grease could contribute to a night out. They simply shuffled aside to create sufficient floor space for my classmate to vent the violence that had been building inside of him all night. All the while, the Lobster Pot staff kept taking orders, manning the fryer, and slinging chips.

It was only after the cab dropped me off on the way home that night that I realized I did not have my house keys. It was close to three in the morning. I was not yet used to the late-night, last family member home routine. The dozen or so pints of lager and cider with flask of scotch-chaser I had downed muted the sense of panic that should have swamped me. I was, as they say in Liverpool, "well bladdered." Leaning against the door post for support, I pressed the doorbell twice, then waited in the darkness for an eternity, until the lights went on in their familiar pattern. Upstairs first, followed by the staircase, and then the hallway, followed by the sound of my father unlocking dead bolt after dead bolt, before the door opened, and he was standing right in front of me, trying to take it all in. I stared back at him, respecting how he had taken a moment to put on a silk paisley dressing gown and tie it fastidiously. I also noticed he was seething with white-hot rage.

When my father was angry, he normally talked forever, delivering judgment like a supreme court justice rendering a verdict. That night he was so incandescent, he could not speak a word. Indeed, he could not bring himself to talk to me for the next seventy-two hours as I slunk around the house, in the shadows filled with guilt for my selfishness and anger at myself for my lack of thought.

Whatever remorse I felt, little changed. I frittered another school week away, cutting class, yukking it up with the boys, and making out with Lisa-Marie on the railway bridge, aching for the release only a Saturday night out could provide. The State kicked off that week. There was a big fight on the dance floor. The bouncers only intervened when one combatant smashed a beer bottle and attempted to stab the other in the eye. They dragged him off screaming and chucked him out of the club. At closing time, two hours later, he was still there in the street, ignoring the rain, thinking only of his nemesis. As the crowd spilled out onto the street, he steamed into its midst, located his prey, and smashed his face in with a series of arcing, furious windmill punches.

Another night of violence. Another cab ride home in startled silence. Yet, once the taxi dropped me off, I felt a sickening shock that would have trumped even that of the State Ballroom's victim. To my horror, and with a searing awareness of my own stupidity, I realized that for a second week in a row, I had forgotten to grab my house keys. The panic was real this time. My memory of my father's recent fury and how long it had taken to subside was still fresh. I would rather be on the end of a smashed beer bottle. Ringing the doorbell was not an option.

Frenzied mathematical calculations unleashed themselves in my head as I attempted to compute every possibility. It was three thirty in the morning. Pitch black, about four degrees centigrade,[*] but at least the rain had dried up. My parents would be up with my infant sister sometime between seven and seven thirty. I decided to brave the cold and sleep outside, despite the fear of being accosted by prowling passersby. I rationalized that my dad might even appreciate the rational decision making, thoughtfulness, and self-sacrifice. I was drunk, of course.

I sat down on the backdoor step, popped up my blazer collar Don Johnson–style (as if Don Johnson was ever stupid enough to do something like *this*), then braced myself to dig in for the long haul. "You can do it," I told myself, stabbing away at the calculator function on my Seiko digital watch, which had been another bar mitzvah gift. "Two hundred ten minutes is only 12,600 seconds. That's nothing." I waited for what felt like an age, resisting the urge to check the watch again. When I began to panic that it was not getting any lighter, I caved, and to my horror, saw that I had only been sitting there for twenty minutes. "Okay. Twenty minutes down, just one-ninety to go."

It was really very cold. Not freezing, but frigid enough for my fingertips to ache and my body to shiver. The chill of the wind was the real problem, and out of desperation, I decided it would be warmer underneath my mother's car, and so I slid beneath the back bumper of her Ford Fiesta, resting my head straight onto the concrete, just out of reach of a small oil patch. Fatigue

---

[*] 40 degrees Fahrenheit.

kicked in, engulfing even the feelings of panic, cold, and fear. I slept fitfully, tortured by fractured nightmares. I tried to calm myself by thinking about the feeling of being on the beach in Chicago, imagining the sun on my back and sand under my feet, only to learn it is true that remembering a time of joy in a moment of darkness only reinforces the sense of misery.

Signs of life percolating out of the back door of my house jolted me awake. I may have been hungover, dehydrated, and unable to feel my extremities, but from the kitchen, I could hear the radio was on, and the kettle was whistling as the water boiled for my dad's morning cup of tea. I was saved. I sprang up as quickly as my aching muscles would allow and knocked tentatively on the frosted glass of the window, which my father's silhouette quickly filled. Again, the satisfying sound of keys at work. The door opened to end my suffering, the comforting smell of breakfast wafting out as it did so.

I wanted a hug. I wanted acknowledgment of my selflessness. A cup of warm, hot tea at the very least. Instead I got shocked confusion. "Roger, what in God's name?" my dad proclaimed. Whenever he used my full name, "Roger," I knew I was in trouble and I could see just how hard he was working to process why his son was shivering and blue-lipped by the back door at seven thirty on a Sunday morning. "Did you just sleep outside?" My head dropping with shame told him all he needed to know. "What an imbecilic, dangerous thing to do, you little moron!" he screamed, pointing out of the room in disgust. "Straight to your bedroom now, you waster." I turned to my mum for solace, but her eyes filling with tears as she stared in my direction made it clear that even she could not save me. "Please go upstairs. Your father and I are at a complete loss with what to do with you at the moment," she mumbled. I headed up to my bedroom, elated to be inside the warm house yet utterly perplexed. Ringing the doorbell made my dad go ballistic. Not ringing the doorbell made him go nuclear. Death by fire or drowning. What exactly was I supposed to do? Remembering my keys in the first place never occurred to me.

My parents may not have known what to do with me, but that never stopped them trying. Cut to midweek. Me doing what I now specialized in at school: cutting class. I was lounging around the Sixth Form Common Room in the company of my motley crew of co-conspirators, Baz Long, Wankstain, and Sally Joyce among them. We were killing time drinking copious cups of tea, blowing cigarette smoke in rings out of a cracked-open window, and playing *Licensed to Ill* with the volume on its lowest so as not to tip off passing teachers. Real rebels without clues.

The dominant topic of conversation at the time was Gripper's latest suspension, this time for beating the crap out of Karl Magnusson, a science dork who had the misfortune of clipping the back of the wrong boy's head with a hockey stick around the hubbub of the lockers at the end of the school day. The ever-quick-to-fury Gripper had reacted by grabbing the stick from the unfortunate Magnusson's hands and battering the side of his face in with it until an enormous egg-sized welt rose up where his eye had once been.

Wank was making the case that the resulting weeklong suspension showed the school administration's woeful misunderstanding of local street justice, when the door to the common room smashed open with a force strong enough to blow it off the hinges. Jaws dropped, cigarettes were hastily tossed out of the window, and the room went silent as the enormous frame of Mr. McNally stormed in, in full-on Fat Knacker mode. He had busted us all dead to rights. Yet McNally ignored the rest of the group. To my horror, he homed in solely on me.

I was sitting, slumped in a lounge chair toward which Knacker charged with his wide, lumbering gait. As he approached me, he stooped for a second without breaking stride, placed one meaty hand over my chest at nipple height, took a grip, and swung me clean out of the seat as he drove my body swiftly upward and back, smashing my shoulders into the lockers, where he held me eye-to-eye. "You're fucking up, Benj," he said with an admonishing tone of anger that was reinforced by his unused hand slapping me back and forth across either cheek to emphasize every syllable. "You're fucking up real bad. Your parents are worried. They asked me to talk to you, Benj. You need to know, these people are malingerers," he continued, jerking a thumb back toward an astonished group of my peers, and using a word I had to look up afterward. "Ignore them. Make them small. Your work is big. Make your future big. Remember the Cod. That is all that matters."

He then let go, condemning me to plunge downward from his height as Mr. McNally stormed out of the common room without ever acknowledging, never mind disciplining, any of my fellow slackers. They sat there mouths agape, staring at my humiliation, sprawled as I was amid the pile of sports bags littered around the lockers.

My parents had mobilized Fat Knacker like some modern-day Golem dispatched to save the day. That fact said more about their level of desperation about my life and its future direction. As did their self-knowledge, that I would not listen to them. So, with some cunning they had recruited McNally as their messenger, and all credit to them, Knacker's message struck home. He, the one teacher who always strove to respect us like men, had just treated me like a little boy. My wounded pride might heal, as would the ache of my single throbbing nipple. But try as I might, I was not likely to shake his words, "Make your life big. Make them small."

"Fat Knacker's a fag," Baz Long snorted.

CHAPTER THIRTY-ONE

The Beastie Boys and the Liverpool Welcome

I continued to ponder that moment with Fat Knacker, but for the rest of my crew, life continued as before. That included the slow death that was Mr. Weakstone's English classes. Our master was in the midst of an hour-long interpretation of Dr. Faustus's downward spiral when the door was smashed open one afternoon. The shock caused Mr. Weakstone to leap a good five inches out of his desk chair. But Gripper had more modern concerns than Elizabethan tragedy. In fact, he had astonishing news to break. "The Beastie Boys are coming to Liverpool!" he screamed, losing all decorum in the enormity of the moment. "The fucking Beastie Boys are going to be HERE . . . playing a gig and everything . . . live and in bloody person." At my desk, I held my head in my hands, unable to process this news.

It was true. My current heroes the Beastie Boys would indeed be rolling into Liverpool on the last night of the short British leg of their Licensed to Ill Tour. "No Sleep Till Brooklyn" was now played so often on the jukebox at the Rose of Mossley, the landlord had taped up a sign prohibiting its selection, a sign that

Gripper routinely ignored, slipping in fifty pence and choosing the song three times back-to-back on repeat.

The Beasties' hold on our imaginations was enormous. And we were not alone. By the time their eight-city swing began, the English tabloid media had worked themselves into a frenzy over the prankster band and their bawdy behavior. Journalists reveled in every detail of the trio's stage set, which featured gigantic Budweiser cans, barely clad female go-go dancers grinding away in cages, and the pièce de résistance, a twenty-foot-high hydraulic pink phallus that sprang open like a crude jack-in-the-box at the climax of the show. As the Beastie circus rumbled across England, from London to Birmingham, up to Manchester, the press were frothing at the mouth at the moral corruption these horrid Americans were spewing. Every article was expertly constructed to make readers like my father, who wanted to be disgusted, seethe as these debased destroyers kept rolling north. Amid tabloid talk of bans and lawsuits, the Beastie Boys' Mike D declared, "We're going by the blitzkrieg theory on this tour: hit hard, hit fast, get out of there quickly, and leave a long-lasting impact." Little did he know how that philosophy would be distilled to its essence on their closing night in Liverpool.

My father's contempt only deepened the love I harbored for the Beasties. Indeed, I was so eager to have my morals debased, I cut an entire day of school with the rest of the Liverpool College breaking crew to snap up tickets the second they went on sale at the box office. We stood in line at the aging art deco concert venue, the Royal Court Theatre, braving the frigid Liverpool morning with four dozen fellow hip-hop heads, trying to look

The day of the Beasties gig. Def Jam T-shirt. Bud hat.
And a skateboard I had no idea how to ride.

streetwise and mean, even while clad in the matching ties and blazers of our school uniform. If enormous inflatable penises were going to explode in my town, I sure as hell was going to be there to witness them. Even Fat Knacker's words of caution could not trump that lure.

With tickets safely acquired, we frittered away the rest of the afternoon by snapping medallions off the front grills of parked Volkswagens so we could dress like Mike D, who delighted in wearing the chrome emblem on a hefty gold chain around his neck. The style was an ironic visual gag poking fun at rappers who fetishized the Mercedes logo. After immense peer pressure from Wank and Tuff, I joined in this act of petty vandalism, snagging a logo off the front air vent of a rusty VW Golf parked near school. The moment the badge's resistance buckled under the pressure of my fingers it conjured a jolt of intense satisfaction fused with a pang of guilt.

The VW emblem was the final detail in an elaborate process I had undertaken to make over my wardrobe of late, into that of an aspiring English break boy, replete with Adidas tracksuit, Puma Clydes, and a Budweiser porkpie hat I had nabbed on special order direct from St. Louis. The fine details of this look were crucial because the Beastie Boys were more than just dumb fun in my eyes. They may have been able to manufacture outrage on demand, but I saw beyond that and drew a sense of identity and inspiration.

There were many aspects of their approach I felt connected to: Their friendship, as three young Jewish kids from New York City who met in their early teens haunting downtown TriBeCa clubs, was the kind of coreligionist camaraderie I craved. The elasticity of their humor was also enticing; being in on the joke, being the joke, ricocheting between bombast and self-deprecation in the span of just a few lines. Indeed, their entire attitude toward music, piecing together a signature sound forged of their schooling in punk clubs, with rock and old-school hip-hop woven in, was an education in aspirational crate digging.

Yes, they were brash, obnoxious wise-asses. The lyrics were violent in a manner I did not physically relate to, and often immensely sexist in a way I could not compute. Yet I rationalized this clumsy, almost cartoonish deviance away. To me, the Beasties were like kids attempting to bring life to a double period of Latin class by blurting shit out to see what they could get away with. That's how the ginormous stage penis had come about in the first place, I discovered. Their record label told the band they could have anything on the stage, to which they responded, "Really. *Anything?*"

Besides, I was fascinated less by their boundary pushing and more by the achievements they had made manifest because of it. They were big-dreaming, big-talking lads who had used their mouths and minds to create something that had grabbed the attention of the world, opening for Madonna, crafting a number one album, and for one of them, dating the ultimate dream girl, Molly Ringwald. The trio's Starter jacket swagger was the wondrously unhindered confidence I had always aspired to, untamed and uncontained by what others thought. "What others thought" was 93 percent of what I actually did think about. So, on school nights, instead of doing my homework, I would circle around my room with headphones on, memorizing the lyrics to the album until I could spit them out like a mystic speaking in tongues.

When I lay on my bed on May 30, 1987, staring at the £5 ticket I had bought for that night's gig, it felt like I had acquired a golden ticket to enter New York City itself, the boom-box-filled five boroughs the Beasties embodied. I pulled on that hat, Def Jam T-shirt, and VW badge (now dangling off a plate-gold necklace I had liberated from my mother's jewelry box) and became King Rog Rock. A man transformed, willing himself to believe that a sense of possibility, adventure, and fearlessness was his for the taking.*

Beastie Boy Adam Yauch had appeared on local TV early that night declaring that Liverpool should be ready to exercise "its constitutional right to be fresh." I did not know exactly what he meant but could not have been more exhilarated. I was not alone. Walking into pregame beers at Rigby's pub was akin to crashing a costume party packed full of fellow B-Boys, clad in shell tops, trucker hats, chunky gold chains, and "fake-vintage" high school T-shirts. By the time we got to the Royal Court the place was heaving. Two thousand fellow fans were stuffed into a sold-out venue. Somehow, though, the energy was off-kilter, and strangely agitated. I expected a communal spirit born of a sense we were all about to experience something special—our version of the Beatles on *The Ed Sullivan Show*, or Hendrix at Woodstock—but the prevailing atmosphere felt nervy and simmering, as if we were a Saxon horde preparing for battle.

We half-dozen members of the Liverpool College breaking crew stood at the back of the packed theater, marking out our territory as we marveled at the stage. Giant tall boys of Budweiser bookended a cage designed to enclose one scantily clad

---

* Reality often proved to be frustratingly different. After I read that the Beasties grew up skateboarding, I instantly went out and procured a skateboard, attempting to teach myself ollies and kick flips in my own driveway. One nasty, involuntary dismount straight into my mother's rosebush persuaded me to carry it around as an accessory in my arms rather than a mode of transport. For three months, I lugged that skateboard around everywhere with me, like Dorothy schlepping Toto around Oz.

female. Center stage featured a pair of DJ turntables on a high riser, alongside a mysterious black box at which Gripper pointed with delight as soon as we walked in. "I'll bet that's where the huge nob springs out from."

The energy surged the second the lights went dark across the venue. I was hit by a hyperawareness that I, King Rog Rock, was about to be in the same room and breathe the very same air as Ad Rock, MCA, and Mike D. This meaningful thought was interrupted by the hoarse tones of MCA booming into a mic offstage, "Fuck you, Liverpool." The second I heard his signature gravelly Brooklyn bark hit the third syllable, a long, drawn-out "Livahhhhhhh . . . ," my excitement was burned away and replaced by the cold, sickening realization that MCA had just made a terrible mistake.

"Fuck you, Livahhhhhh-pooooooooooooollllllllll."

This riff might have been standard Beastie Boy stage patter, swagger that worked perfectly well in Los Angeles, Chicago, Brighton, or Birmingham. But Liverpool is different. You simply can't roll into town, say that, and expect to escape a beating. It does not matter who you are. Those are fighting words, akin to insulting someone's mum in front of her face.

The three Beasties, however, were blithely unaware of the sin they had just committed. They pogoed onto the stage, grabbing their crotches and spraying cans of beers on the crowd, as banks of light illuminated the cage, now featuring a bikini-clad dancer writhing against the bars. Yet even as the shiny bald-headed DJ Hurricane spun the opening beats of "Slow and Low," something irreparable had broken in the crowd. As the fans crushed forward, all of them were suddenly seething, ready to show the Beasties that the pupil had become the master.

"Let it flow, let yourself go . . ."

After the first beer can spiraled toward the stage, exploding upon impact, a dozen more followed its arc, causing Mike D to exclaim, "Suck my dick." This invited fans at the front to spew forth a sea of spit, coating the bouncers, who were now desperately linking arms in an attempt to push the hordes back. The entire floor of the theater became a blanket of furious two-fingered V-signs. The Beasties were being given a true Liverpool welcome.

They had not made it halfway through their first song and now were in danger of completely losing control of the show. A barrage of cans began to fly down from the balcony. MCA barked for stagehands to turn up the houselights, a move that only pushed the Scousers to do something I had hitherto believed was unthinkable: waste full cans of beer, preferring to defend their city's honor by flinging them angrily at their now fully exposed prey rather than drink.

I watched in horror at the surreal scene unspooling around me. The go-go dancer, who had probably turned up at the gig believing this night would be one of the most exhilarating of her life, was now cowering for cover at the back of the cage as lagers exploded all around her. A lad standing to my left, clad in a freshly purchased Beastie Boys concert T-shirt, hurled his Bud with the one-in-a-million accuracy of a proton torpedo aimed for the Death Star. The can traveled a high trajectory, spinning end over end until it clipped a stunned DJ Hurricane flush in the center of his shiny bald pate, sending the chunky mixmaster tumbling backward off his platform.

Roadies and bouncers careened across the stage in panicked damage limitation mode. One stagehand shook his head and mimed shooting at the crowd, as the rest used their own bodies to shield the Beasties from incoming fire, guiding the beleaguered stars toward safety.

A moment of pause ensued, but regrettably, it proved only temporary. Ad Rock refused to be cowed. Something told him the wise move was to storm back onto the stage, armed this time with a baseball bat instead of a microphone. At first, he stood defiantly, a gesture that brought on a fresh fusillade of cans. He then swung his body into a slugger's stance and began to take his licks, smashing three or four cans back into the audience as if the entire theater was just a batting cage dispensing beer cans instead of fast-pitch baseballs.

It required at least half a dozen roadies to perform the extract-and-rescue operation, as they courageously smothered Ad Rock and carried him off, dragging and screaming against his will. With the stage now clear, the set lights went black, a symbol of surrender that inspired a cry of "We tamed the Beastie Boys" to arise spontaneously among the crowd, resounding around the auditorium in thick, defiant, victorious Scouse tones—a football-style chant as delirious as any I had heard on the terraces, even on cup final days.

Yet, emasculating the Beastie Boys and dispatching them inside of twelve minutes was not enough for this angry mob. Like many a triumphant army, they now wanted to pillage and hellraise to commemorate their moment of victory. With no other outlet, the throngs elected to vent their fury upon each other. Chaos erupted all around us. Strangers started to wrestle each other to the ground, haymakers were thrown, and pint glasses were smashed.

Gripper was never more in his element than when surrounded by anarchy. "Get back," he said to us calmly. Without having to exchange a word, Stevie Tuffnell stepped up alongside him and the two of them began dropping anyone unfortunate enough to stumble into our vicinity, unleashing a ferocious battery of uppercuts, hooks, and the occasional headbutt. The brutality they dispensed was sickening yet effective, creating a protective force field around our crew. Even as violence exploded across the theater floor, we never feared for our safety. Instead, I was able to scan the room, which now resembled a gladiatorial battle royale. One man picked a stranger up above his head then flung him, full body, onto the stage; a group of feral teens stomped on a limp-bodied victim; a desperate woman glassed an assailant who seemed hell-bent on choking out her boyfriend.

Then our throats constricted. A tightness gripped my chest. Breathing became impossible. "Fuckin' 'ell, tear gas," the cry went up. "The Bizzies* 'ave gassed us."

A stampede formed as the crowd moved from fight to flight. Every man for themselves, bodies colliding in every direction seeking an escape from the fear, burning, and the sudden absence of oxygen. Concertgoers jumped down from the balcony; others crawled along the floor, hoping to dodge the gas by dragging themselves over the beer, glass, and bloodstained carpet. I stumbled backward, half searching for a way out, half dragged by the wave of bodies crashing through the exit. Suddenly I was spat out into the street, a scene of carnage and confusion. People were doubled over, retching, fighting to breathe. A girl ran past me, her face shocked, scalp matted with blood, bits of glass still caught in her hair.

The blue lights of police cars and ambulances flooded the scene. I collapsed onto the curb opposite the venue, gulping

---

* A common, derogatory Scouse name for the police.

down the glorious fresh air, simply relieved to have survived the madness. "That was mental." I heard a group of lads begin swapping exaggerated narratives over what had just happened. "Total aggro. One of them bouncers fired a pistol at us from the stage, like," they boasted. "They ran off stage like a bunch of wimps. Best night of me life."

Cold, heavy rain started to pour from the sky, as an exhilarated Liverpool College breaking crew reassembled. The only injury to report was a cut on Tuff's knuckles, apparently the result of his socking some kid who had braces on his teeth. "We'll always be able to say we were there," a hyped Gripper declared while bopping his head back and forward like a fighting cock. "Let's get to the State right now," he commanded. "We got to tell people our war stories before idiots who weren't there start bullshitting that they were."

There was no way I was going to the State. There was no way I could celebrate what I had just witnessed. Liverpool had not "tamed the Beasties." We had merely brought them down to our level of hopelessness. I did not want to be with Gripper. I did not want to be with any of the crew. I was honestly relieved when they agreed to leave without me. I stayed on the curb and watched them march off into town, chanting "We tamed the Beasties" as they danced and pumped their arms in the rain. I was done. With all of it. The drudgery, fear, fists in the face, and doner kebabs and everything of late-night Liverpool life. I felt only a debilitating sense of disgust and sadness. It wasn't the violence; I was numb to that. It was the emotional whiplash of the twelve-minute Beastie Boys show. It felt like it was the embodiment of what English life had to offer. Two thousand people had paid for tickets to enjoy a once-in-a-lifetime experience, only to realize they would gain more pleasure from destroying it.

This is what Casey had meant when she said that the English derive pleasure from tearing others down. Usually it was just each other. On this night, it was those "most illingest B-Boys," the Beasties. I sat there in the rain listening to my countrymen milling around outside the venue bragging to each other about what they had just experienced, and the gun became bigger and bigger with each telling.

CHAPTER THIRTY-TWO

We've Got to Make a Decision

Tracy Chapman saved my life. The folksinger with the soft yet fierce contralto voice was a healing, defiant, and inspiring presence at a time when I desperately needed all three. The Beastie Boys concert scarred me. Yet, it ultimately proved to be necessary. It was a turning point that compelled me to separate myself from the people in my life who believed that preventing others from enjoying themselves amounted to the "best night ever." It forced me to finally accept that what Fat Knacker had said to me was true.

The Liverpool College Sixth Form Common Room remained a chaotic hot mess of hormone overdrive, alcohol-fueled decision making, and strange priorities. I withdrew in the hope I could imagine a different future. I drifted away from the Rugger Buggers. At Rigby's, Stevie Tuffnell used to toast the first drink of the night, "To beers, the Boys, and birds." The Beastie Boys' experience made me realize I wanted no part of that worldview, so I faked excuses for a couple of weeks as to why I could not hang out, then the invitations simply stopped coming. Our relationship frayed slowly at first, then suddenly, to the point where I fell back into the anonymous pool of nobodies in the common room, pawns who in their eyes did not merit recognition.

I also broke up with Lisa-Marie. Okay. She broke up with me. One Monday morning, I arrived in the common room to find a letter taped to the front of my locker. The heavy stench of white musk was a clue that it came from her. The fact she had ornately calligraphied my whole name, Roger James Bennett, on the envelope was a signal I should brace myself.

The letter was long but it boiled down to this: Sandwiched in between such twee Zelda Fitzgerald quotes as "Nobody has ever measured, not even poets, how much the heart can hold," Lisa-Marie explained that she felt that "I had changed and preferred to use school as a place of study," which was a fair point. She signed off with more quotes ("Do not seek the because—in love there is no because, no reason, no explanation, no solutions"—Anaïs Nin) and added a lipstick kiss as a final flourish. I did not feel much, even as she proceeded to start dating her way through other members of the Liverpool College breaking crew. Rather, what was left of the Liverpool College breaking crew as the idea lost momentum after the Beastie Boys concert and quickly became defunct. One final victim of the Royal Court debacle.

Thankfully, I was not alone. I had Jamie. Granted, our friendship had become strained, mostly on account of me totally ditching him. Blinded by the opportunity of running with a fast crowd to which I had long dreamed of being part of, I had sacrificed our relationship. Being seen talking to someone as lowly as him might have made me uncool by association.

Chance brought us back together. More specifically, Jamie hitting Stevie Tuffnell in the head with a rugby ball one night outside the school changing room. I was walking to the bus with Tuff late one afternoon. Jamie was still in his games gear, horsing around with some mates. I had ignored him as we walked past, but then he tried to replicate a Joe Montana touchdown play that had won the NFC championship game. Unlike Montana's, Jamie's pass was wild and overthrown by about ten yards, and it smacked Stevie Tuffnell in the back of the head with a sickening thud.

Tuff dropped his games bag and stormed toward Jamie, intending to deck him in the name of retribution, per standard protocol. I watched Jamie back off with his hands in front of his face begging for mercy. "Sorry, Tuffnell. I did not mean to . . ." he pleaded. I ran after Tuff. He readied himself, clenching his fists, as Jamie cowered, eyes closed, ready to receive his punishment. "Forget it, Tuff. He's not worth it!" I shouted, hoping my words, while cruel in the moment, could save Jamie by giving his attacker an honorable out. Tuffnell panted heavily for a moment; his eyes filled with hate. Looking at the teachers patrolling nearby, he nodded silently and gravely, picked up his discarded bag, and stormed away from both of us without saying a word.

Overwhelmed with relief, Jamie rose from his knees. As I watched him brush clods of mud off his legs, I realized just how much he *was* worth it. Here was my noble, fun-loving, big-hearted friend.

"Missed you, Benj," he said with a grin, tucking his shirt back into his shorts.

"Missed you, too, Jamie," I replied, and without having to discuss the matter further, we fell back in together as if we had never been apart, savoring every episode of *Cheers* and *It's Garry Shandling's Show*, and cruising around Liverpool at the weekend in the red Ford Escort his dad had bought him for his seventeenth birthday secondhand. Saturdays quickly became a pattern of late-night poker games with the King David boys in which I never learned the rules but bluffed every single hand.

I returned to Mr. McNally and his Data Resource Room.

Under his guidance, I rededicated myself to academics, straining every sinew to prepare myself for my A-levels* exams like Rocky pounding frozen meat before the big fight. "It's your passport out of here," Fat Knacker often said as he tapped away on the keys of his beloved Commodore 64 computer. "A year of grind is a small price to pay for a life of meaning, Benj." Luckily, I hadn't wasted much of my final year at the College. I still had time to right my ship.

I lived to goad Mr. McNally into storytelling mode. It was not hard to do, to prod him into losing himself in tall tales from "the Cod" in which he claimed to have gone kayaking with James Taylor or bought beers in an after-hours bar at which Meryl Streep was ordering a sloe gin fizz. "It's a land of freedom and possibility," he would say, snapping himself out of his reveries with a sigh when he realized he was back in the reality of his boxy little office. "A place where you can create without being judged, Benj."

In moments like those, he would always drag himself up from his desk and snap a cassette tape into the small book box kept on the bookshelf behind him. We would sit in silence and savor the sounds of Joni Mitchell, Television, or the Velvet Underground. "Listen to this, Benj," he said one day, opening a cassette box with a gold-hued cover and slipping it on.

"Tracy Chapman."

"Never heard of her."

"You mean, you never heard anything *like* her."

Few songs grab me the very first time I hear them. Normally, I have to listen to the lyrics a few times and let them grow on me. But there was something about the tenderness and honesty

---

* English finals.

of this voice that instantly overwhelmed me. The tone containing both vulnerability and strength was beautiful. A tremendously satisfied Fat Knacker put his enormous feet up on his desk, yanked his meaty arms behind his head, and closed his eyes.

That afternoon, I walked home from school, forgoing the bus so I could stop off at Penny Lane Records and acquire my own Tracy Chapman cassette. Somehow, I summoned the willpower to wait until I had finished my homework before listening to it, so I could give each track my complete attention. I stared at the cassette box after pressing play: Tracy, head down, with her short dreadlocks, too modest, humble, or shy to look straight at the camera, wanting her music to do all the talking.

The album lasts just thirty-six minutes and eleven seconds. Yet Tracy stuffs a world of social ills, desperation, and injustice into those eleven songs. The sound was devastatingly pure and courageous and in stark contrast to the synth bands and hip-hop acts who dominated the charts at that point by bringing the noise. Tracy chose to craft her message. Her voice embodying tenacity in the face of suffering.

"Fast Car" was the single most human track I had ever heard. The flickering cymbal giving way to the hypnotic guitar riff, the storytelling so patient, wise, and empathetic. Every line was a study of stoicism in the face of struggle. By the time the drum kicked in to lift the chorus, Tracy sounded like she was smoldering with introspection and truth, almost burning up in the process. I tried to play the song for the boys at the Saturday-night poker game, but it was laughed off halfway through. "Is that a man or a woman singing?" Mike Nagel snorted. His disdain made me love Tracy all the more.

Tracy's career was as inspirational as her music. Most of the songs on the album had been written when she was a student, busking for coins on the streets of Boston. She became a global darling in the course of one night—during Nelson Mandela's seventieth birthday tribute, an eleven-hour celebration broadcast around the world live from Wembley Stadium, headlined by Whitney Houston, Sting, and Eric Clapton. Tracy was merely a filler act, playing early in the day, but just when Stevie Wonder was due to perform in prime time, a piece of his sound equipment malfunctioned, and the organizers hastily flung her back onstage.

I watched on in horror in my living room at home, as the single performer I loved most in the world stumbled out in front of the 72,000 confused, drunk English fans who packed the field in front of the Wembley stage. They had expected to be rocking out as the musical legend crooned "I Just Called to Say I Love You." Instead they had been served up a twenty-four-year-old unknown who timidly strolled onto stage alone, dressed in a black turtleneck and armed with just an acoustic guitar for company. I genuinely feared for Tracy, knowing what kind of cruelty my countrymen could inflict. While she was tuning up, an angry roar crackled around the bowl as the fans started to chant impatiently for Stevie Wonder. His sound check continued in the background despite her presence on the stage. There were an estimated 600 million viewers watching the live broadcast around the world. I looked down at my cup of tea and thought about going into the kitchen for a refill to avoid having to witness this potentially disastrous spectacle unfold in real time.

Tracy leaned into the microphone and broke out that opening guitar riff. So patient, wise, and eternal. Her voice began floating above the crowd's roar, initially with trepidation, but by the time the first few lines had been sung, she appeared to have drawn mystical strength from her own lyrics. And then, by standing there, being herself, singing her truth, she proceeded to silence the English fans with her own power, transforming a packed, noisy arena into the most intimate, magical setting.

At the end of "Fast Car," Tracy sings, "I had a feeling I could be someone." Overnight, she was. The Mandela performance made Tracy a global superstar. In the past, I had been jealously protective of the bands I revered, falling out of love with them when they became too popular because it felt like they had violated the strict confidence of our personal relationship. Tracy's rise, though, felt enormously validating. Her message in every interview was a map I knew I now had to follow: stay in touch with your emotions in times of both light and darkness; be willing to act and make big, bold changes to your reality; attack life with courage. And above all, get out while you can.

I aspired to live by Tracy's code, attempting to bring the big, bold changes she relentlessly preached into my own life. I moved into the tiny bedroom my brother had vacated when he left for university. Nige was very much a minimalist. His room contained only a bed and a desk, which, besides my tape player, were all I needed as my senior year regimen became borderline monastic, revolving around study, sleep, and more study.

Occasionally on school nights, a car of intoxicated classmates would drive round and attempt to coax me to come out to the pub. I would watch on from high through the window by my desk as my father answered the front door and sternly informed them I would not be joining. This sudden swing to abstinence would make me feel a stab of sadness in those moments, compelling me to turn up the volume on my cassette player and cue

Exam results had just come out. It was the first time we had all smiled in about ten months.

it to the bold promise of "If Not Now . . ." But it also reinforced my determination, unlocking a tenacious focus I honestly did not know I had inside of me.

Do I need to tell how this ended? That everyone in my class fucked up? Our grades were a total collective wipeout, a school-wide shame from which only two of us emerged with credit: James Kay and me. Almost everyone else had to scramble and hurriedly recalibrate their plans for higher education. To this day, part of me still believes that I benefited from some clerical error. My parents, though, were elated. Both at my success, and its hardworking style, which validated their core sense of reward and punishment. The night the results came out, my father opened some bottle of Bordeaux he had been saving for a special occasion and poured us both a glass to make a toast. "Do you think the past two years have been easy for me?" he said. "They have not," he continued, without waiting for an answer. "I have hated every second. But I am not here to be your friend, Roger, I am here to be your father, and they are two very different things."

Luckily for me, I still had a singular friend. And I confided in Jamie one rainy Saturday night in which the two of us had ended up in his red Ford Escort, thundering around the empty parking lot of a service station on a highway just outside of Liverpool. Sometimes, when we had nothing to do, Jamie liked to entertain us by what he called "driving as if we had just nicked the car"— acting as joyriders who had stolen a vehicle. This essentially involved speeding around doing handbrake turns and wheel spins until the inside of his Escort stank of burned tire rubber. "Fast Car" was on the dashboard cassette player as we sat there gasping for breath in the dark with the windows open, staring out at a large illuminated McDonald's sign across the puddle-filled, deserted parking lot. As Tracy sang, we knew. We had to make our decision: leave the place where we'd lived our whole lives to that point, or die this way.

I knew my answer.

Epilogue

"The great privilege of the Americans does not simply
lie in their being more enlightened than other nations,
but in their being able to repair the faults they
may commit."

—*Alexis de Tocqueville,* Democracy in America, *Volume I*

"Be kind. Be hopeful. Be optimistic. Never get down.
It's all gonna be okay. . . . We're one people. We're one
family. We all live in the same house."

—*John Lewis*

I became an American on June 1, 2018. Excitement levels
were high on the way down to the swearing-in ceremony in
lower Manhattan. I risked embarrassing my wife and four
kids and gave the driver good cause to knock a few points off
my Uber rating by subjecting everyone to repeat plays of Neil
Diamond's "America" on full blast through my tinny iPhone
speaker. "Far . . . We've been traveling far," Neil groaned with
that gravelly yet triumphant baritone over and over.

I am well aware of the widespread consensus that considers
this song to be unlistenable, cheesy kitsch. But "widespread consensus" never lip-synced along to Neil Diamond's self-assured,
world-wise crooning on countless occasions with Mr. McNally

in his Data Resource Room. I swear to you, few tunes have reso-
nated with me more than this one in that moment. Our minivan
cruised past the Empire State Building, the very same skyscraper
my grandfather once had on his fireplace mantelpiece in replica
form. I felt my heart begin to pump blood so furiously that if my
Uber driver had stopped, I could have leaped over the real thing
in one bound.

My grandfather's souvenir Empire State Building now sits
on the nightstand in my apartment on the Upper West Side of
Manhattan. Though miniature, it was regretfully too big for me
to bring to the courtroom, but still my suit pocket bulged with
a Smithsonian exhibit's worth of memorabilia: the harmonica
from my Bruce Willis fanboy phase; William "Refrigerator"
Perry's rookie card; and a photograph of Jamie and me together
as curly, mop-haired teens. On my right hand, I wore my grandfather Sam's wedding ring, which I also keep by my bed, impaled
on the slightly bent spire of that mini Empire State Building.

Once we had reached the Pearl Street courthouse, I constantly patted down this inventory of keepsakes to calm my
nerves as we waited outside in a lengthy security line consist-
ing of fellow soon-to-be Americans of every race, ethnicity, and
human form, all of us poised to become newly minted citizens
of the United States. In stark contrast to the stress and mania
typically associated with security lines at airports, where TSA
pre-check tends to bring out the worst of humanity, the vibe felt
joyously carnival-esque. We had all come so far to reach this
point, a few extra minutes of waiting meant nothing.

When we neared the metal detector at the front of the line, I
took a moment to look back, marveling at my company: 162 in-
dividuals hailing, as I would later find out, from 47 different
nations around the world. Some of these people had literally

journeyed to be here, trekking huge distances across deserts or frigid mountain ranges to earn a place in line. Others had survived wars, famine, or refugee struggle. All of their stories put dodging a few bare-bottom canings from Mr. Stott and the threat of being beaten up in some late-night chip shop into perspective.

I had reached America on September 10, 1993, some five years after making my Tracy Chapman–inspired vow with Jamie. Upon landing at JFK, I drove to the Midwest, headed for Chicago. Within two days of my arrival, Michael Jordan, the man whose poster had graced my bedroom wall for seven years, announced he was retiring from the Bulls, a devastating occurrence that rocked the entire city, and that I internalized as somehow being my fault.

MJ angst be damned. I had practical needs, money first and foremost among them. Like any new arrival, I hustled to find employment anywhere that would take an English bloke with a law degree and no work visa. Soon I was grinding out my days on the predawn shift at a bakery, afternoons as a librarian, and evenings as a well-meaning but hopelessly absentminded waiter. Within a year, Jamie arrived to join me, and the two of us moved into Rogers Park, an area we had never visited but chose because the name sounded like it was our destiny. We charged out into the city wide-eyed, chasing down the kind of distinctively Chicagoan wonders we imagined Ferris Bueller himself might savor: listening to bebop at the Green Mill, marveling at blues jam sessions in the Checkerboard Lounge, or devouring movies at that jewel of an art-house theater, the Music Box.

The four years I spent in Chicago were golden. I was witness to the back half of the Bulls' dynasty, the 1994 World Cup, and the daily mundane astonishments that any new immigrant experiences upon first moving to America: the immense size of gas stations; the startling variety of mushrooms on offer in spectacularly wide-aisled supermarkets; and the novelty and casual convenience of a land where there are coffee shops on every corner. If you have watched the early scenes of *Scarface* or the last ones of *Yentl,* you will gain a sense of the naive wonder with which I rode the El or explored the city's streets. This wonder was enhanced by my happiness at living in the city my great-grandfather had aimed for but somehow missed.

Above all, I embraced the opportunity to take one leap into the unknown after another. From afar, Mr. McNally remained my guide. I can be honest with you now. Back when I sat in the front row of his economics classes as a kid, part of me thought Fat Knacker was bullshitting. Don't get me wrong. His stories were always entertaining, but it often felt like we were listening to a bloke who was encouraged by the presence of a captive audience to burnish his own nostalgic memories. Yet, everything my teacher promised has come true. For me, the United States has proven to be a land so free, you even allow bald blokes with accents to appear on television.

I have now spent more than half my life in America. The entire experience has been a dizzying one, akin to Vito Corleone's in the *Godfather* but without fencing stolen dresses and a five-family gang war. I live in Manhattan and every night go to sleep looking out at the very same skyline George the handyman once painted so clumsily onto my bedroom wall. I have had four kids with a wife whom I adore even more than Duckie loved Andie. There is not a morning I do not wake up without thanking the Old Gods and the New for the good fortune that led me to her, and to live in the magnificent metropolis that I hear awakening around me.

Each of my kids has an American accent, a reality that

My first week in America. With dreams as big as my hair.

has not ceased to provide me with a giddy thrill every morning around the breakfast table. The weekend before my citizenship exams, we all celebrated by visiting Coney Island to ride the Cyclone, the legendarily creaky roller coaster that has terrified riders since 1927. After rattling around its wooden tracks, we settled our stomachs by strolling down the boardwalk. Having rammed down far too many hot dogs at Nathan's, we came across a huge Stars and Stripes blowing magnificently in the sea wind coming in off the Atlantic, a wind that, like me, may well have started in Liverpool but ended up all the way across the ocean.

I mentioned that thought to my wife, and she encouraged

me to do what any dad would under the circumstances: force my kids to pose for a photograph against their will. I needed to capture the family I had the vast good fortune to create since arriving on these shores alone. As we stood there attempting to cram our bodies around my large cranium, with the flag snapping in and out of our faces, I thought of the fact that after three years of interviews, background checks, and the mundane tactical bureaucracy that is the immigration process, I was about to experience a life change of immense symbolic proportions, one that was born in Liverpool, blossomed in Chicago, and flourished in New York.

At the swearing-in ceremony, the judge led us through the oath of allegiance. I put my hand on my heart and stared down at my grandfather's ring. Four generations on, I had completed his father's dream. This was the dream we had discussed together in exhaustive detail over so many afternoons playing chess on his leather sofa. Yet, as the judge proceeded to talk about the rights and responsibilities inherent in citizenship, my eye drifted to the side of his bench, where a photograph of then-president Donald Trump loomed. The judge proceeded to acknowledge this lurking presence, as he regretted that we are living in an era in which not every American welcomes new immigrants openheartedly.

The truth of these words would be proved correct in jarring and immediate fashion. The second we exited the ceremony, I tweeted a photograph of myself on the courthouse steps, beaming as I held up my freshly earned certificate of citizenship. Hundreds of congratulatory replies rolled in. Among them were a nasty strain of followers who felt the need to praise me for pursuing "the legal pathway to citizenship," in contrast to those they reviled for entering America illegally. This assumption was made because I am white, funny, and on television, and ignored a truth that I had first arrived here on a three-month tourist visa and simply never left.

That toxicity intruding into such a personal and emotional moment was a stinging reminder that division has always been churning under the surface of the America I idealized. The rupture was made explicit in horrific fashion by the Charlottesville march, the Tree of Life shooting, the Brett Kavanaugh hearings, the first Trump impeachment, and George Floyd's murder.

The fact I had become a citizen at the very time the United States became so turbulent and chaotic was crushing. There is a running joke among viewers of the *Men in Blazers* television show that the star players I interview often experience an instant loss of form or an injury. Our fans call it "The Curse of Rog." As the America of my ideals, of my dreams, gave way to outrage, unrest, and confusion, I was reminded of all the division I had experienced in the England of my childhood. That realization was as if I was trapped in the ultimate Curse of Rog.

Like millions of Americans I continued to wrestle with a bewildering sense of dislocation during 2020's summer of protest, turmoil, and suffering, one in which the fear of COVID melded with the long-aching agonies evidenced by the Black Lives Matter movement. As we descended into the chaos of the 2020 presidential election and the *New York Times* saw fit to run articles such as "7 Ways You Can Save the Democratic System," the confinement of the pandemic bubble made everything feel all the more hopeless and suffocating.

Obsessively, I began to reexamine my own journey. It was clear to me that the America of today is not the America of the 1980s that I fell in love with. In fact, the America in my head may never have existed. So where exactly did that leave me?

At first, I tried to persuade myself that home is where those we love live. And just as the idea of America had given me courage in my life, I now hoped America itself had that same courage to grapple with what it had become.

Then I voted in my first presidential election. I woke up at 5:30 A.M. to do so, hoping to avoid the long lines predicted at the polls. I stumbled through the chilled early-morning gloom of late fall Manhattan, unsure of exactly what to expect at a polling station in the time of COVID. Nothing prepared me for the sight I found. Preparing to vote was a long line filled with fellow Americans of all shapes, sizes, and backgrounds, creating a fiesta-like atmosphere. Just like at the citizenship ceremony, the energy was akin to a bottle of Coke that had been shaken before opening.

I took my place behind a ninety-three-year-old African American woman in a wheelchair covered in American flags. She told me she had urged her caregiver to make sure she was first in line because she was so excited to vote. So many of the people I spoke to, both young and old, told me that this was the first time they had ever been inspired to vote. I returned home that morning filled with an immense optimism and an "I Voted" sticker. One I wore for the next four days, long after that optimism had burned off, as my family and I anxiously braved endless Steve Kornacki–filled hours waiting for the results to trickle in.

Joe Biden's victory was not announced until the following Saturday, around lunchtime. I was preparing to watch a Premier League game when the news spilled out across the airwaves. Chelsea was about to kick off against Sheffield United when Lester Holt interrupted proceedings. The broadcast then returned to the football, so I immediately had to repress my emotions, adopt what passes as my game face, and work on through the afternoon.

At the final whistle, I had to race to a meeting in Montclair, New Jersey. I ran to the parking lot to find New York City filled with Americans celebrating in the streets. Strangers were congregating together, lining the avenues and dancing as passing cars honked their approval. The sound of pots and pans banged in triumph echoed from apartment balconies, a ritual that had started when the city was gripped by the fog of the pandemic to celebrate essential workers, now reclaimed to mark a moment of full-throated joy.

It was dusk as I pulled my car onto Broadway and headed for New Jersey. I was exhausted. Not only because I had worked all day, but from the fear, hope, confusion, and relief I had experienced during an emotionally tumultuous election week. Seeking a distraction, I flicked the car's sound system on. I possess one single, sprawling, eclectic Spotify playlist that is the subject of mockery for my children. It contains hundreds of hours of music, ranging from Icelandic hip-hop to Maori chanting. I love to play it on shuffle, flicking through a dozen or so song intros before I land on the exact tune that reflects my mood in that moment. This night, though, as I headed toward the West Side Highway, the perfect song came on within three spins. It was "The Rising" by Bruce Springsteen, an anthem written amid the darkness of the September 11, 2001, attacks.

As I drove past streets filled with exuberant celebrations, I savored the themes of the song—selflessness, resurrection, unity, and above all, optimism in the face of challenge.

"Sky of blackness and sorrow (a dream of life)," sang Bruce knowingly. The line caused me to purse my lips and furrow my brow, which I do whenever I am trying to suppress tears. It also forced me to think once more about my own experiences, sewn by a family story, sharpened by the welcoming pages of Richard Scarry books, Scooby Doo's detective stories, the joy of *The Love Boat*, the swagger of *Miami Vice*, the allure of Molly Ringwald, the issue after issue of *Rolling Stone*, reinforced by hundreds of prank calls made to Chicagoans during Bears games, and the combined poetry of John Mellencamp, Public Enemy, and Tracy Chapman. What had the last four years done to those dented dreams?

I had reached the Garden State Parkway when my phone buzzed with an incoming WhatsApp call. I did not have to look to know who it was. Even though Jamie has long since moved back to London, we speak to each other every day. My childhood friend has remained a constant presence in my life. He is also an obsessive American political junkie, so on this day of all days, I expected his call. There was a sense of wonder in Jamie's tone as he dove straight into an analysis of Philadelphia's suburban voting patterns. As he turned his attention to the shifts in Allegheny, Lackawanna, and Erie counties, I could hear muffled explosions in the background of the call.

"What's going on? You in a war zone, mate?" I asked.

"Fireworks," he said. "Whole neighborhood is celebrating tonight."

"What exactly are they celebrating?" I asked, somewhat bewildered.

"We have an America we can dream about again," he said with a note of astonishment, as if this should have been totally obvious.

"But that American dream you and I had when we were kids..." I said hesitatingly, "...what if we were wrong this whole time?"

"Benj," he said calmly, "there are parties all over the world right now. Across Britain. Berlin . . . hell, even Paris. They had a public prayer service in India, for God's sakes."

"Why, though. Why?" I said, raising my voice. "All that time, weren't we dreaming about something that never existed?"

"It might be flawed," my dear friend answered. "That doesn't matter. We all need something to believe in and it's the best thing we have," he said. "The entire world is a better place when we can all dream about the U.S. . . . ."

God bless America

Coney Island, the week I became an American. I am overwhelmed by an immense sense of gratitude for all this country has given me.

Acknowledgments

This entire book is really one long acknowledgments section, so I will try to rein myself in and focus on the practical. I am immensely thankful to everyone at Harper/Dey Street for the kindness, wisdom, and joy with which they have partnered on this project. My editor, Carrie Thornton, is one of my favorite people in the world. Savvy, intelligent, and generous. I worked with her on my first book, *Bar Mitzvah Disco*. A lot of life has happened to us both since then. We are, mostly, all the better for it. The day after Carrie read this book's proposal, she said, "You wrote this with me in mind, didn't you?" And she was absolutely right. Thanks also to the magical Peter Kispert, assistant editor; Ben Steinberg, associate publisher; Kell Wilson, marketing manager; Heidi Richter and Maureen Cole, publicity directors; Elsie Lyons, art director; Michelle Crowe, designer; the magnificent Dan Vidra in sales; and mighty Liate Stehlik, president and publisher.

Book covers stress me out, so Yeon Kim is my hero. I am also indebted to the legendary Peter Mendelsund for his guidance. I admire how he sees the world and engages with it, as well as his Marvel Comics superpower: being able to articulate emotions and images and then make them real.

My agent, David Larabell, is a mensch, a pillar, and a CAA man of action. A bottle of Laphroaig turned into human flesh. Thanks also to the incredible Steve Herz and everyone at the

Montag Group, especially Gideon Cohen and Michael Sones, who have changed the way I see the world.

In my real life, I am lucky to have found a job I adore, and a hardworking team I revere and respect. The *Men in Blazers* podcast is, I hope, at its heart, filled with love and friendship. So many of the stories in this book have been shaken loose from the crevices of my memory by conversations with Michael Davies. We did not meet until we were both in our thirties, but our shared appreciation for the wonderful weirdness of England, and a deep reverence for the idea of America, make us feel like we were childhood friends. My production partner, Jonathan Williamson, is one of the most talented and nourishing collaborators I have had in my life. To story-tell with him is to really appreciate all that is good in the world. May Ipswich Town Rise Again. Thanks also to Jordan Dalmedo and Jonah Buchanan, who are the Kevin De Bruyne and Bukayo Saka of production, and to Scott Debson, whom I have bonded with over a mutual adoration of mint vintage Starter jackets. Our live producer John Johnson is Broadway Olivier Giroud.

I could not do anything without Miranda Davis, who produces every project I work on. She is brilliant, meticulous, and the owner of what we would call in Liverpool a "proper funny" sense of humor. There are 330 million people in America, but I am willing to wager no one knows more about the release dates of 1980s American television shows on British television than she.

For the book itself. Thanks to the iconic Courtney Holt for his title suggestion, Daniel Rose for his Flemish mastery, and Mireille Silcoff for her early read, encouragement, and insight. O Canada. Brian Koppelman sat me down and advised me to "write what you feel and write what you know." A recommendation I taped to my desk and tried to follow.

I owe an enormous debt of thanks to Jeff Owen and his parents, Bobbie and Buddy, for taking me in during that life-changing summer in Northbrook, Illinois. I shudder to think where my Sliding Doors journey would have led me without it. Writing the book reconnected me to Jeff and his family and I am incredibly thankful for that. Buddy has sadly passed away since then. He was a sweet, wonderful bloke who used to slip away mysteriously at night. I did not understand why until I mustered the courage to ask him two weeks into my stay. He told me to come with him, which I did. We drove out for an hour, early evening on a warm Chicago night, until the suburban homes and malls were left behind. We arrived at a lake in the middle of nowhere. After parking up, we boarded a boat. His pride and joy. A tiny bathtub of a craft that puttered out into the middle of the lake. We cracked open a cold beer each. It was dark then, and all I saw were the lights at the backs of dozens of other boats just like ours, bobbing up and down. We drank our beers quietly, then headed home. That was it. I realized Buddy's happy place was his boat, and that everyone has to find their happy place in life. New York City has been mine. I raise a beer to Buddy Owen's memory.

I have now lived more of my life in America than I did growing up in England. To arrive here with no support network has been occasionally terrifying, but always gratifying. In terms of my American journey, I owe a debt of thanks to all those who have helped me along the way with acts of generosity and kindness: Beth Berkowitz and her family, Lew Kreinberg, Bettylu Saltzman, Leon Despres, Studs Terkel, Norman Rosenberg, Ann Hoffman, Alex and Caren Goodman, Lynn and Jules Kroll and the whole family.

Thanks also to the Chicago Bears, the Chicago White Sox,

the Washington Capitals, the Tulane Green Wave, and, above all, Everton Football Club, for providing me with the sporting narratives that accompany my existence like a joyous bass line. For all of them, glory is a precious, rare emotion. I appreciate that, as it is a reflection of life itself. Moments of joy are fleeting and must be savored. Never take a second for granted. Make memories while you still can. I am indebted to Primo Levi, Philip Larkin, and Tracy Chapman, whose poetry has reinforced that sense.

The older I have become, and the more worldwide pandemics I have experienced, the more I realize the people in my life I wish I could spend more time with. Silky and Holty are both in there, along with Dan Harverd, Rachel Levin, Michael Cohen (not that one), Eli Horowitz, and David Katznelson.

In Liverpool, I am grateful to the cast of wacky characters I grew up with, especially the Epstein, Moryouseff, and Berman families. My aunties, especially Simmy, and her late husband, Eric Kirsch, and now Joe. Shirley and Lenny Wolfman were a constant source of books and ideas. I am grateful to Katie Bickerstaff, Queen Kate Soul, who kept a treasure trove of our photographs and memories, and with whom I was able to check so many of the tiny details of our past with. She is a truly wonderful, creative soul. Proper Blue. I have also adored my correspondence with James Kay, "Hammily Sammily." It is wonderful reliving so many memories with him, remembering Latin lessons past and debating what, technically, constitutes a "Goatcock."

Mr. McNally saved me. He really was a giant of a man who taught at the College for twenty-seven years with the emotional intelligence and force of will to penetrate the lives of hundreds of self-involved, cynical teens who had no respect for authority. I have a photograph of him in my office as a reminder that

I live in the country that provided Mr. McNally with so many of the stories he delighted in regaling us with. Every step I have taken to make it here has been a leap into the unknown. Leaps that were propelled in large part by an economics teacher's life lessons. Mr. McNally passed away in 2006. I wrote to Eileen, his widow, and in her letter back, she said, "There is a fear that not only his talent, but also his very being has been forgotten as time passes." I hope this book plays a small role in assuaging that fear.

Thanks to the Glassman family—the incredible Hilary, Paula, and the late Irving Glassman. Their generosity and hospitality gave Jamie and me all the room we needed to lose ourselves in our imaginary world, then make it real. Jamie Glassman! When I was married, my brother and Jamie were joint best men. They began their speech by admitting it was an easy decision, "as Nige was my only brother, and Jamie was my only friend." A joke that is true. To be honest, it is a friendship that runs so deeply, I have never needed more. I am telling you this decades too late, but your leg warmers were pretty cool. So were the mirrored sunglasses you bought which had eyes on them. I hope we can continue to play chess against each other every day for the rest of our lives.

Finally, my family. Nige, you are still the coolest and street savviest. It is funny how life has made us now look like twins. I love how much pleasure it gives you when people meet us together and guess that I am the older one. Big love to Rebecca and the kids. Amy, I am so grateful for the two important years we shared with you and Jonathan when you lived in America. Huge love to your whole London clan. Mum and Dad. This book is written from my perspective. I cannot wait for yours where you tell the story of how you had to parent a kid who thrived in his imaginary world, but in the real one was a bit of a disorganized mess. Mum, thank you for your patience and love and immense reservoir of empathy. Dad, you are a remarkable character. I admire your enthusiasm, eternal optimism, and undented passion for Liverpool and England. Thank you for the work ethic and the modicum of discipline you were able to inculcate in me. I love you both.

To my children. Samson, Ber, Zion, and Oz. This is my story. May you write yours differently and better in your own voices. Vanessa, how I met you is a different tale entirely. A beautiful one. I love you as much as I do America.

About the Author

Roger Bennett is a broadcaster and podcaster and half of the duo Men in Blazers. He is the co-author of the *New York Times* bestseller *Men in Blazers Presents Encyclopedia Blazertannica*. Born in Liverpool, England, he now lives in New York. You can find him on Twitter at @rogbennett.